RULES OF THE GAME

ASIM QURESHI

Rules of the Game

Columbia University Press
New York

Columbia University Press
Publishers Since 1893
New York   Chichester, West Sussex
Copyright © 2009 Asim Qureshi
All rights reserved

Library of Congress Cataloging-in-Publication Data

Qureshi, Asim.
  Rules of the game / Asim Qureshi.
    p. cm.
  ISBN 978-0-231-70124-2 (alk. paper)
  1. Terrorism—Prevention. 2. Terrorism—Political aspects.
  3. Terrorism—Government policy. 4. Globalization and terrorism.
  5. Muslims—Civil rights. 6. Muslims—Crimes against. I. Title.

HV6431.Q95 2009
363.325'16—dc22

2009032502

Columbia University Press books are printed on permanent and durable
acid-free paper. This book is printed on paper with recycled content.
Printed in India

c 10 9 8 7 6 5 4 3 2 1

References to Internet Web sites (URLs) were accurate at the time of writing. Neither
the author nor Columbia University Press is responsible for URLs
that may have expired or changed since the manuscript was prepared.

Dedicated to

Shaqira, Aniqah, Aaliyah, Jamal, Shakeel, Amaan, Lily, Eman,
Hanna, Lamah, Zahraa, Saif, Haytham, Duhaa, Thania
and Anusheh.

This book is written in the hope that your world is safer than ours.

What I'm trying to do here is, and this will be followed up with the action in the next few weeks as I think you will see, is to send a clear signal out that the rules of the game have changed.

Tony Blair—former British prime minister

CONTENTS

ACKNOWLEDGEMENTS

In the name of God, the Most Beneficent, the Most Merciful.

Rules of the Game belongs to those who have suffered the most throughout the 'War on Terror'–the victims and their families. It is the courage of these individuals who have spoken of their experiences that has opened the door to human rights organisations such as Cageprisoners to investigate into Guantánamo and other prisons around the world–without them we would still be in the dark about most of the atrocities taking place.

The book has come into fruition due to a chance meeting in Khartoum with my friend Scott Baldauf from the Christian Science Monitor. He will appreciate the providence of that meeting leading to an invitation to speak at a conference in Johannesburg where I met Tarak Barkawi, who proceeded to propose the book over a steak dinner. I would like to thank both of them for the role that they have played in conceiving this work and further to Tarak for his guidance and comments in helping to shape its direction.

To my publisher Michael Dwyer and the entire team at Hurst I owe many thanks for the time and effort that they have put into making this book something worthwhile for the public.

Great thanks are due to the team at Cageprisoners who have given me opportunities and the necessary direction to help those who come within our organisation's remit. The team has given me a free hand to pursue investigations around the world and much of the information that I have provided comes from their support in doing so. In particular I would like to mention Maryam Hassan, whose knowledge of detentions in the 'War on Terror' is second to none–those within our organisation and outside of it rely on her encyclopaedic knowledge of these issues. Also I would like to thank from the team Moazzam Begg, Adnan Siddiqui, Saghir Hussain, Makbool Javaid, Fahad Ansari and

ACKNOWLEDGEMENTS

Yvonne Ridley–they have all played their roles in helping to promote my work while keeping me grounded as an individual. There are of course many volunteers and helpers who support our work unfortunately too numerous to mention by name–I thank you all for your contributions.

The work that we have done over the last six years would have been very difficult had it not been through the support and advice of our friends and partners from the human rights world. I would first like to mention Victoria Brittain, who has never failed to give exactly the right advice on many situations when it was needed the most. Friends also take the form of entire organisations such as the International Justice Network, Amnesty International, the Center for Constitutional Rights and the Center for Human Rights and Global Justice–friends and colleagues from all these organisations have played crucial roles in helping our work.

One organisation however stands out for me personally, and that is Reprieve. Clive Stafford Smith and his team have been a constant source help as we have cooperated with one another to achieve similar goals. From the organisation I would like to mention Zachary Katznelson who I had the benefit of travelling to Pakistan with–a gentleman and tireless campaigner. Also Clara Gutteridge, who in many ways is my opposite number, our travels and work together have really convinced me that those at Reprieve do go the extra mile for their clients.

This book is in many ways about identity and I would like to thank Shaykh Haitham Al-Haddad and the entire team at the Muslim Research and Development Foundation for their advice and thoughts on the manuscript, and more importantly, for helping me discover my identity.

To my parents, Ami and Abu, who have instilled in my brothers and I the importance of putting others first. I cannot fail to mention my twin older brothers and role models, Usman bhai and Imran bhai, for all the encouragement they have given me. No man is an island, so it would be remiss of me not to mention Saliha bhabi, Sadia bhabi, Sohaib, Haaroon, Ami, Tanvier bhai, Naima bhabi, Abdur Rahmaan bhai, Sahir bhaji, Zahier bhai, Zahida bhabi and Qamar.

Above all those in this world, I owe my thanks to my wonderful wife Samira and our son Haytham–the single most joys in my life. They have given me renewed energy and insights into the work that I do and provide the strong platform that I need in order to help others.

ACKNOWLEDGEMENTS

The time that they have given me away from themselves to work on this book and to work on all the other projects I am involved with is something that cannot be simply returned–inshaAllah it will come back to them manifold and I thank them for all the big and small things that they do for me.

INTRODUCTION

"I felt that they were trying to use certain parts of the defendants' lives to support the charges of terrorism, I think probably in the hope that we would be affected by the media coverage, and by playing to our prejudices. They used the fact that they were Muslim against them, the fact that they attended the Finsbury Park Mosque..."[1]

Juror from the Ricin Trial

On 5 February 2003, the United States secretary of state, Colin Powell, addressed the United Nations Security Council in order to make the case for collective action against Iraq. Part of the testimony emphasised the link between the Iraqi regime and the suspected use in Britain of the poisonous chemical ricin as part of an alleged terrorist plot.[2] The ricin plot became a factor in the 'legitimisation' of the invasion of Iraq when the US and her allies sought to enter the country having failed to secure the backing of the Security Council. The reality of the situation turned out to be completely different. There was no ricin, there was no plot, and after three years of being held in detention without charge the suspected men were finally acquitted unanimously by a jury.[3] Their story however does not end with their acquittal; rather it has become symbolic of the way in which governments have chosen to subvert their own legal systems in an attempt to counter terrorism.

The last seven years of counter-terrorism strategies have produced a plethora of commentaries looking at the legality of government policies, whether they relate to the wars in Afghanistan and Iraq, Guantánamo Bay or the use of secret detention and torture. The aim of this book, however, is to present the stories of those who have been personally affected by the ill-conceived reaction to the terrorist threat of the United States and her allies. It is about policies that have been implemented worldwide in order to justify abuses of human rights and the

1

degradation of the law, but conveyed through the voices of those who have suffered. The US has led the way in the War on Terror, but in doing so, it has lowered the threshold of acceptable human behaviour to such an extent that even countries such as China find the moral authority to point the finger back.

The narratives of those detained as a result of these policies come from all over the world—from the west coast of the US to China there are thousands of people imprisoned due to suspected links with international terrorism. It has touched the Muslim world in ways that were never expected, and with almost two billion Muslims in the world today, crossing all inhabited continents, Islam is now the largest suspect community ever to have existed. The purported counter-terrorism measures employed by various governments or regimes highlight the extent to which this is the case.

It is difficult to present this worldwide problem. The divergence in counter-terrorism measures and their subsequent abuses of law and human rights are vast. The stories themselves are important, but what is at the core of the matter is the value of fundamental norms, and how those norms have been laid by the wayside through the treatment of detainees. By concentrating on concepts that are important in any system of justice, it is hoped that the voices of those most affected will demonstrate how these principles have been lost.

It is in the post-9/11 world that we can begin to understand how the most fundamental rights have been cast aside in the global War on Terror. On 16 September 2001, Britain's former prime minister, Tony Blair, indicated the philosophy that would drive efforts worldwide to deal with the threat of terrorism:

"Whatever the technical or legal issues about a declaration of war, the fact is we are at war with terrorism."[4]

The United States of America, the most potent superpower in modern history, was attacked on her own soil. What resulted was a form of legal blindness that struck the entire international community, including legal scholars around the world.[5] Unequivocal statements made by the Bush administration made it very clear that there was no option other than to agree with a US-centric counter-terrorism response: "In this conflict, there is no neutral ground."[6] From such statements began Operation Enduring Freedom, opening a Pandora's box of legal manipulation.

INTRODUCTION

United Nations Security Council Resolution 1373 aimed to grant self-defence rights to those states affected by terrorism[7], however it was not envisaged by legal scholars that the vagueness of 1373 would constitute an approval for military action in the eyes of the US administration.[8] It was thus that the legal fraternity became anxious over the use of anticipatory self-defence, sometimes referred to as pre-emptive strike.[9] These legal obscurities found stretched validation through 1373 and a commitment by the legal advisors within the White House to find someone responsible for the World Trade Centre attacks.

Afghanistan was not the first point of strike in the US retaliation efforts. Two weeks after the 9/11 attacks two young men in Bosnia, Nihad Karsic and Almin Hardaus, were kidnapped by US military agents, subjected to sensory deprivation, beaten and finally held and interrogated in metal shipping containers. The same techniques would later be used on those captured in Afghanistan and placed on rendition flights to Guantánamo Bay and other secret prisons around the world.

The detentions of Karsic and Hardaus in Bosnia began the erosion of fundamental norms that fifty years of developing international law had aimed to protect. When the US, one of the world's leading advocates of international standards of human rights, took the decision to place winning the War on Terror above all else, the world began to repeat the horrors of the early twentieth century and the Cold War.

The rules of accepted rights are best embodied in the Universal Declaration of Human Rights (UDHR). Reflecting customary international law, the document has come to be known as one of the most important guides to establishing international human rights and humanitarian law.[10] It is in the UDHR that one will find more detailed references to the aforementioned principles:

- Article 1—the right to freedom.
- Article 3—the right to life, liberty and security.
- Article 5—the rule against torture.
- Article 9—the rule against arbitrary arrest, detention or exile.

The UDHR sets out those very basic norms that for centuries have been identified by tribes, states, empires and civilisations. Of course it would be wrong to claim that the UDHR codifies all the ways in which human beings should interact with one another, but the very vagueness of its provisions helps to establish the wide reach of the rights within its text.

As with any positively enacted legislation, such a law can only ever find its meaning through the way in which it is implemented and the respect it is accorded. To our everlasting shame, since the declaration was made, human beings have sought to manipulate those provisions that exist to protect human life in order to justify policies that take life. Reagan, Bush and Clinton have used legal justifications such as 'humanitarian intervention'[11] and 'torture lite'[12] to circumvent these strongest of principles.

The need to articulate fundamental norms of behaviour did not stem from vague pronouncements made by the gentry, but were a response to the horrors perpetrated by imperialism and dictatorships. The UDHR was formed as a result of the atrocities committed during the Second World War; but the document began to gain more relevance in the post-colonial era, when abuses were still manifest. Despite the clear wording of the UDHR, apartheid in South Africa was still very much backed by the United Kingdom government, and in the United States the black civil rights movement was only beginning its long campaign.

"With the help of many nations, with the help of 90 nations, we're tracking terrorist activity, we're freezing terrorist finances, we're disrupting terrorist plots, we're shutting down terrorist camps, we're on the hunt one person at a time. Many terrorists are now being interrogated. Many terrorists have been killed. We've liberated a country. We recognize our greatest security is found in the relentless pursuit of these cold-blooded killers." President George W. Bush, signing the Homeland Security Act 2002

Counter-terrorism measures in the War on Terror have fast become associated with abuses of human rights on a global scale. Terms such as arbitrary, detention, incommunicado, torture and secret are being coined wherever one finds policies aimed at tackling a terrorist threat. The rules have indeed changed, but who is changing the rules, and what effect is that change having on the global conscience?

In the context of the global War on Terror, past practice plays a crucial role in understanding counter-terrorism measures and how they relate to suspect communities. During the Second World War, Japanese Americans faced internment at the hands of their countrymen simply due to their origin. Later during the 1970s and 1980s, the Irish would fall victim to those same policies in the United Kingdom. The threat of terrorism is not new, and neither are the reactionary measures that are used to combat it.

INTRODUCTION

The War on Terror cannot be seen as individual acts separate from one another in an effort to rid the world of terrorism—rather they must be seen as pieces of a jigsaw puzzle which, when placed together in their correct positions, produce an holistic picture. The first piece that needs to be understood is that of profiling. Muslim, the first chapter in this book, attempts to show the diversity of the profile of the Muslim terrorism suspect. There are many non-Muslims in the world who have converted to Islam and retained their names and choose not to don attire of Islamic appearance—these people would be very difficult to identify. How to distinguish John Smith, a Muslim convert without facial hair or Islamic clothing, from any other John Smith? Similarly, Muslims from the American, Asian, European, and African continents could come from a multitude of backgrounds and ethnicities. Yet this profile remains—simply based on the perception that acts of terrorism today are primarily[13] perpetrated by Muslims.

Those in the most remote corners of the earth suffer directly from the use of profiling based on religion. In the far north-eastern corner of Kenya, refugees from Somalia were interned when Ethiopians attacked the Union of Islamic Courts (UIC) for being an extremist group, simply because of the Somali heritage they shared with the UIC. These Somalis have been in a refugee camp for seventeen years and had no tangible links to Somalia—and yet Kenya placed them under internment following the breakout of war between Somalia and Ethiopia. In the words of the Somalis themselves, they felt as if they were in Guantánamo Bay because they were Somali Muslims. Removed from any semblance of media, communication or access to the outside world, these interned Somalis shared the plight of those detained by the US in Guantánamo.[14]

The nature of profiling has also had a devastating impact on the lives of individuals. Of particular note, Jean Charles de Menezes, the young Brazilian man killed at Stockwell Tube Station in London by Metropolitan Police who suspected him of being a Muslim terrorist.[15] The stark implications of profiling are only too clear in the killing of this young man, and yet one must consider the reaction that may have followed had Jean actually been a Muslim. The Muslim community in Britain is not a homogeneous entity by any means. There are those at the extreme end of the spectrum in terms of their practising of the religion, yet even those who are not outwardly observant of the prescriptions of the faith are affected. This should make profiling an even less

5

appealing tool; unfortunately the opposite approach has been taken. Muslims, regardless of their religious motivations, are questioned about their political views on Palestine, Iraq, Kashmir, Afghanistan and Chechnya when entering or exiting a port.[16] While abroad, religious and irreligious Muslims alike are often detained at the request of their home country to circumvent domestic detention procedures.[17]

In 1215 the Magna Carta was issued and marked legislative change in securing the rights of individuals. This was to support the existing common law concept of habeas corpus, quite literally the right to the body—a remedy against unlawful detention. This principle, although common sense to many who consider it the very core of justice, has been deeply entrenched through various forms of positive legislation around the world, because of the need to protect its importance. The right to a fair trial, the right to answer allegations, the right to defend your honour, are all norms that have been protected; and yet, these most basic norms are the ones that are now under attack. Chapter two, Guilty, brings together the testimonies of detainees from around The world who have been subjected to various forms of detention without charge and have not been able to mount an adequate defence for themselves.

Detention without charge has seen many faces throughout history. The various permutations that have existed resulted in the need for habeas corpus to be protected beyond all other measures; without it justice within the courts could never be guaranteed. Despite the acceptance of habeas corpus many groups underwent forms of detention without charge: the Jewish people in Germany, blacks and coloureds in South Africa, Kenyans ruled by British, Algerians under French rule, Japanese in the US and even the Irish in the United Kingdom. These are some of the more infamous examples of detention without charge, they are largely known due to the wide scale of the abuses that resulted.

The second chapter also looks at the use of incommunicado detention globally. A concept that is wholly contrary to the norms of international human rights law, it is once again finding a place within international legal frameworks as a tool in the fight against terrorism. The general theory that surrounds this form of detention is that it will stop the possibility of the suspected terrorist getting instructions to others from his/her cell and can help to garner information that might otherwise be hard to obtain. Incommunicado detention was frowned upon because of the likelihood of abuse, yet it has found its way back in current counter-terrorism measures. A few countries, such as Spain, have chosen to legalise it[18] in order to maintain a veneer of legitimacy while others—in the developing world—have been kidnapping suspects off the streets and using the process in an ad hoc manner. In early 2007 the thirty-day detention and interrogation of four-year-old Hafsa Swaleh Ali and the detention of Millie Mithounie Gako, a Christian grandmother in Kenya, brought to the world's attention the unethical nature of such techniques.

Detention without charge in the global War on Terror has taken on a completely new identity. Although using the same mantra of justifications for such policies from the past, the process of detaining an individual has in some cases become far more nuanced. Citing various national security concerns, powerful democracies in the world such as the United States and Britain have been able to pass legislation in order to detain individuals under such conditions. The detentions of Algerians, Libyans, Jordanians and Tunisians in Britain in 2002 and 2003 led to indefinite detention without charge being introduced in Britain for the first time since the Irish 'Troubles'. After three years imprisoned without charge or a single question being asked of them, their detention was ruled unconstitutional.

The men were eventually released under draconian sets of control orders but were rearrested after the 7 July bombings—even though none of them had been implicated in the crime—and detained for a further three years, after which they were released under extremely strict conditions. Detainees such as Detainee U[19] are effectively being held under house arrest as he is not permitted to leave his home at any time of the day.

This notion of being guilty without any charge continues into Chapter Three where the phenomenon of the control order is examined. Used as a tool when detention is not possible due to a lack of evidence, governments issue control orders to detain individuals while they build a case against them. The humanitarian aspect of these measures is problematic, with families affected deeply, both physically and psychologically, by the conditions they are forced to live under. In some cases, the conditions of detention are so corrosive to the well being of the individual that they feel under intense pressure to abscond from the order in order to make life easier for their families, as well as themselves. The situation becomes ever more unfair when the lack of judicial oversight is considered. These policies have mainly been used in

Britain; however other states have begun to adopt them with equally devastating effects.

The United States of America has long held itself to be the bastion of human rights and democracy and the protector of the rule of law. Many of the statements uttered by President George W. Bush revolve around the values of the rule of law and how the struggle of the War on Terror is one related to those values.[20] It is in the US itself, however, that the greatest contradictions in human rights standards exist. Legislation has swept through the US since 9/11 making it almost impossible for suspected terrorists to have a fair trial—the burden of proof has been placed squarely in the corner of the defendant. Chapter Three aims to identify problematic methods used by western democracies to detain suspected terrorists and more worryingly, to try them. The testimonies highlight the various ways in which the attack on human rights and civil liberties has taken place and the resulting consequences.

The chapter entitled The Rule of Law brings forward views from those living in the western world. Cases such as those of John Walker Lindh, Mohammed Harakat and Sabri ben Kahla highlight the extent to which Muslim detainees in the western world are undergoing extreme difficulty when defending their cases, with severely disproportionate sentences being administered. Legislation has centralised power to make it easy for prosecutors to bring about convictions through tools given to various state departments.

"No State Party shall expel, return (*refouler*) or extradite a person to another State where there are substantial grounds for believing that he would be in danger of being subjected to torture." UN Convention against Torture (UNCAT), Article 3

Chapter Four, Foreign Exchange, follows on from the theme of detention without charge by looking at the international transfer of detainees. The removal of citizenship, extradition and the process of deportation have been radically altered over the last seven years. Previously, *refoulement* (the rule against transferring an individual to a country where they may face harm) was considered absolute in its illegality due to the implications for the human rights of those facing torture or ill treatment upon removal from a place of sanctuary. The suspicion of terrorism is used to circumvent carefully established principles of the rights of those facing harm from another state. For example, both Bosnia and Britain have implemented rules that seek to strip people of citizenship in order to have them sent to other countries where they may face the prospect of ill treatment. Similarly, by claiming that states can enter into Memoranda of Understanding with one another to protect those being returned to their countries of origin goes well beyond the protections envisaged within the UDHR and subsequent international legislation on the rights of foreigners.

The enactment of the Extradition Act 2003 in Britain allowed for a new relationship to be formed with the US—this relationship permitted the US to list allegations against anyone in Britain and meant that person could be sent without having the opportunity to answer a prima facie case first. The stories of Babar Ahmad, Talha Ahsan and others who face extradition to the US, highlight the importance of having the chance to answer a prima facie case in the country of your residence before being sent abroad. It has been questioned whether such extraditions could be akin to *refoulement*, especially when being sent to the US.

For many, Guantánamo Bay became the face of the War on Terror; it has become the embodiment of everything that was wrong with US foreign policy and the way that it is attempting to deal with its enemies. Human rights NGOs have taken Guantánamo Bay as the starting point; it was and still is the most well-referenced detention facility used by the US administration and its allies in combating terrorism. Once Guantánamo was taken as the reference point, the abuses in other prisons quickly began to flow from the stories of those detained there. Soon the world learned that the Pakistani government[21] sold human beings to the Americans from $5,000 to $5 million per individual; that these men were sent to Afghanistan, and from there to countries such as Egypt, Morocco and others before being set down in Guantánamo Bay. While on their travels, the detainees would often meet others being held by the US or her allies as part of the War on Terror. Stories have been told of children as young as six or seven being held in the worst conditions imaginable.[22]

Despite the knowledge that former detainees from Guantánamo have been able to reveal to the world, there remains a vast amount of information that has yet to be released—human rights lawyers are slowly making their way through the secrecy and evasiveness of various governments. However, the picture always results in being far bleaker than ever imagined—the detentions at Abu Ghraib are a testimony to that.

The chapter Guantánamo Bay in many ways typifies the War on Terror's detention strategy. Many books have been written by the former detainees at Guantánamo Bay[23] and their lawyers and it would not be beneficial to replicate the vast amount of information that already exists. Rather, this chapter aims to understand the statements of the former detainees, their families and lawyers in light of the effect that Guantánamo Bay has had on the global War on Terror and on the psyche of those affected. As with the Somali refugees in the most isolated region of Kenya, the name Guantánamo Bay resonates certain concepts which connect all the issues that are discussed in this book. Incommunicado detention, torture, detention without charge, disappearance, rendition and even *refoulement*—all of these and more are covered by the policies implemented at the camps at Guantánamo Bay.

The election of President Barack Hussein Obama heralded the hope that there could be a major shift in US foreign policy, especially in terms of the War on Terror. Early indications have shown that the new US president is willing to make the changes that are needed through orders to close Guantánamo and CIA black sites—however the surge of troops into Afghanistan and the message that the use of rendition will in all likelihood continue, may indicate that these hopes will be shortlived.

"More than 3,000 suspected terrorists have been arrested in many countries. Many others have met a different fate. Put it this way, they're no longer a problem to the United States and our friends and allies." (applause) George W. Bush, State of Union Address, 2003

The chapter entitled Darkness was very much inspired by investigative work conducted in Pakistan. Hundreds of individuals have been kidnapped in Pakistan by the security services and 'disappeared'.[24] Enforced disappearances are illegal under international law and contravene the Article 9 rule against arbitrary detention or arrest. Rendition and disappearances in the War on Terror do not discriminate, but have taken men, children, women including the heavily pregnant and even the elderly. Commentators will often refer to the concept of extraordinary rendition, however this description in itself is problematic. Rendition itself has no legal precedence anywhere in the world except for the US and Israel, and even then it was under limited circumstances. It is the process of kidnapping an individual and taking them to another territorial jurisdiction. It is in direct contravention of international human rights law. It is the statements of those affected by such processes that best explains why such a process is deemed illegal.

The chapter also introduces the practice of proxy detention. Traditionally proxy detention relates to the sending of an individual to an allied third party country where they can be detained and interrogated. Many of those held in Guantánamo Bay underwent forms of proxy detention as they were sent to countries in the Middle East to be interrogated and tortured before their arrival in Guantánamo. Over the years, however, the nature of proxy detention has changed as countries are less willing for their hands to be seen in the same room as the torturer. Many citizens and residents of western countries have been tortured and interrogated by other countries due to cooperation that takes place between security services behind the scenes. This has become an extremely dangerous innovation in the tactics that are being used, as the guiding hand behind the detentions is often not known until much later. Of particular note in this process is the Syrian prison Fara' Falastine which has been used on numerous occasions to detain individuals such as Maher Arar, Abdullah Almalki, Muayyad Nureddin, Adam Brown, Mohamed Hamid and many others. These men are convinced that their home countries requested their detention.

"Torture is one of the most evil practices known to man. Once torture has become acclimatised in a legal system it spreads like an infectious disease, hardening and brutalising those who have become accustomed to its use… Views as to where the line is to be drawn may differ sharply from state to state. This can be seen from the list of practices authorised for use in Guantánamo Bay by the US authorities, some of which would shock the conscience if they were ever to be authorised for use in our own country." Lord Hope, House of Lords, 2005

The final chapter, Torture and Abuse, deals with one of the most tragic aspects of the 'war': that being the complete disregard for one of the strongest norms to have universal agreement, the rule against torture. Article 5 of the UDHR is one of the best-known principles in international law, "No one shall be subjected to torture or to cruel, inhuman or degrading treatment or punishment." Very few articles have had the same level of replication as Article 5, thus reflecting its status as one of the strongest peremptory norms. Photographs and testimonies taken from US-administered prisons around the world strongly indicate that torture and abuse are prevalent in the processing and securing of detainees. However, it is not just Abu Ghraib that is a problem, the legal invention of torture lite by US government lawyers has opened the floodgates of abuse for the rest of the world, which

11

had previously seen the position of the US as being, at least officially, unequivocal.[25]

The testimonies in this section provide a very real and stark perspective on the nature of torture and abuse. Those detainees held in Guantánamo Bay have been subjected to a number of interrogation techniques which many have considered to be torture, however they were also subjected to conditions far worse in prisons in Afghanistan and elsewhere in the world. The British soldiers involved in the death of Baha Mousa in Iraq further highlight the cost of harsh detention and interrogation techniques.[26] The statements of those involved provide the most telling reason for the strength of international condemnation of torture and abuse.

Abuse at the level of the military is only one stage in the global deviation from this most basic human right. The demonization of Muslims as potential suspected terrorists has led to beatings, shootings and killings by police as well as clandestine agencies. The climate of fear and suspicion has been heightened greatly, human rights have been displaced by security, and the result is abuse without control. The chapter aims to look at various types of abuse and how they correlate with one another in terms of a climate of fear that has been created by the War on Terror.

The impact of the worldwide policies of the War on Terror is best understood through the voices of the people who are most affected: the detainees, their families and the lawyers, all of whom are on the front lines. With the release of many of those detained in Guantánamo Bay and the work of brave legal scholars and practitioners around the world, more is being learned about the new era of detention after 9/11. Despite this there are thousands of individuals still being detained and thus the world is at a critical juncture; where it can accept responsibility for the way in which legislation and policies have destroyed the lives of thousands of innocent people and bring a stop to it, or decide that this price is worth paying for the sake of international peace and security. It is important to note that even in the short term, it is unlikely that international peace and security can be achieved through the abuse of human rights.

The perceived dichotomy between human rights and security must be understood through the perspective of the victims. If a numbers game is played, then many more innocent people have died due to counter-terrorism measures since the World Trade Centre attacks than have died in terrorist attacks[27]—however the purpose of this book is not to count numbers, it is to highlight the human value of what is taking place in the hope that those voices will appeal to the public and administrations to reverse the current trend. Without the voices of the victims, we cannot know the extent of the global problem, so it is only fitting that they are the ones who should speak.

1

MUSLIM

"What it means is if your intelligence in a particular area tells you that you're looking for somebody of a particular description, perhaps with particular clothing on, then clearly you're going to exercise that power..."[1]

Hazel Blears—Home Office Minister

"Intelligence-led stop and searches have got to be the way ... We should not waste time searching old white ladies. It is going to be disproportionate. It is going to be young men, not exclusively, but it may be disproportionate when it comes to ethnic groups."[2]

Ian Johnston—Chief of British Transport Police

On 11 September 2001 the FBI launched a program known as the Pentagon/Twin Towers Bombing Investigation (PENTTBOM). In the history of the United States of America there has never been such a large criminal investigation. The FBI dedicated 7,000 of its 11,000 special agents and thousands of its support personnel in a bid to identify the hijackers and any possible supporters they may have.[3] By June 2004, official figures recorded that over 500,000 leads had been uncovered and over 165,000 interviews conducted. After having pursued all these leads, the terrorism task force detained 762 aliens, but these men were held mainly on immigration charges and the suspicion of terrorism.

Different classifications were given suspects according to the alleged danger they posed. The classification "of interest to the September 11 investigation" was however, rather broadly interpreted by the FBI. Agents who went into the field to detain an individual on whom they had been given information at a specific location would in fact detain all those without proper immigration status at that location. Thus a wider net was cast than the stated intelligence-based searches had intended. No distinction was made between the subjects of the lead and other individuals at the scene, for the FBI wanted to make sure that not one 'terrorist' was left to slip away.[4]

On 15 June 2005, the United States Senate Committee on the Judiciary convened in order to take evidence on the subject of the treatment of detainees. One of the aspects of US detention that the Senate was keen to investigate was that of the PENTTBOM detainees. Speaking before the Senate, the inspector general of the United States Department of Justice, the Honorable Glenn A Fine, highlighted the way in which the FBI had conducted the investigation of those detained through PENTTBOM by stating that:

...the Department instituted a policy that any detainee on the INS Custody List had to be detained until cleared by the FBI...this 'hold until cleared' policy was clearly understood and applied throughout the Department.[5]

The Office of the Inspector General in their report on the PENTT-BOM detentions criticised the arbitrary manner in which the detentions took place. The policies were carried out indiscriminately against those who simply had visa irregularities as well as those who may have been ethnically profiled as suspected terrorists.[6]

The treatment of immigrants in the US sparked a global practice that has continued until today. There is now a profile that exists of the 'Muslim terrorism suspect' and policies implemented around the world reflect that profile.

It must be considered however, what the profile of a Muslim terrorism suspect is. There are close to 1.6 billion Muslims in the world today; they span all races, societies and inhabited continents, so how can they be defined? It is impossible to say that the superficially adherent Muslim—the one with the long beard, turban and Arab or Asian style clothing—is the one to watch, especially considering that those who carried out the 11 September attacks were cleanshaven and in western clothing. More importantly though, how can John Smith, who turned Muslim and decided to carry out an attack against civilians, be profiled? Unlike other communities of the past who were suspected of terrorism, the Muslim profile is amongst the most difficult to identify due to the sheer number of ethnicities the religion crosses.

As a policing and security policy, profiling has been used in a multitude of circumstances across the world and history. Whether it was the Jews in Germany, blacks and coloureds in Apartheid South Africa or the Irish in the United Kingdom, profiling was used as a technique to target groups and ethnicities. Gareth Peirce, the celebrated human rights lawyer who defended the Guildford Four during the Irish Troubles and now represents Muslim detainees in Britain, explains:

We should keep all this in mind as we look at the experiences of our new suspect community. Just as Irish men and women, wherever they lived, knew every detail of injustice as if it had been done to them, long before British men and women were even aware that entire Irish families had been wrongly imprisoned in their country for decades, so Muslim men and women here and across the world are registering the ill-treatment of their community here, and recognising, too, the analogies with the experiences of the Irish.[7]

A shared experience between suspect communities[8] has brought with it a common understanding about the way in which the threat of terrorism from specific communities should be understood. The diversity of the stories told in this section highlights the broad way in which Muslims around the world have been profiled. Refugees, students, activists, and even non-Muslims have accidentally fallen victim to assumptions about the profile of a Muslim terror suspect. This chapter points to the difficulties that are faced when implementing profiling as a counter-terrorism policy.

Beginning in Bosnia

Operation Enduring Freedom was initiated after the 9/11 attacks. It caused shockwaves all over the world as the US carried out its very public attempt to catch Osama bin Laden and retaliate against Al Qaeda. What were not known until much later, were the covert methods with which the US military and security services carried out these activities. Far removed from the battlefields of Afghanistan or the World Trade Centre, the US military began this covert operation in the small Balkan state of Bosnia and Herzegovina.

On the night of 24 September 2001, and during the following day, a series of kidnappings took place at the behest of the US military that began the malignant policies that would make their way to Afghanistan, Iraq and secret detention facilities around the world. That first night, a 69-year-old man, Abdel Hakim Khafagy, and his business partner were kidnapped by German and American agents and taken to the US military base at Tuzla before being placed on rendition flights to Egypt, where they were tortured.[9] The next day, Nihad Karsic and Almin Hardaus[10] found themselves victims of the same random detention policy.

During their studies in Bosnia both Karsic and Hardaus had wished to work in aid agencies to help Bosniaks (Bosnian Muslims) through the Saudi High Commission for Relief, an organisation established by the Saudi government in order to help orphans living in Bosnia. Both men decided to opt for very mundane roles within the commission—as kitchen hands or guards for the commission's office.

Most of those suspected of hijacking the planes in the Twin Tower attacks were thought to be of Saudi origin, and so a high level of alert was placed on Saudi-related activities. As a hub for international troops and agencies, with a US military base in its territory, Bosnia became well placed for the US and her allies to begin covert investigations into any activities funded out of Saudi Arabia. Nihad Karsic comments:

In my school year of 2001-2002 I got employment in the Saudi High Commission for Relief—I was working with war orphans. My office was placed in Ilidja in a house; I was working there in the kitchen as a kitchen hand. This was the main office, we were sending money to other offices in the rest of Bosnia and I was with my friend Almin Hardaus, he was my work colleague.

We noticed one black car passed the house and we noticed flashes from a camera and when we went out the car was leaving. We thought that someone was taking pictures while the car was moving. This happened a few times over the space of a few days.

We had a call in the morning between 4-5am it was someone mumbling, he was obviously a foreigner and was not a Bosnian and he cut the line after a little while. In the afternoon I went to the bakery, I think it was 25 September 2001, we bought bread and when I was coming back three people wearing civilian clothes came in front of me wearing hand-guns. They told me to get into the back of a car—I assumed it was the same car as before as it was the same in size and colour.

With the security services of the world placed on extreme alert, rules related to detention and suspicion were completely thrown aside. For Karsic and Hardaus, their affiliation to the Saudi High Commission was considered enough of a link to possible terrorist activity to warrant immediate kidnapping and interrogation. Both men were extremely troubled by the manner in which they had been taken and the questions that were being asked of them. Almin Hardaus continues:

Nihad was arrested in the day and I did not know what happened to him. I heard some cars, some running, I stood up on the window and I saw some soldiers fully armed. Some of them had masks on their faces. I came back inside in the room—it was lighted, soon they smashed the door, I heard some shots from a gun and I stayed down. This room was in the basement and this house was on two floors, they ran to the upper floor and smashed every room and the doors. After a few minutes, I heard a soldier coming down to the basement and I saw a red dot on the door. I said something so that he could hear me and he stopped and called for others. They were Italians Carabiniers.

I stopped and called for others, and when they came, I lay on the floor, then they entered in and when they entered, they didn't shoot, they searched me. They handcuffed me and threw me on the floor. They started to interrogate me with various weapons pointed at me. They asked me questions like where are the weapons, where is the safe, where are the keys etc? While they were interrogating me, I heard a noise in the upper floors, I heard them take our safe from the upper house. I was on the floor for half an hour. They lifted me up, hooded me, two kicked me on my sides and they took me out.

They put me in a kind of van. I noticed that there were five or six in a van with me. After 10 minutes of driving, they stopped the van and took me out and were whispering, and then the Americans took me.

Karsic and Hardaus were assumed to be terrorists; they were immediately treated as such, not even as suspects. The men understood by the accents of the voices they heard that they had been taken by members of the Italian S4 Security Force stationed in Bosnia as part of the peacekeeping force. With the help of Bosnian translators, the Italian military police questioned them intensely about their involvement with international terrorism while threatening to hand them over to the US military. Karsic recalls:

One of the officers from the Italian Caras arrived, then he asked me questions like, "Where are the terrorists, where are the explosives?" They were repeating these kinds of questions all day long. All of the questions were very general. I asked why they had kidnapped me, is it because of my beard or my appearance, the officer replied, "No, it is not randomly, there is a reason for it." I then asked where the Bosnian police are, but I do not recall what he answered. The officer then accused me of not cooperating with them; he said that they are a serious army. They offered me money, safety and studying abroad in exchange for cooperation and information. I replied to them that even if I want to work for you, I do not have any information.

This interrogation lasted for four or five hours. The Italian officer said again, that if you do not cooperate with us, we will send you to the Americans.

They did not beat me at all, the Italians did not touch me; they only kidnapped me.

For the detained men, kidnap by the Italians would only be the beginning of their ordeal. To this day, detention at the hands of US army personnel is still painful for them to recall. For Karsic and Hardaus, the War on Terror did not begin in Afghanistan, but rather on the streets of Sarajevo, and for them simply because of their connection to Saudi Arabia.

Military action by the US and Britain in Afghanistan officially began on 7 October 2001. One day later in Sarajevo, US military intelligence again used a technique of profiling in order to identify individuals who would be detained as suspected terrorists. Saber Lahmar, an Algerian who graduated from Madinah University in Islamic Studies, joined the Saudi High Commission for Relief and was sent by the commissioner to Bosnia to aid humanitarian efforts in the latter part of 1996. During his time in Bosnia the Saudi commissioner moved him from his administrative position to run the library in the newly formed Saudi Cultural Centre.

On 8 October 2001, Lahmar's friend, Bensayah Belkacem (who would later join him in Guantánamo Bay) was arrested by the Bosnian police. Days later it was Lahmar's turn, but this time the US personnel aimed to use an alternative tactic. Speaking of the events as they happened, Lahmar's wife, Emina[11], explained the background behind her husband's detention and how keen the US were to show that Algerians were behind a secret plot in Bosnia:

My father was working in the US Embassy and before anything happened to us, he was called by US officials to the Embassy for informal questioning. For Bosnian personnel this is a common thing; every six months this happens. At the time it seemed to my father that it was obvious that they knew about my husband, regardless of whether or not they were asking any direct questions, it was obvious they wanted him.

My father was working six years in the Embassy on maintenance and because of the threats in these days, the US Embassy was closed, and even though it was closed, they still asked my father to come. Literally they locked him in the Embassy; they didn't allow him to go out saying that there were threats on US personnel. They took his phone and they prevented him from calling anyone.

It was three days after the arrest of my husband that my father decided to speak to me about what took place in the Embassy. The US had asked him, would you like to sacrifice your son-in-law for the sake of your job? My father replied yes, if he is guilty then he should be sentenced, but if he is not guilty then I will never have something like this on my soul. They said that was enough for them and they fired him.

I have articles from newspapers from that time that the American Embassy warned Bosnian officials that if they did not give them the Algerians, they would withdraw all diplomacy from Bosnia.

The detention of Bensayah Belkacem by the police was far more direct. Belkacem, an Algerian by origin and married to a Bosnian citizen, ran a business importing clothes from Turkey and had not previously been suspected of any crime, including by the Algerian government. The trouble with the authorities began when the police came to his family home on the pretence of document irregularities. His wife Kobilica Anela commented about the events after his initial arrest:

The questions they were asking were whether he [my husband] was Yemeni or Algerian, there were no questions about terrorism, just his nationality. They charged him because of this. They interrogated him for eight hours and also the police took me for interrogation and wanted to speak to my children as well, but I argued with them. The police took me and left the kids with my father.

They interrogated me for four hours. Who did he socialise with? Who were our guests? It was just provocation as I was the only wife to be interrogated out of all of them. They asked me to confirm that he was Algerian, and then asked me to sign, and because it was late I signed. When my husband was arrested, already on TV it was saying that the police has captured the first Al Qaeda officer in Bosnia.

For the first nine days no one mentioned terrorism during the interrogation of him, after nine days a lawyer called me and told me that he was charged with attacking and destroying the US and UK embassies in Sarajevo. In the next few days they arrested another five Algerians. In the media they already started saying that they were the Algerian Al Qaeda group.

At the time I had a legal fight with the court in Zenica due to the Yemeni forgery and also in Sarajevo over terrorism. In the Sarajevo case they did not even have one single piece of evidence. The biggest role in their prosecution was that the *New York Times* said he was an Al Qaeda officer in Europe.

The attacks on Afghanistan had not yet even begun and US intelligence claimed they were able to crack the Algerian and Saudi groups in Bosnia. Assumptions based on ethnicity and the history of the conflict in the Balkans caused the US and its allies to take drastic and illegal steps that would have tragic consequences for those that were unlawfully detained. These early policies were to set the tone for what was to follow.

British nationals detained in foreign lands

In a story released by the *New York Times* in May 2007, the secretary for US homeland security, Michael Chertoff, called for travel restrictions to be placed on British citizens of Pakistani origin due to concerns about international terrorism.[12] Chertoff's assumption was that British citizens of Pakistani origin were the main profile of suspected terrorists (possibly due to the ancestry of those involved in the 7 July attacks and the alleged 'Airline' plot), and as such they should have a special visa procedure before entering the US. Speaking to the British press, the US secretary explained, "We need to build layers of protection, and I don't think we totally want to rely upon the fact that a foreign government is going to know that one of their citizens is suspicious and is going to be coming here."[13] Such a position advocated by a senior figure within the US was only indicative of the mood that already existed around the globe.

Adam Brown[14] and his wife settled in the city of Damascus in Autumn 2005 in order to study Arabic. To do so, he had to register with the Syrian authorities and the British consulate as a British citizen living abroad. Already Syria had become known for its famous prison Fara' Falastin, where a number of Canadian citizens had been detained and tortured including Maher Arar[15]. As for Brown, it was his ethnic appearance which first attracted attention while walking the streets of the city:

I was stopped in central Damascus, asked for proof of identification, which I didn't have on me at that time, after giving a bribe which the undercover police officer was asking for he then left me alone. When I went to leave after he told me to wait at the spot which he didn't return to, thinking he was happy with the little bribe he received, I left but then five non-uniformed police officers jumped upon me and beat me. They handcuffed me and put me into a blacked out vehicle.

In the beginning they were trying to get me to admit that I'm not actually British. They thought that because from my parents I'm of mixed race origin, which they don't really seem to understand. They thought I was from Saudi Arabia, and I was trying to hide my true identity. That was the initial sort of reasoning they claimed for grabbing me and then from that they took me to a centre for military intelligence, it's called Fara' Mutaqa, there I was blindfolded and kept handcuffed.[16]

Just prior to the invasion of Iraq, the Syrian authorities gave a level of discretionary freedom for mosques within its territory to preach the importance of resisting foreign invasions, especially when a neighbouring Muslim country is being attacked. The government, usually known for its tight control over the sermons of its country's clerics, took an open view of this preaching[17] and also allowed those who wished to defend Iraq to go through its deliberately semi-permeable border. By allowing people through, while not allowing them back, the Syrian government hoped to rid itself of those committed to jihad.[18]

Playing on some of the ideological stereotypes, the Syrians attempted to profile anyone they deemed a possible suspected terrorist by forcing them to admit certain traits in their ideologies. By doing so they would be able to claim credible reasoning for detaining an individual, rather than to simply allege that they had apprehended a terrorist. The Syrians attempted to prove by all means necessary that Adam Brown was there as a fighter on his way to Iraq:

They didn't handcuff from the beginning. The first method to get you to talk will be to make you lie face down. I believe that they must have thought I was British at the beginning so they weren't going to risk it so all my beatings were on the soles of my feet so as not to leave marks. But to the people that I witnessed, they would beat them all over their bodies with electric cables. The beginning of the interrogations were to sort of ascertain where I was from and what I was doing in the area. They claimed that I was in the area where all the mujahideen [Islamic fighters] get picked up to go to Iraq. But it was the main tourist area of the entire city. All the hotels, all the money changes any tourist would make in Damascus would have visited that area. So that was a bit ridiculous, especially when they obviously must have gone away and checked at the immigration because I was living there fully registered, my house was registered, I'd applied for a residency and I was registered at Damascus University.

When they found out I was a British citizen then the questioning turned to, "Oh you must be a Salafi" and I later found out that they want you to admit that you are a Salafi, if you admit you are a Salafi then they want you admit you're a Takfiri and if you admit you're a Takfiri then you'd have to admit you're a Irhabi or a terrorist.[19] So they were sort of pursuing that line of questioning and wanted to know what I'd been doing for the last year-and-a-half in Damascus and brought names of several people that I had never heard of. They asked me do I know these people and this sort of questioning continued for the first six or seven days, up until the time of Eid.

Brown's situation would not improve for many months as he went through various forms of detention. For many, Muslims or non-Muslims, the best way to study Arabic or any other language is to spend time in a country where that language is spoken. For those Muslims keen to learn the language of the Qur'an, if they have the time and means, Syria and Egypt exist as the centres for Arabic learning in the Middle East. Brown's choice was Syria in the hope that he would be able to peacefully pass his time in the ancient city of Damascus. Others, however, choose to go to the Arabic language centres in Egypt, which is where Tanweer Sheikh and Mohammed Suleman Latif decided to go.

Finishing their studies for the year, the friends travelled to Andalusia with a larger group intent on learning more about Islamic history and culture in different parts of the world. Starting their journey in the south of Spain they made their way down to North Africa and after spending some time in Morocco went east to Egypt. Sheikh and Latif had previously decided to remain in Egypt where they would study Arabic. With some time to spare during their course, the group of friends made their way to Mount Sinai to visit the famous site where Moses brought the Jews of Egypt. It was there that the Egyptian authorities first stopped them:

31 August 2006. It was that Thursday morning that they held us and began our interrogation. Initially we were at the top of Mount Sinai, this is where one officer came up to us and asked us for our passports and he checked them. He asked us if we spoke Arabic and we said no. We started our descent and he tracked us all the way down the mountain and at the bottom he took us to the appropriate authorities who subsequently arrested us.

At first I didn't even realise that we had been arrested, I thought it was just questions. Asking what we were doing in Egypt, why we were there, who we had been travelling with, who had arranged our flats. All these kinds of questions, so we tried to answer as best as possible without giving too much away and getting anyone else involved.

When they took our passports, they told us to come back. They were questioning at this time at the Tourist Police Office which is at the base of Sinai. They let us go back to our hotels and told us to have some breakfast etc and we went with our drivers. The hotel was St Catherine's which is just five minutes from Sinai, and so we were under the assumption that we would come back and get our passports without any problem.

When we got back to the hotel, I made a quick call to our tour manager and let him know the situation. I asked him for advice about what I should do and how I should answer the questions. He advised me not to be nervous and to answer as best as possible, to tell the police that we are here for the purposes of study which can be confirmed with the institution.

The police officers came to our hotel to try and hurry us up, they told us to pack our bags and searched our flat while we were there and throughout our rooms. Initially we were a little cocky, like we were saying to them, what are you doing, questioning them, and helping them to search our different pieces of luggage. We told them that they were wasting their time.[20]

We went with them expecting our passports back but soon realised that this may not be the case.

Their identities as British-born Pakistanis soon caused concern with the Egyptian authorities who viewed them with great suspicion. As with Adam Brown, the desire to learn Arabic in an Arabic-speaking country led to the suspicion that they were there for covert purposes:

We were suspicious that they would not give our passports back from the time that they asked us whether or not we spoke Arabic, simply because they viewed us suspiciously after that. We had come on the 23rd June, so we were there nearly two-and-a-half months just for tourism, so for them this was something that was particularly worrying. The local police were not particularly interested in verifying with the institution whether or not we were there for the purposes of studying.

At the beginning we didn't emphasise the fact that we were studying, this was because we had always been told that if we were ever questioned by the police, then we should deny knowing any Arabic and reaffirm our British identity at all times. After I spoke to our course organiser, he was the one who recommended that we tell them we were studying, as the Arabic we knew was so little that it was of no consequence. When we were taken back this time, we did mention the fact that we were doing a course.

They were not interested in that at all though. They would keep on asking us what we were really doing there. Why we were really in Egypt. Really tricky types of questions to deceive us and make us say something wrong. The kinds of questions they would ask for example, would relate to the books that they removed from our bag.

The two books they had removed were the Qur'an and a book called 'Don't be Sad' which has nothing mildly dodgy about it. They were very suspicious of the 'Don't be Sad' book flicking through the pages and reading parts of it from time to time. They also made a big deal out of possessing a copy of the Qur'an. He said why do you carry this Qur'an, why do you read this Qur'an? He started asking what other books we have at home, he asked what do you read with this Qur'an, what other books do you keep under it? They were trying to imply that we might have some dodgy books at home.[21]

Assumptions have been made by the security services around the world of the traits of a suspected terrorist and things they are supposed to believe. With these assumptions there are often cultural realities that are ignored or misunderstood due to the basis of the questions being asked. It is well known that across the sub-continent nearly all Muslims know how to the read the Qur'an, they are able to read the Arabic script fluently, but many cannot understand its words. For many Arabs who speak the language naturally, it is inconceivable that anyone would be able to read Arabic script fluently without understanding. Mohammed Suleman Latif explained how they became subjected to a profile that was assumed the moment they were detained:

I was questioned for about two to three hours, just me and him alone. The first thing he said to me, was that he was not going to leave the room until I started speaking in Arabic to him. He said I was going to be there for days, weeks, months and years if I did not cooperate and admit to speaking Arabic. I just kept on reiterating that I do not speak Arabic, so once we got over that the questioning continued. He started asking me questions about who I know in Egypt, what was my real purpose for being there, still trying to imply things. He tried to put words in my mouth, especially in relation to the groups I might be associating myself with.

After I kept on giving him the same answers, and even started saying I'm telling the truth and wallahi. He said you are not telling the truth to me, and that is when he started threatening me. Basically he kept on saying to me, no, tell me the real reason you are here. I said the real reason I am here, is to do a couple of Arabic lessons and to look around Egypt. He kept on repeating himself, then said, please, please, I don't want to hurt you. As I stuck to my story, he said, that is it, you have now destroyed yourself.

He then started asking me about the people I knew in Egypt. I said that other than the ones I knew in the institution, I knew no one else. He kept on going on about the Qur'an, asking why I read that book. He would then ask me about who taught me about religion, who taught me how to pray, how I knew how to read the Qur'an and why I did not understand it.

At one point I got very direct with him, as I somewhat lost my patience. He kept on calling me a liar, and despite all my protestations to the contrary he would continue down the same line. So I simply stopped communicating with him, as I could not be bothered to speak to him any further. He asked me if I had any more to say, I said nothing because every time I tell you something, you do not believe me.

There was a time about half-an-hour before the end of the interrogation where they kept on telling me, think about yourself, have you got anything more to say. At that point I said no. He would ask this question every ten minutes for about half-an-hour. He then repeated the fact that I had destroyed myself, and then ordered two officers to take me away. They finally took me away to the same place as my friends.[22]

Brown, Sheikh and Latif all travelled to the Arab world with the aim of studying Arabic and as a result were amongst a number of foreign nationals who were detained without due cause. Studying Islam and the Arabic language are not the only reasons that Muslims travel abroad for long periods of time, for some it may be business while others may go abroad to be involved in humanitarian work and aid efforts.

After the major earthquakes that took place in Kashmir in 2005, Rangzieb Ahmed travelled from Britain to Pakistan in order to aid his own people who had been affected by the disaster. Having registered with Al Qasim, a humanitarian non-governmental organisation based in Islamabad, Ahmed was involved with the distribution of corrugated iron sheets in order to help set up temporary shelters for those displaced. After a couple of months of being involved with the relief effort, Ahmed made his way back to Islamabad on 20 August 2006, where he was kidnapped by the Pakistani security services:

I left Balakot after dawn at approximately 7am. I travelled from Balakot to Mansira by bus. Mansira is where you commission a taxi. I arrived at approximately 8am and commissioned a taxi to take me to Islamabad. About 45 minutes to 1 hour into the journey the driver...decided to stop in a town called Haripur to buy cigarettes. He got out of the car and went into the shop. As he went into the shop within seconds three vehicles with approximately fifteen males came out. I was sitting in the front passenger seat at the time. I recall that five/six males approached the passenger side of the vehicle, opened the door and one male grabbed both my hands and pushed them together and pulled me out of the car. I was pulled out of the car and made to stand facing them with my back to the vehicle at which point two males searched me.

The male on my left who was the one who pulled me out of the taxi began to talk to me in Urdu. He told me not to worry and they just wanted to ask me some questions; that they would then feed me and let me go...I recall that I was asked if I was a foreign national to which I replied yes, that my father was from Kotli, Kashmir.[23]

Having been kidnapped off the streets of Haripur, Ahmed found himself cuffed and hooded and taken to a secret location. Over the previous four years, the Pakistani security services had kidnapped hundreds of foreign nationals on its streets, many of whom ended up in Guantánamo—it is claimed that 85 percent of those who are detained at the base camp in Cuba were sold by the Pakistani government to the US at a price of $5,000 each[24]. Being a foreign national in the northern regions of the country, Ahmed found himself in a particularly precarious situation, with his captors looking for a reason to brand him a terrorist. He recalled:

I was led into a room and sat on a chair at which point one set of handcuffs and one set of shackles were taken off. The hood was then also removed a few minutes later…The two males who took me into the room left and a few minutes later two males came in wearing shirts and trousers. From this I assumed that they were ranking officers.

I was asked my name and whether I was from Pakistan and what I was doing in Pakistan. I told them that I was assisting the earthquake relief. They asked me which Islamic organisation I worked with to which I replied none. They asked me what my plans were and what Al Qaeda was up to. I told the man that I had no dealings with any such organisation and that I had nothing to say. They then left the room after asking these questions.

A short while later, someone came from behind me and put a hood over my head. A few minutes later another male came in, slim, very dark skin, black moustache and took the hood off. He then took off my handcuffs and the leg shackles. I was then told to take off my clothes and to get changed into some bottoms and sweatshirt which were dark orange in colour. This reminded me of those detained in Guantánamo Bay.

I got changed into these clothes and the same individuals brought some forms and began to ask me some questions…[they] asked me what terrorist organisation I worked with and again I denied working with any such organisation… They asked me who had sent me to Pakistan and I told them that I had come on my own and no one had sent me. They also asked me who took me to North Waziristan. Again I replied that no one took me there as I had never been there.[25]

Countries use profiling to serve a more cynical purpose than that of attempting to identify suspected terrorists. Rangzieb Ahmed's detention allowed the Pakistanis to show that there is a problem with international terrorism and with foreigners crossing between countries, and further that they are doing something to fight the threat. Even more cynically, when this takes place in the western world (as will be discussed) it is often to help perpetuate a climate of fear so that the public can see physical action being taken against unknown threats.

Unlike the others mentioned in this section, Alam Ghafoor, a British businessman, had no religious reasons for travelling to Dubai. By his own admission not a regular adherent to his religion, Ghafoor was detained in Dubai while on a business trip with his partners. Having arrived there just before the attacks in London on 7 July 2005, security agents picked them up, seemingly in order to question them about their activities, though they were already presumed guilty:

We went over [to Dubai] on the 4th of July, that was myself and my colleague Mohammed Rafiq Siddique. I had a stubble and I decided to go over there with a goatee and have some carvings done, have some tramlines put into my sideburns without any consideration as to the consequences. By 7th July we were at the hotel. We saw the British news and at first they were claiming power failures on the underground, however as the story progressed, it was actually confirmed that there had been bombs. Concerned, I phoned home in order to speak to my family in Huddersfield and I said that I've seen there have been bombs going on in London, have there been any going off anywhere else? Are there people coming around being angry? Those are the immediate reactions that you expect.

Wednesday evening we went out for a meal and went to an Indian restaurant. It was half-past-one in the morning and the early hours of Thursday. Our other friend, Zee, he was making a phone call so he was on the phone outside; he came back into the restaurant with five or six guys. They just grabbed us and took us outside. They took us into the foyer, in plainclothes and into the lobby of the hotel, and they said to us, "Give us your phones and give us your keys". I said, "Look, what's going on?", They said, "Be quiet, don't speak". A couple of them had mobiles and walkie talkies. I really did not know who they were and I did ask; I kept on saying to them, "Tell me what is going on". All they kept on saying was, "Be quiet".

Some cars pulled up outside, and they threw two of us into the back of one car and two of us in the back of the other. These were plain cars. They reached into the back and handcuffed us. The guy in the front reached into his glove compartment and started messing around with some guns. My initial reaction, and it was the same reaction as the others, was that we're here in the Middle East, these guys have just picked us up and they are going to take us into the middle of the desert, and they will shoot us in cold blood. They didn't say who they were and I didn't know who in the hell they were. I was absolutely terrified. They drove on to a deserted car park, and they reached into the back again and blindfolded us. They drove around again; they eventually stopped somewhere and dragged us out of the car. I thought this is the point; maybe I am going to be shot now.[26]

With no understanding of where they were being taken or what was going to happen to them, the men became even more terrified with each passing second. They were taken to a building for interrogation and faced a familiar line of questioning tailored in such a way as to force them to admit that they were Al Qaeda operatives in the United Arab Emirates and had in fact orchestrated the London bombings themselves:

I was taken into a building, put into a room, sat down, and there was this deathly silence. All of a sudden the door flies open, someone comes in the room and slaps me around the head and whips the blindfold off. I am surrounded by six or seven Arabs, two or three are shouting in English, two or three are shouting in Arabic, and one of them is trying to speak in Urdu. There are all these fingers pointing with them saying to me, "You are the bomber, you are linked to London bomb, we want information from you now". I was totally gobsmacked, I was like, "I don't know anything about this". They said, "No no no, we have been told to pick you up by the British intelligence". I said "Look, there has been some kind of mistake, I am a British citizen, let me speak to my Embassy". They said, "No no no, they have asked us to pick you up, you are here because you are tied up with the bombing campaign in London and you have fled to this country to hide." There was so much screaming and shouting going on from these guys; they were so angry and agitated, pushing me around, threatening to hit me and threatening to punch me. This went on for some time and then they left.

After a little time, some of the guys came back, and they asked me, "What is your name?" I replied, "Alam Ghafoor". They said, "No, this is a lie, you must have a third name". I said again, "No, I am Alam Ghafoor and that's it". They said, "What is your nationality?" I said, "I am British". This said, "No, this is a lie, what is your real nationality?" I said, "I am British, check my passport". They said, "This is a lie, you cannot be British, where do your parents come from?" I said, "My mother comes from Pakistan and my father comes from the India side". They said, "Then you are Pakistani". I repeated, "No, I am British, I was born in England and I am known as an English person". They said, "No, no", one of them jumped up and slapped me and he said, "You are Pakistani, we know you are Pakistani and you are denying it". He went outside and this other guy came in and started questioning me.

As for my friends, similar treatment was given, however luckily one of my friends was thrown straight into a cell, so they did not start on him until Friday morning. With me, it was these questions about my name, nationality, what I knew about the London bombings, how I was involved and when did I come to Dubai. I said I came to Dubai on the 4th July and when they asked for what purpose, I said it was part business part pleasure. They told me "No, you came to flee England before you gave the command for the bombs to go off". I said, "I am not linked in any way, I run a business in England in a mini market and beyond my family I really don't have contact with anyone else". I just could not believe it.

"No, no, no, you are a liar, they said, you have been on training camps in Pakistan and Afghanistan and you have set up a training camp in the UK, and you have some involvement in the US." "I have not been camping in any way whatsoever; it is totally unappealing to me." I said, "Look, the last time I went to Pakistan was in 1993 and I went for six weeks and that is the one and only time I have been there. I will be going later this year as my father is buried there and I must go to pay my respects." "No, no, no", they said, "your passport is false, and you are lying to us."

Someone else then entered the room, and he started speaking to me in Urdu. He said to me, "Look, we know that you can speak Arabic and Urdu, so he said I will speak to you in Urdu". I said, "No, you're mistaken, I speak in broken Urdu and what is Punjabi with my mother, the rest of the time I speak in English. So if you are going to ask me questions in Urdu, I am going to be very childish and stupid in my replies". He said, "No, we know that you are very fluent in Arabic and in Urdu, and we will talk in Urdu."[27]

A profile exists for Muslim men travelling around the world that makes it often difficult and sometimes impossible for them to go about their business without being stopped or detained. The case of Alam Ghafoor, especially when taken in the context of his treatment later on, highlights the tragic ineffectiveness of this use of profiling. The stories of these men are illustrative of a widespread policy that is being implemented around the world and which has abused the rights of many. Particularly in the case of British nationals travelling abroad, until their embassies are forced to act on their behalf, there is very little that can be done to help these detainees, as they are held outside the law.

Foreign nationals detained in Britain

International law has generally failed to provide protection to one particular group of people: those who flee their countries of origin in fear for their lives. Even if those who seek asylum are given a layer of protection by the host country, their interests still remain unprotected, especially if they travel abroad. After the World Trade Centre attacks, the position of the British government in relation to asylum seekers and those with British residency turned to one of extreme suspicion. In the counter-terrorism policies put forward as early as 2001, it was foreign residents that were first affected, for their rights were seen as dispensable.

Counter-terrorism policing based on fear had been seen in Britain following the bombings in Kenya and Tanzania in 1998. The security services of the world went on their first major mission to uncover Al Qaeda terrorists around the world, except legislatively there was not the same climate of fear. One victim of these policies pre and post 9/11 is Detainee E. In 1998 he was arrested by the British authorities and although he was cleared of any charges, and compensated for his arrest, this mistaken association with international terrorism continues to haunt him today. In 1998 he was arrested for allegedly being involved in a plot to build bombs for attacks at the football World Cup in France at the time. The authorities were forced by the courts to pay

Detainee E £18,500 as compensation when they found him completely innocent of any crime. He explains how that was not the end:

They found us to be completely innocent. Despite the compensation success, they broke my life with this arrest, that money means nothing because since those false allegations, my life has been broken. In 2001 they arrested me again because already they had my name on their systems which had blacklisted me.

The difference between me and you is that you are British, they cannot treat you like they treated me. They are allowed to do what they want. If I had a British passport, they could not do what they are doing. I am guilty simply because I am not from this country, because of my language and my skin, and they wanted to use that to scare people—for me the key thing is that they wanted to use us. I believe that the government wanted people to be scared of learning about their religion by treating us in such a way—this would make Muslims too scared to learn about their religion in case they become criminalised. It makes me laugh because some of the brothers want to learn Kung Fu, but they find that they cannot as if they do, they may be accused of being terrorists—that is our situation. They think it is ok and it is normal for the British, but it is not normal for us, we are the ones that are suffering from these laws. I have one friend in Belmarsh, they arrested him do you know why? They found in his car a screwdriver, pliers, electricity wire and the timer for a boiler, he is an electrician! They said he is a terrorist! This is exactly what they said about him.

What means terrorist? They don't want to explain what this means. It is my dream to know what this word means. I know how they use it, but people just hear this word and get scared, but no one knows what it means. For me a terrorist means that you have a long beard, skin that is not from this country, that the person wears Islamic clothes and maybe a little fat around the waist. They do not realise that we are a people that have feelings, we are crying, we are smiling, we are playing and enjoying ourselves and we like to enjoy ourselves and we have kids—you know what it means to have kids—we know how someone feels if they lost their father, mother or son...but why they want us to feel that feeling for them, and not feel that feeling for ourselves?[28]

Detainee E's profiling from his previous arrest and release speaks directly of the tactics that were used by the British government to detain foreign nationals and show the existence of Al Qaeda within Britain. Many arrests were made across the Algerian and Libyan communities, particularly in the attempt to use legislation enacted in 2001 to hold the men in detention without charge (see Chapter 2).

The Algerians detained in 2002 were arrested without any charge being brought against them. At the time they were confused as to why they were being held and for months they were kept in total ignorance.

They were not allowed to ask any questions, and nor were any questions asked of them. The British authorities eventually revealed their suspicion of a ricin plot for which the men were all accused, tried and acquitted.

Mouloud Sihali escaped from Algeria in order to evade state-sponsored killing through conscription in the national army. He eventually sought asylum in Britain but became an illegal immigrant when the British government refused to give refuge to those who left Algeria. Quite by accident, he became a victim of the War on Terror through the ricin plot. The only reason for his initial detention was his ethnicity as an Algerian, irrespective of any articles they found in his home which were unconnected to his arrest:

They arrested me actually quite by mistake—they had not thought of arresting me at all. What happened is that I had a couple of Muslim Algerians staying with me as you do in our community, if you have a bit of space you would rather let someone stay in your room under the radiator than under a bridge when they come new to this country. I came here new to this country with one of the other guys, Omar Jadid who has now returned to Algeria. He was staying in my place without my even asking him about any questions of his past; it is not the done thing to ask such questions when someone is asking for help. I didn't know, but he had absconded from an immigration detention centre and was pending deportation. He didn't tell me these things and I had not asked. He had nowhere to go so he asked if he could stay for a few days or weeks in my place to which I said no problem.

Back then there was the first Iraq dossier being introduced before the House of Commons and Tony Blair had told the security services to arrest anyone who might be a threat due to Britain going to war. That was back in September 2002, so they started to pick up people who were fundraising or gathering money or collecting charity money, or anyone. They didn't however go after any British citizens or residents, they only went after the asylum seekers or the ones living illegally. They started picking such people up.

They simply held us and then started trying to make links to us through our phones and other means. They went through everyone I called and know. They found one guy who allegedly had some papers in his possession which had a print out of some chemical processes which I don't know what he would be doing with those anyway, but he said he was holding them for a friend. They linked me to him because they said that previously we had shared the same room in the same place. The link was there, and they linked me to Omar Jadid and they linked me to another guy who was Meguerba and because I may have come across the men in various ways, they assumed I knew other people as well. This is how they linked all of us in the ricin case, it was a technical link rather than a physical one and it was all to show that there was some kind of cell.[29]

The detention of Sihali seems questionable when considering his lack of religious adherence. He admits that his interest in religion before his arrest was negligible and he was more surprised than anyone else at being detained. Sihali's profile as an Algerian immigrant was considered enough to place him in detention, and this is just one example of many of how the government has sought to use counter-terrorism legislation in order to apprehend individuals without due process. Hurt by his treatment, he explains his own feelings about the last seven years of various forms of detention:

I would say something to the Muslims living in the UK—if they think they are safe, then they should think again. If they think that they won't be touched or that they are untouchable then they should think again, because I used to think the same way. I never thought that something like this could ever happen to me. Why would it happen to me? I hardly even prayed from 1997 to 2002, I was going out and doing all of the forbidden things which I am not proud of and may God forgive me, but I was a regular person and I did things like anyone else would.

I never thought I could ever be accused of such things, but look at the mess I have been left in. Nobody is safe, it can happen at any time, you can be mistakenly taken for any reason. Once they accuse you of something, they will never back down and will haunt you for the rest of your days. Once they put a black mark on your name and you get linked somehow mistakenly in your community, that is it, you are done. First they used to pick up the asylum seekers and residents, now they are picking up full British citizens born here.[30]

Sihali is one of many Algerians who faced detention due to their origins; but later another ethnic group was targeted by the British authorities—Libyans who the government claimed were a threat to national security. Having fled Libya to escape the regime of Colonel Gaddafi, these men have been the subject of a series of allegations that they are involved in efforts to overthrow the Libyan dictator through links with the Libyan Fighting Group. The detention of these foreigners was easy for the government due to the lack of protection that they have as immigrants in Britain. Detainee DD, one of the Libyans who faced deportation to his country of origin, explained how his political activities were first praised and then criminalised by Britain:

I left Libya because I opposed the regime of Gaddafi. I came here as a political asylum seeker. My opposition to the Gaddafi regime was purely political; it did not involve the use of any sort of violence or force. This point is acknowledged by the British authorities too. The Libyan government has sentenced me to execution by hanging. When I sought asylum, I did not have any documentation to prove that such a sentence has been passed on me. However, when the British authorities decided to deport me, they wrote to the Libyan Government, asking them to clarify their intentions regarding me. The Libyan Foreign Ministry wrote back stating that, should this person be handed over to the Libyan government, he shall be sentenced to death. I have this document with me now.

When I sought asylum here, I gave them access to all my personal information; my name, address, even my thoughts, what I do, everything. I remember on my arrival at Heathrow airport, on the same day, I didn't leave the airport; MI5 sat with me and asked me some questions. I then asked whether my proposed political activities in opposition to Libya were against any British laws. They replied that the country is open to you for this purpose. They now view me as a threat to the country. If I intended to engage myself in any such activities, I would not have given them files of information about myself. I would have stayed undercover and done what I intended to do. My point is that all my files are very, very clear; that my activities are purely political and focussed only against the Libyan regime.[31]

The schizophrenic relationship that the British government has with Gaddafi's Libya and the manner in which the British Libyans have been treated highlights the desperation with which the British government has conducted its counter-terrorism policies. Using the grievances that asylum seekers have with their countries of origin, the security services were able to profile foreign nationals in order to highlight the risk of terrorism. Profiling in such circumstances has proven to be far from bona fide as those that have been detained have been so because of their status as immigrants, rather than because of any actual evidence of wrongdoing.

2

GUILTY

"Everyone is entitled in full equality to a fair and public hearing by an independent and impartial tribunal, in the determination of his rights and obligations and of any criminal charge against him."

Article 10, Universal Declaration of Human Rights

Being considered innocent until proven guilty ensures that justice is served for all human beings—it is a necessity in order to administer the law fairly at all levels, not simply a judicial requirement. The War on Terror has sought to change that universal understanding; governments around the world are ready and willing to sacrifice human rights and civil liberties in the name of security interests. An endless media campaign by mainstream networks perpetuates the climate of fear that allows policies to be legislated without checks and balances.[1]

Amongst the oldest principles of judicial fairness is the right to a fair trial or hearing. The above quote from the Universal Declaration of Human Rights has long established the international obligation on countries around the world to ensure that anyone detained has protections in line with the spirit of Article 10. The emphasis on such provisions is so entrenched, that a multitude of international legal instruments have protected the same rights in all circumstances, whether during peace or war time.

After 9/11, the United Nations Security Council passed Resolution 1566:

States must ensure that any measures taken to combat terrorism comply with all their obligations under international law.

Those countries that are keen to bypass the rule of law have used this provision within the resolution; they consider that as long as they

37

can prove that their actions are consistent with international law, they are free to use measures to combat terrorism. The overstretching of provisions such as 1373 and 1566 has become a feature of the way in which various countries around the world have sought to go beyond the law. The customary norms of international law have attempted to entrench principles such as non-*refoulement* and the rules against arbitrary detention and torture. However, it is these very norms that have become vulnerable in the quest for stricter counter-terrorism provisions.[2]

Guantánamo Bay has become the most potent symbol of detention without charge in the world today. The base is synonymous with abuse and unlawful detention. Due to the complexities of this specific case I will analyse the issues surrounding the base later in a dedicated chapter. In this chapter, it suffices to say that the treatment of detainees at Guantánamo set in motion behaviour elsewhere which seeks to undermine the rule against arbitrary detention and the right to a fair trial. With legal innovations such as 'enemy combatant' being forced into legal language, others are taking their lead from the US and applying those same concepts to detain suspects without recognised legal precedents.[3] This was seen in the Horn of Africa when refugees fleeing from Somalia to Kenya were placed on rendition flights to Ethiopia, where they were accused of being 'enemy combatants'; a phrase first coined by the US.

Assumptions have been made by more powerful countries that, in the War on Terror, less developed countries have a greater ability to bypass due process and can detain suspects without charge or trial. Bosnia serves as one early example of how the law was bypassed in order to detain suspects illegally in the name of security. Whether the detention took place domestically within Bosnia or whether individuals were in fact sent outside its borders, the fledgling sovereignty of the Bosnian government has been preyed upon in order to circumvent the judicial system and detain Bosnian citizens without charge.

With the East Africa bombings in 1998, countries within the Horn of Africa began the process of developing counter-terrorism measures in order to detain suspects. Countries with stronger civil society, such as Kenya, warded off attempts to introduce detention without charge, despite permitting the presence of western security services. However, after 9/11 this all changed and there was renewed pressure on the East African countries to involve themselves in the global War on Terror.

By 2007 Ethiopia had invaded Somalia and those suspected terrorists detained in the Horn of Africa were subjected to various forms of unlawful detention reminiscent of Guantánamo Bay.

For the countries of the Middle East and Asia arbitrary detention has been a normal legal practice for many years. Often the security services will detain an individual under state security laws then subject him to ill treatment. Dictatorships and despots declare perpetual states of emergency which in turn are used to justify arbitrary detention on the pretext of national security. The War on Terror gave these same countries further means of legitimising their policies and led to their using international events to further their actions domestically.

Furthermore, the War on Terror has brought with it an unprecedented level of complicity between those Arab and Muslim nations accustomed to using arbitrary detention and other countries less able to do so. As will be discussed in later chapters, western countries have begun to use the security services in such nations to detain suspected terrorists for longer than they would be able to under their own laws.

This chapter looks at these policies of detention without charge and how they have been implemented around the world. Some governments, such as Britain's, have attempted a veneer of legality by trying to argue the need for such measures; while others, such as Pakistan's, have resorted to far more covert techniques of detaining individuals. Those countries with previously poor records have increased their activities. However, even countries with far better human rights records have resorted to implementing incommunicado detention, and where detention is not possible, governments have introduced alternative forms of incarcerating individuals without charge or evidence against them. In these cases the most popular method used is the control order.

Hooded and shackled

Detained at the offices of the Saudi High Commission in Bosnia, Nihad Karsic and Almin Hardaus were taken to Butmir Base by Italian peacekeeping forces to be interrogated about their involvement with international terrorism. At this stage neither man had heard of the US detention facilities in Afghanistan and Cuba, and when told that they were being handed over to the Americans, they were hopeful that they might be dealt with justly.

RULES OF THE GAME

As soon as the US soldiers took them into custody, they were subjected to a process of sensory deprivation that came to public attention after pictures were released of the detainees held in Afghanistan. Placed in a cage like that used later at the Bagram detention facility in Afghanistan, Karsic explained how they were treated by the American troops in Bosnia:

> In that place, one American agent interrogated me with a translator. The agent had a moustache, eye glasses, around 45 years old; he told me that he was a geologist by expertise. During this interrogation the agent kept on telling me that he didn't believe a word I said. He asked me everything, what I was eating, about my faculty, who I was meeting, where are the terrorists.

> This agent then said to me that I was not cooperating with them and that I was going to be sent to the US base in Tuzla. This was the same day, just in the night. The next day they arrived again, they handcuffed me, hooded me, and placed headphones over my ears.

> They handcuffed me with plastic handcuffs, and they put me in a helicopter and they took me to Tuzla. I had these ski glasses, but blacked out, and a hood over my head. I had a problem with breathing due to this but they didn't want to respond. I complained but they would not listen to me at all. They placed me in a container that was used as a prison cell—it was an improvised prison cell. All the American bases, they were built using shipping containers I assumed—when they made their bases they had many of these.[4]

Many detainees who have been placed in US custody around the world have described being housed and interrogated in these metal shipping containers. The most notorious of these was used in the massacre at Dasht-i-Leili,[5] where it is alleged that between 1,000 and 3,000 Taliban troops were stuffed into shipping containers by American soldiers and shot at. Inside such a container, Hardaus found himself face to face with a US interrogator keen to extract any information related to the 9/11 attacks:

> They took me to a kind of container—I was handcuffed—they searched me again. I was hooded all night long, but I felt there was a person standing near me, I had a feeling that it was coming to daylight when two men approached me, they elevated me up and put me on a chair. They took the hood off my head and I saw a table in front of me, then I saw a soldier and from the appearance I could tell he was an American. This soldier began to speak to me in Arabic, I told him a few times I told him I cannot speak in Arabic, but he continued to do so. I told him I cannot speak in Arabic, I told him I know a little English, but I didn't know any Arabic. When he saw I didn't know Arabic, he began asking questions in English. He asked me if I knew what hap-

pened in the US, and kept on asking me where the weapons were. He kept asking me which Arabs I knew here in Bosnia and these kinds of questions.

After that they hooded me and put earphones on me and placed me on a helicopter. After 40 minutes of flight or less we arrived at a base, at that time we did not know where, but later I found out it was Tuzla. It was US Marines; they were quite obviously expecting for us to arrive, they were all huge men. All this time we didn't see each other and they placed me in a cell made from a shipping container.[6]

The incommunicado detention of these two men was only the beginning of US operations in Bosnia. During the nineties many foreign fighters entered Bosnia, keen to help the Bosnian people repel Serbian forces whose ethnic cleansing program had led to widespread atrocities against innocent civilians in the Balkans. Based on the assumption that Al Qaeda had been involved in the jihad of the Bosniak people, the US military immediately saw any ties to Saudi Arabia or other Muslim countries in the region as suspicious. For that reason Karsic and Hardaus, despite being Bosnian citizens, were forcibly kidnapped off the streets.

The Algerians living in Bosnia were immediately taken to be possible members of a North African Al Qaeda cell. US intelligence based in the country was keen to prove that there was a threat to security and that operations in Europe were the work of many of those foreign fighters who had arrived in the nineties; and so it was that six innocent Algerian men became the subjects of US interest. Saber Lahmar's wife Emina explained the circumstances of his unlawful detention in light of the political moves being made by the US at the time:

Bosnian police came and they took my husband that night and they came with a warrant to look for false documents, weapons, drugs and money. The police, they were very kind, they searched in our books and notes, we had coffee easily and no one mentioned any arrest. Even we had a conversation with the police officers and one Serbian policeman in the Bosnian police said that if my husband is guilty then he is guilty too...After the search they asked my husband to go with them to sign some papers at the station...They took him however and never came back.

At the time it was Clifford Bond who was leaving the embassy and Thomas Miller was supposed to arrive. In these few days there was no Ambassador. There was a secretary in the embassy and he was an extremely bad man—he became the Charge D'Affaires. He was extremely keen to make this link between the Algerians and Al Qaeda.

We didn't have any possibility to see my husband because they didn't have any legal document that he is in the interrogation prison as the State prosecutor did not want to write any charge on him. They had no legal means to charge. I had information that Alija Behmen—premier of Federatia of BiH—from the Social Democrat Party arrived with one American and he told the state prosecutor to write charges even if they have to pay until the end of their lives compensation to the families, it was enormous pressure put on by the Americans.[7]

The testimony of Emina Lahmar illustrates the immense pressure that the US was placing on the Bosnian authorities to produce results to show that they were countering Al Qaeda in the Balkans. The Algerian detainees were clearly unconnected to any terrorist activities and despite numerous efforts by the police and intelligence services to connect them, they were not able to charge them with any crime.

Boudella Haji, one of the Algerian men who was eventually sent to Guantánamo Bay, arrived in Bosnia in the nineties as an aid worker. During the conflict he was left seventy percent disabled by an exploding mine that destroyed his left arm and burnt his muscles. Despite his injuries, Haji continued in aid work by joining the humanitarian NGO Human Appeal. He soon became the head of the organisation, which looked after war orphans living in Sarajevo.

When requests came from the US to imprison the six Algerians, the Bosnian authorities were keen to find ways of demonstrating their compliance without having to go too far beyond the law. So they stripped the men of their Bosnian citizenship. It was felt that they would be able to circumvent much of the law if they were dealing with foreigners, rather than their own citizens. As Haji's wife, Nadja Dizdaravic states, the next step was to attempt to remove them to Algeria:

After the revision of nationalities, the Bosnian government asked Algeria to take the six on the condition that they would imprison them, but Algeria refused to do so. Algeria said that they would refuse to imprison them if they sent them back there.

My husband was arrested on 20 October 2001—he was arrested but they did not find anything on him. Here by the law, you are supposed to be held for three days by the police after which time the judge can allow for an interrogation in prison for 30 days, but this is only supposed to be conducted by judges. They decided that because they suspected him of planning terrorism in Bosnia and because of that wanted to criminalise him and revoke his citizenship.

After I made a charge on the court against them, they gave my husband his nationality back and also the Bosnian government gave him a ten year stay in Bosnia. The Human Rights Chamber also cancelled all decisions against him.

Regardless of the decision of the Supreme Court that they must be released, the American Commander of S4 (security force for peacekeeping in Bosnia) John Sylvester said that regardless of the decision of the Supreme Court, the men would be deported to Guantánamo.[8]

The US undertook a vigorous media campaign in order to incite fear of the Algerian detainees[9], making constant references to their links with Al Qaeda in order to sway public opinion against them and thus make it easier to act outside the law. Despite strong opposition by the courts to their rendition, events conspired against the Algerians and they were forcibly taken to Guantánamo Bay, despite having proven their innocence many times over. Kobilica Anela, the wife of Bensayah Belkacem, described how the prosecution attempted to link the Algerians to Al Qaeda:

In the court in Sarajevo they proved there was no telephone link between him and Pakistan and Afghanistan, there was no link whatsoever to Abu Zubaydah as had been claimed. Bosnian officials were asking the US if the six are on the warrant list for terrorism, but they were not. When I went to visit him prison officials kept me out in the cold on purpose in order to make it difficult for me.

After everything was over with the court and there was no case left against them—the lawyer told me that this was all politics and that the law has nothing to do with this.

When I went to visit him after he had been cleared by the court, I was treated normally. I had a source that told me that my husband was about to be deported to Guantánamo. I asked the prison to see him and they allowed me, but this time they became tough again and really checked over us. When we entered to see him, he knew that he was being deported as I had brought the children. So he asked me if he was but I couldn't say as I had been warned by the police not to say anything at all. The Americans warned the Bosnian officials that if you do not deport them after the release, we will arrest them.

16 January 2002 they moved my husband from Zenica to Sarajevo at 9pm in the evening without informing anyone and on 17 January 2002 people began to gather in front of the prison. I found out from the media so I went with my lawyer to Sarajevo. I was standing in front of the prison all day and all night. At midnight they tried to take him out of the prison, there were around 3,000 people in front of the prison as the six had been give the decision of release and we went to receive them.

That is when the trouble started—the police tried to take them out but there was a huge mob who had tried to stop them from leaving. The police put hoods over the men and took them out of the prison. In one moment they opened the window and I shouted to my husband I was there. At 4am I saw a

French policeman again who was in charge of the European police in Bosnia; when he left the police began to beat us hard. It was all the Bosnian police forces, they beat us really hard.[10]

Despite the perception that legal processes had been involved in their detention, the decision to have the men removed from Bosnia as suspected Al Qaeda terrorists was made long before they spent a single day in court. With the US keen to prove the existence of a North African cell in Europe, the men were kidnapped and taken away despite having been acquitted of all charges. They were finally released from Guantánamo Bay in early 2009 after political pressure from the Bosnian government, by which time they had been in unlawful detention for seven years.

The African front

The presence of Al Qaeda in the Horn of Africa became clear in 1998 with the twin bombings of US embassies in Nairobi and Dar-es-Salaam. In the Nairobi attack 4,000 people were injured and 201 Kenyans and 12 Americans were killed; Dar-es-Salaam left a death toll of 12 with 85 injured. Despite the attacks, the Kenyan government made no overt changes to its legal system and did not try to push through anti-terrorism legislation, mainly because there was general acceptance that the targets were in fact US citizens, rather than Kenyan.

9/11 changed things dramatically in East Africa as the heightened tension around the world forced African governments to play their part in combating terrorism. In 2002 missiles were fired by suspected terrorists at an Israeli aeroplane in the Kenyan coastal city of Mombasa and although the missiles missed the plane, it was only minutes later when a car bomb blew up the Paradise Hotel, at a beach resort in Kikambala which was often used by Israeli tourists. The car bomb blast killed three Israeli citizens and ten Kenyans, leaving eighty people injured. These attacks drastically changed the character of counter-terrorism in Kenya and soon the whole of the Horn of Africa.

After attending Friday prayers in his local mosque in Mombasa on 1 August 2003, Omar Syed Omar went shopping for new clothes for his soon-to-be-born child. While shopping two plainclothes police officers approached him claiming that they needed to ask some questions at the Mombasa central police station. Not being told why he was wanted, Omar agreed to go with the men, assuming that whatever misunderstanding there had been, he could quickly clear it up. While at Mombasa police station, he was told that he would be taken to Port police station, where he was kept until midnight.

The police ordered Omar to take them to his house. He became suspicious of them at this point as they did not even know where he lived and so questioned the nature of the intelligence that they had on him:

I took them to my house in Machengo; when we arrived there they took position and told me that I should speak to my father-in-law as I live with him. When he came, he came with his wife and they thought I was alone. I told them that I was with the police and that they should not panic and just open it. While they opened it the police rushed inside pointing their guns. I kept on shouting to not worry as I was afraid my wife would panic and hurt herself and the baby.

They took a lot of our things; they took my ID card and also took my wife's ID card. I was then taken back to Port police station. At about two in the afternoon I was taken to Moi International Airport where there was a small police aeroplane. Then I was put in this plane and then tied to my chair and taken to Nairobi Wilson Airport.

I was blindfolded by the Kenyan police and taken to an unknown location which I learned later was the General Service Unit (GSU) headquarters. It is on Thika Road and I was put there. When I arrived at that place that night, they told the personnel to switch off the camera, as they did not want anyone to know I was there. There were two cells and I was put alone in one—there were two officers already stationed there. They told me that I should get some sleep.

The next morning they came to interrogate me. They took me in a car pretending to take me somewhere far, but it was actually in the same place. I was taken to a room which was downstairs somewhere. Then I was interrogated for about five days. They were asking about my background; where I was born, where I went to school, what kind of people I hate.

After five days they told me that there are some foreigners who want to interrogate me. I told them that I need a lawyer; I cannot be questioned like this alone. They said that as long as I am in their territory, they know what they are going to do to me.

My family didn't know where I was, they thought I was still in Mombasa and were searching for me there. Nobody knew where I was. In fact I was kept in that kind of situation for about 48 days. I was being kept incommunicado—I didn't have access to my lawyer, no friends or relatives. I stayed in GSU until 19 September 2003.[11]

Omar believed that his situation would quickly improve with the presence of foreign personnel. He was informed that the FBI, Scotland Yard and Mossad were all interested in speaking with him and thus felt that he would have an opportunity to be released from his incommunicado detention.

After the five days the Kenyans questioned me, there was a man who came to do the same thing. I don't remember his name but I am sure he was Mossad. He interrogated me for almost two weeks. The situation was not good, I was kept on a stool that was tall and had my hands handcuffed behind my back. He would keep me there for a long time and it would become unbearable. He would have a book with photos in it and he would ask if I knew the names of the people. He would ask if I had been travelling abroad anywhere, what kind of people I hated, the hobbies I like, etc.

The man never told me directly that he was from Israel—but I remember that one day there was a confrontation between me and him and that I would not speak more. If they believed that I had done something then they should charge me as this was against the law. When I started talking like this then he started to harass me. He grabbed me by the scruff of the neck and threatened me—but a senior officer on the Kenyan side told him to stop. He said to the Mossad agent that if you want to speak to him, then speak to him softly as he has been talking to you for two weeks. It was at that time that I heard some discussion outside that the man interrogating me was from Mossad—from the accent I could detect where he come from. The FBI introduced themselves to me, they showed me their cards when they came. They asked the same questions as the other people. It was three men who came.

When they first arrested me—they said that a lady had been robbed so they wanted to question me. They wanted to do an identification parade but when I arrived at the police station there was no lady. It was only when I arrived in Nairobi that they told me that they had suspected me of terrorism—in relation to the bombings of an Israeli hotel in Kikambala—they booked me as a suspect. They hadn't told me it was in relation to the bombing of the hotel at the time.

It was 18 September 2003. I was taken to the high court where I was charged with the Kikambala bombings. I was taken to Committee Maximum Prison—that day is when I saw other people with whom my case would be consolidated. The case proceeded until 9 July 2005 when I was brought before the court and acquitted.

When I returned back to the prison to collect my things; as I was being released I was rearrested. I was charged with the possession of firearms. I was surprised as according to Kenyan law if you are charged with a crime, you are supposed to be tried in one go. They brought it two years later. I think there might have been some pressure somewhere, maybe these people didn't do their work and wanted to show the outside world that they charged someone with something. Maybe that is the picture they wanted to create.[12]

Omar Syed Omar's situation is an early example of detention policies that were later to be implemented across the whole of the region, but even before his original arrest, the groundwork for such detentions had already been laid. Within a year of the attacks on 9/11, the US began to transfer troops to the Horn of Africa. It was with their deployment that the Combined Joint Task Force for the Horn of Africa (CJTF-HOA) was established at Camp Lemonier in Djibouti.[13] Joining with forces from neighbouring countries such as Ethiopia, Kenya and Somalia the purpose of the task force was to deal with the emergence of terrorist threats in the region. On 12 September 2002, US soldiers finally arrived in Djibouti, heralding a new front in the War on Terror, and with it, more detentions of suspected terrorists.

The Joint Task Force never acknowledged a time limit for its presence in East Africa; rather it was established in the region as a counter-terrorism force until the threat of international terrorism was removed.

The US claimed that its presence in the Horn of Africa was to aid its allies against the threat of terrorism, rather than being an occupying force in the region. But later, with two other fronts in Afghanistan and Iraq, the US army found itself spread very thin and turned to its 'allies' in order to prosecute the War on Terror.

It is ironic that US allies in the region, such as Ethiopia, are noted amongst the worst human rights abusers in the world—a fact acknowledged in a US Department of State's human rights report.[14] On the pretext of tackling international terrorism, Ethiopia turned its sights to Somalia with the backing of the US.

Sponsored, trained and equipped by the CJTF-HOA, at the end of 2006 Ethiopian troops joined with deposed Somali warlords under the guise of the Somali Transitional Federal Government (STFG) to invade Somalia, then de facto controlled by the Union of Islamic Courts (UIC).[15] On 24 December the Ethiopian Prime Minister Meles Zenawi declared that Ethiopia would actively engage in hostilities with the UIC, stating as its justification the protection of Ethiopian sovereignty, despite this breaching Article 2(4) of the UN Charter. The charter specifically prohibits any act of aggression and only allows for self-defence where hostilities have already been engaged. Beginning its campaign of aggression against Somalia, Ethiopia began an illegal war in the Horn of Africa.

With the backing of US forces, Ethiopan troops quickly overpowered the UIC and by January 2007 had deposed them and installed the

Somali Transitional Federal Government, which immediately enacted emergency laws.

US involvement in the Horn of Africa brings to mind the 1986 judgement of the International Court of Justice in the case of Nicaragua v USA, in which the court held that training, equipping and giving logistical support to a state in its aggression against another country is tantamount to aggression itself.[16] The level of logistical support provided by the US military to the Ethiopian troops put it in the position of effectively pushing for the invasion of Somalia, thereby breaking US obligations under international law. Furthermore, the US bombed suspected Al Qaeda targets from the air during the Ethiopian offensive.[17]

With the outbreak of war a mass exodus of refugees began to make its way towards the borders of neighbouring countries. The immediate bombing of Mogadishu International Airport stopped any flights out of the country by foreign nationals or those wishing to flee the conflict zone by air. Many of those who were in Mogadishu decided to flee south towards the Kenyan border where they would find security and, for the foreign nationals, their embassies. Travelling on the southern road from Mogadishu, the refugees made their way through Jilib where they were joined by others on their way to the coastal town of Kismayo.

But US ships patrolling the coastal waters of Somalia made it impossible for Kismayo to be used to escape the conflict zone. All those who had fled south away from the fighting now had to go even further, to the southernmost tip of Somalia, Ras Kamboni. Ras Kamboni was on the border with Kenya, and became the last point of escape for all those fleeing Somalia. With Ethiopian troops sweeping across the country, the refugees were forced to use Somali guides to take them through the jungles between Somalia and Kenya and onto the town of Kiunga, where they hoped to find security.

A group of women and children of various nationalities, attempted to escape from Somalia after being split from their families. They made their way through the jungles at the border to reach Kiunga where they sought help from the local people. Halima Hashim explained how they were detained after their arrival:

Salim [the guide for the women] went to Kiunga town to speak to the chief about our situation, that we were Kenyans who had documents to prove that. Salim insisted to us that we had to go and see the chief. In the morning he took us to the chief's office. We told him about our situation. He said we had to go to the police station where we were told to wait and gave our ID cards. In Kiunga there were ten of us in a cell, eight women and two men.

We were just in the cells and they started interrogating us, asking us how we reached Kenya, what made us go there to Somalia. We were there for five days before they decided to move us to Nairobi at which point we were moved to the Inland Container Depot.

We were held in the depot for three weeks. At that point it was so cold, I was pregnant with no mattress to sleep on and had become very sick which made me cry a lot. I constantly complained that I needed to go to the hospital but they would not listen to me, forcing me to take whatever medicines I could.

Soon enough word managed to get out to the Kenyan public that we were being held in detention without charge and it was at that point that my mother came to see me in prison. When she arrived the Anti-Terrorism Police Unit (ATPU) took her aside and interrogated her for twenty minutes. After that they called me in and shouted at me, asking how it was that people outside had found out I was there, they were very angry about this. It seemed that somehow a petition for habeas corpus had been launched for us and the courts demanded our immediate release. One of the ATPU officers said, "I have a letter here from the government, and we are the government. The Muslim people and the Human Rights people are not going to do anything for you." When I questioned why they were detaining us, they said, "You will stay with us for a very long time, because you have not told us anything."

Due to the mounting pressure from outside by Muslim organisations, the ATPU decided to move us again to keep us from being found—they took us all to separate police stations. The ATPU questioned me again in this station, they were claiming that Issa Osman Issa [a suspected terrorist] was intimate with me and that I was carrying his child. They kept on bringing me pictures saying that he was my husband, they were extremely rude to me. This made me cry a lot, because they knew already that my husband had been killed by the indiscriminate shelling by the Ethiopians in Somalia.

There was a lot of pressure on the ATPU to find us guilty of being terrorists or to get us to admit this thing because we all knew that the CIA or FBI were willing to pay money for foreign nationals who had been in Somalia.[18]

Hashim was detained alongside Fatima Ahmed Abdur Rahman and her four-year-old daughter Hafsa Swaleh Ali who had also left Somalia to escape the fighting. Both mother and child found themselves at the mercy of the Anti-Terrorism Police Unit who cared neither for their status as refugees nor for Hafsa's tender age. Fatima Abdur Rahman recalls their experience:

On 7 January 2007 we were arrested in Kiunga in Kenya. We were never caught and arrested; we went to report ourselves. We were kept in Kiunga prison for five days and were forced to sleep on the concrete floor without mattresses—this included the children.

We were split into two groups and transported to Malindi and from Malindi to Nairobi. The guards told me that there was not enough space in the plane for Hafsa so for the journey between Kiunga to Malindi she was left behind— they said that they would bring Hafsa with the second group; however it was not until the following day that we were reunited.

After having been taken to Malindi we were taken to the airport for half-an-hour and then taken to Nairobi. I was kept in a prison in Nairobi for twenty-five days with Hafsa. She had lice and became sick—we all had lice. The cell they had placed us in was a mixed cell with men, women and even other children—they did not try and keep us separate to the men.

Since our release Hafsa has developed a cough which she doesn't seem to be able to shake. She has trouble sleeping and gets up at night out of fear. Whenever Africans walk the streets wearing uniforms, she runs to me and hides because she is scared of them. She doesn't want to go to Nairobi at all as she remembers what happened to her there. They had interrogated Hafsa and she remembers that—they even asked her if she knew where her father was as they suspected him of being some kind of terrorist.[19]

In their efforts to capture Al Qaeda militants in Kenya, the ATPU spread across the country in order to detain anyone who might seem suspicious to them. Under pressure to produce results and to gain favour with the US who were running aid trucks into the country, the Kenyan police concentrated on remote, predominantly Muslim regions. On the road north-east from Nairobi, heading towards the Somali border, the town of Garissa became the focus of attention from the ATPU. There an aged Islamic teacher, Shaykh Mahmoud Adam Salat, found himself the victim of allegations that he was recruiting for Al Qaeda:

I am a teacher at Al Faruq Centre which has over 300 orphans and I am the Imam of Masjid Sunnah here in Garissa. I am married but am disabled in one leg due to a childhood accident.

When I was doing my normal work I heard that the police were looking for me here in Garissa. The police found me at my home and told me that they didn't want to arrest me but that they had heard some allegations so they wanted to speak to me. This was on 17 January 2007.

There was apparently a young man who had told the police that he had been fighting alongside the Union of Islamic Courts (UIC) who alleged that fourteen people including him were recruited at the Masjid Sunnah mosque and were given money to go and fight. They asked me to verify that. I told them that this was not true and I had never heard anything like it. They told me that the young man had not given his name, but had given the name of another Imam called Omar. They wanted me to help them find this Imam. I said I did not know anything.

They asked me if I knew Al Qaeda; if they had ever been to my mosque, if they had ever tried to do any recruiting there. I answered everything to the negative. I told them that I am a Kenyan and I have never been outside of Kenya and I do not know what you are talking about.

When I couldn't confirm any of these allegations they told me that they were going to take me to court. When they took me they did not bring any case against me, but instead remanded me in custody to bring me back to the court the following day.

On the following morning, they took me to court, I was told that I and others had recruited young men to fight with the UIC. I refuted that allegation in court through my lawyer who accompanied me. The prosecutor requested the court to remand me as they said they had a serious case—due to allegedly having trained people to fight abroad. Of course even if this was the case—it is not even illegal in this country.

For seven days I was kept in jail while I awaited their further investigations. After the seventh day after the police could not produce any evidence, they had to release me at the bond of 200,000 shillings. After several summons to the court, they have finally said they have nothing on me.

I suffer from gastric problems and during that week I suffered a lot. As I do not have any money, I cannot pursue anything against the government for what they did to me.[20]

Having travelled with Hashem and Abdur Rahman as far as Kismayo, seventeen-year-old Safia Benaouda stopped there to help another refugee go to the hospital. Both women were heavily pregnant and were supporting one another in their escape to Kenya. When the groups of foreigners and refugees made their way to Kenya, Benaouda was accidentally left behind and was not able to find her husband who was forced to travel with another group. Finding herself another group of women to travel with, Benaouda made her way from Dobley towards Kenya, trying to navigate through an extremely thick forest. One of the women contracted malaria and died on her way across and it was three weeks before they were found and arrested:

When we were arrested, we had just prayed Fajr. It was quite early, about 5am, so we lay down again to rest. Suddenly we heard bullets everywhere. I was sitting next to one woman and the rest of the women ran towards us, and we all covering the kids. There were three United States soldiers and about ten Kenyans. The Americans were wearing military uniforms. They were white and their flag was on their shoulder...That was when the Tunisian woman was wounded. One of the soldiers shot her in the back. The American soldiers stayed with us until a helicopter came which was a couple of hours after our arrest. The Americans asked us all questions—our names, age, about our husbands, and our nationality. They were asking us what we were doing there. They showed us some pictures and names and asked if we recognised anyone. One of the women told me that she saw an American soldier take mine and my husband's passports from my belongings.

We had two little American girls with us whose mother had died. We told the American soldiers that Rahma and Sumayyah were Americans but they did not seem to care.

After our arrest, the Kenyans took us by helicopter to a little airport where we were put on a plane. My husband and some other men were also on that plane. I only found that out afterwards as I was blindfolded on that plane ride. When we were taken off the plane, we were taken to a police station in Nairobi. The women were taken to a separate police station from the men. We were in that police station for five days and six nights.

Later on, in the cell in Nairobi, Rahma the four-year-old had a distended tummy. Her eyes were distant. She looked as though she was in another world. She looked at you and just looked through you. Her mum had died, her dad and brother were missing. She was just there with her little sister, Sumayyah, the baby…They were so cold; their noses were running and they were sneezing. We were afraid they would get pneumonia. The baby had a bad nappy rash. She was bleeding with big blisters. They had bad diarrhoea. We were begging the interrogators to give them medical attention. They did not care at all. We felt so horrible…Sumayyah was screaming so much because she was in so much pain.[21]

Swedish national Safia Benaouda was kept in incommunicado detention with the other women until the ATPU decided it was time for them to be taken away. Outside the prison, human rights groups such as the Muslim Human Rights Forum were beginning to place pressure on the government to have these women and children released. As a result of this pressure, those who came from Somalia would be taken out of their prisons, but only for their situation to deteriorate.

Panicked by the influx of foreigners from neighbouring Somalia, the ATPU began to increase its activities and spread its resources further south towards Mombasa and Malindi, thinking that the threat of Al Qaeda may come from the south now as well. Fearing all foreign nationals or those who may have been involved with them, even non-Muslims were arrested and detained on suspicion of terrorism.

Grandmother Millie Mithounie Gako was employed by two Arab businessmen from Oman in order to aid their business affairs in Mombasa. Gako, the two Arab men and their Emirati translator Kamilya Mohammed Tuweni took time to relax in the beach town of Malindi one day before their meetings. After having checked into the Eden Lodge Hotel they went to their rooms to unpack their bags when banging on their doors alerted them to the fact that the ATPU had arrived:

There were about nine people and they said that they were security and wanted to know who was in our room. I told them that it was myself a Kenyan national, and the other was Kamilya from Dubai who is someone that is almost like a sister to me. I told them that we had come for business as we had an appointment in Mombasa and that we were in Malindi for a holiday.

They checked our passports and went through all of our bags—they went through absolutely everything. We did not have a needle, not even a razor blade with us. We had nothing with us except for our clothes and our personal belongings.

They then asked us about Hassan and Ahmed—we told them that they are in the other room. Neither of the two can express themselves in English or in Swahili—which is why we had brought Kamilya—to act as an interpreter. We knocked on their door and Hassan opened. The security went in and they checked everything. They could find nothing—their documents were clean. I know their documents were clean because I put up the money for their visa initially as they did not have US dollars, I gave them $100-they took for Kamilya $50 for 3 months, they took $20 each for transit and gave me the remaining $10. They had booked their return for the 11th and so were only going to be in the country for 3 or 4 days.

Around 7pm they came again and told us that they are going to take us to Nairobi. We said why are you taking us to Nairobi? What offence have we committed? For some reason they then said that they were taking us to Mombasa. We were told to take our luggage and place them in the vans and they also searched us. The whole time there was not a single female officer helping to search us. We came out of the hotel and there was a Land Cruiser waiting for the police officers—in the end there were around 30 police people.

They then took us to Nairobi and we arrived at 3pm in the afternoon where we were taken to the Anti-Terrorism police station run by the Anti-Terrorist Police Unit (ATPU). By this time they had started calling us all sorts of names in order to pretend that they had caught some terrorists. A terrorist I questioned to myself, how could they call me a terrorist? I am a Christian, and a grand-mother, what kind of terrorism would I do? I suspected that because Ahmed and Hassan were Arab, they assumed that they were terrorists, even though I know them to be good people, and because of that consider me one.[22]

What began for Gako as questioning by the ATPU in order to extract a bribe, soon became the nightmare of incommunicado detention as the four colleagues were transported by road from Mombasa to Nairobi:

In Nairobi they began to interrogate us at 7pm-8pm, however this did not last long as they came to take us to Killilayshowa police station. They did not let anyone know that we were there, they would just keep on coming to us with questions. There was even a time when they came to photograph us with only our knickers—they did this to Hassan, Ahmed and the four boys from Akooda. When it came to my turn I told them that there was no way I would stand for being held naked and that I had seen no claim that would result in that end. I told them that I have been all over the world and never had any claim against me—I am not a terrorist at all. There was just no way I was going to stand for them photographing me naked with only my underwear on so they agreed not to photograph me.

Kamilya however was forced to take off her blouse and she was photographed—the surprising thing was that it was a man who was doing the photography. Even with Ahmed and Hassan—they were forced to take their pants off, and you know with Muslim men it is something very bad to be standing there naked like that.

We were kept in that prison for 17 days, but the fortunate thing was that someone there had a mobile which they let me use—I immediately called one of my daughters who got in contact with different human rights groups and Mr Maloy who was the person we had an appointment with. Mr Maloy took the flight to Nairobi—he paid money for our lawyer and said that if that was not enough he would be willing to pay whatever in order to help them. Muage Kigo, our lawyer, went to the court and filed a petition for habeas corpus. On 23 January he served the Police Commissioner and on 24 January he served the Commissioner, the Attorney-General, the Commander in Killilayshowa and everyone else.

Once they had all been served they came on the night of 27 January at 3am. They called me out of the cell and I refused to comply as I was aware of their brutality. Sometimes they can take you and shoot you and then tell people that you were trying to run away. I kept on saying that I was not going and then they came into the cell and said that they had to take me; I just said fine, if you want to kill me you can, just don't harass me anymore as people know where I am and what you have done.

They took me at 3am and dropped me in the middle of Mombasa. Imagine that at 3am, without having anything on me, they dropped me there. I didn't have anything at all. From there I went to the taxi people and told them my name and what had happened to me and they were sympathetic to me so they gave me a phone to call my son who came for me at 3:30am.

At 4am I went back to Killilayshowa after having prepared tea for my colleagues, when I arrived there I found out that they had taken Kamilya. I found out that they had taken her to the border with Tanzania as she spoke Swahili.

That night Kamilya managed to get a call to me saying that they had taken her to the Tanzanian border but the Tanzanians were not taking her as she was not one of their citizens as she is a citizen of Dubai—I have passport photocopies that prove this.

They moved Kamilya again and she was next spotted on the 27th in Agriba police station but by the time I got there they had moved her again.

As for Ahmed and Hassan—they had been taken to the airport and put on a plane to Dubai and around 1pm they called to say they had arrived safely. Although it was good that they were safe, their deportation was contrary to the court order which stated that they should either be charged or released. The Police Commissioner should have appeared at the court and should have questioned why we had not been charged.

There is no law in this country, the police can just arrest you, they have got a lot of power. The deportation of Ahmed and Hassan was not according to the law—these people had passports, they had visas and a return ticket.

Later we found out that they had taken Kamilya to Somalia, and I wondered how they could have done such a thing? They could have taken Kamilya back to her home—but they sent her to Somalia. She is a citizen of Dubai—why take her to Mogadishu? In Somalia there is no government, there is war and there are so many things happening.[23]

After the invasion of Somalia by Ethiopia, a completely new front in the War on Terror opened up, but with that front came the policies and practices of detention that had previously only been seen in Afghanistan and Iraq. With the mantra of the War on Terror and the invocation of the name of Al Qaeda, men, women and the youngest of children were kept in incommunicado detention without any charges being brought against them. Scared of the repercussions of such actions by a strong civil society in Kenya, the authorities found alternative ways to rid themselves of the problems they had created.

Foreign Muslim

The practice of incommunicado detention in Asia and the Middle East has long been known. Immediately after the World Trade Center attacks, Pakistan was declared a hub for international terrorists linked to Al Qaeda. The majority of those detained in Guantánamo Bay have been kidnapped from the streets of Pakistan and sold into US custody.

An Italian citizen of Moroccan ethnicity, Abou Elkassim Britel, travelled with his Italian wife (herself a Muslim-convert) to Pakistan in order to establish a business which involved the translation of Islamic books from Arabic to Italian. They hoped to open the world of Islam to the Italian speakers and felt that this could be achieved cost effectively from Pakistan. Britel's wife, Anna Lucia Pighizzini spoke of her husband's detention in Lahore at the hands of the Pakistanis and all the troubles that befell him as a result:

My husband disappeared on 10 March 2002. I had spoken to him on the phone that day. In the evening, he was stopped in Lahore at a police road block while he was travelling with his luggage on a taxi. As soon as they saw his Italian passport they told him it was false and took him to the police station. Then he disappeared until 11 February 2003.

He was transferred to Islamabad on 5 May 2002, to the Pakistani secret services. He was then taken four times, tied and blindfolded, to a villa where he was interrogated by US agents.

Kassim was never allowed to meet or talk with the Italian Ambassador, which was something my husband kept asking for, since the day he was stopped by the police. He wanted to prove the authenticity of his passport. He kept asking both the Pakistanis and the Americans.

I believe that the Italian Government was aware all along of this situation because in the scripts I have noticed that it was mentioned how Italy had run an investigation about my husband and me. Furthermore, the interrogators knew a lot about our life in Italy.

Kassim was interrogated four times in a villa where the Americans were based. He was taken there blindfolded and under great secrecy. He said he wouldn't talk to the Americans because of the illegal nature of his situation, and also because they wouldn't allow him to meet with the Italian ambassador. On the contrary, they claimed that the ambassador didn't want to meet with him, "because he was a terrorist".

A senior Pakistani secret service agent was present, and threatened to torture him. At that point Kassim said he would have them tried in The Hague, so they offered him money in exchange for information about Osama bin Laden. My husband persisted in asking to speak to the Italian Ambassador. His attitude angered his interrogators, provoking them to swear against the Italian Ambassador, Italy, Europe and more subtle threats towards his family. On the last occasion, the interrogation was performed by a new person, who introduced himself as 'David Morgan'. He said he had just arrived from Washington and wanted to know why Kassim was refusing to talk, to which my husband replied by reiterating that he wanted to speak to the Italian Ambassador. Once again they told him that the Ambassador didn't want to talk to him, so my husband asked them to bring him the phone and let him speak to him directly. They refused to do so because he was, "a prisoner". At this stage, Morgan asked him several questions about his life and filled in a form. He informed him he would meet the Moroccan Ambassador, rather than the Italian one, but that meeting never took place.

After a few days the Pakistanis told him he would be going back to Italy.

I understood from an NGO report that the Americans were paying very well for non-Pakistani prisoners, perhaps, because of this, my husband, like many others, was 'sold'.[24]

Britel's story is one that is familiar all over the Muslim world. Pakistan is not the only country to have taken part in the new wave of detentions across the globe as the US has sought to use its influence to encourage counter-terrorism measures. Britel's presence in Pakistan was considered sufficient to legitimately profile him as a suspected terrorist and despite the multitude of reasons for foreign nationals being in Muslim countries, others were detained with similar justification.

When the invasion of Iraq took place in March 2003, Mobeen Muneef, a British citizen, made his way to Iraq in order to help with the aid effort. Despite his good intentions he was detained by US forces as a suspected terrorist and insurgent and was eventually sent to the notorious Abu Ghraib prison. His arrest and subsequent detention was explained by his brother Amir Muneef:

He was going to Baghdad to help out with humanitarian aid efforts [but it is] not completely clear [how he was detained]. The US Forces have given apparently two different accounts, which in turn differ with Mobeen's account.

[With regard to the allegations that he had small traces of gunpowder on him] Apparently, if a person comes into contact with people who have gunpowder residue on their person, the gunpowder can be transferred onto another person. For example, the soldiers who apprehended him would have been in contact with gunpowder via the weapons they were carrying. Also small arms are very common in that part of the world especially Iraq and it would have been difficult not to come into contact with people or items which had gunpowder on them or were carrying small arms.

He was interrogated [at Abu Ghraib]. We are not exactly sure of the conditions he was kept under. However, from the stories that came out in the media, one can only be worried about those conditions. [He was interrogated] every day, for a period of two weeks. It is not certain how often every day, as he was disoriented. He had been kept in a darkened cell, 1 metre by 2 metres at Balad. He was detained in Balad before being moved to Abu Ghraib.

Camp Bucca is a purpose-built detention facility. It is built to house 2,000 detainees but currently has approximately 5,000. They are housed in a series of wooden huts surrounded by wire fences and watchtowers. There are 300 third-country nationals detained in the facility. Mobeen is the only British national being detained there. He is sharing an accommodation block with around fifty other third-country nationals. He sleeps on plastic mats with underlay and blankets.

No direct contact has taken place. The only contact has been through third party sources. Basically, we have received one letter through the Red Cross and communication that has come through the British consulate. Basically in the part that was not censored, he talks about how he is and conditions in the detention facility.

On the first visit, he was brought in wearing blacked out goggles and handcuffs. These were taken off during the interview but two soldiers and one American in civilian clothes stayed during the meeting with the consular officials. The Foreign Office told us he was alright.

At Balad, he had stomach pains and tightening of the chest. He also passed out a few times. At present, to our knowledge, he is not taking any medication.

It has been put to us that Mobeen is under US jurisdiction and thus Britain has no power to intervene, even though Britain is a major coalition partner. One Briton, although apprehended by the US Forces, was handed over to the British for transfer to England.

In the first instance, [he should] be transferred to the British authorities in Iraq and then transferred to England. If they think he has a case to answer for then they should try him under the British legal system in England. It appears Tony Blair thinks the British legal system is inferior in some way.

It is well known that under any civilised regime that you do not just lock people up but if they are detained that you give them a trial. Under the American constitution this is enshrined in law, as far as I know. This is also currently a cornerstone of British law.[25]

Muneef's case is one of many where involvement by the US and UK has resulted in unlawful detention in third-party countries. The lack of due process and the long period of detention without charge have become endemic in the fight against global terrorism. Countries in the Arab world have a long history of arbitrary detention but have come to use the mantra of the War on Terror in order to excuse long standing policies with comparisons to the actions of the United States and their western allies.

Tunisia has one of the worst human rights records amongst the Arab countries in terms of detention without charge.[26] Many Tunisians fled the country in order to escape religious persecution at the hands of a Tunisian government fond of mock trials and arbitrary detention. One Tunisian well known by his government, Sayfullah Ben Hassine, fled the country in order to escape religious and political persecution for

GUILTY

not agreeing with the government's dictatorial regime. Using the War on Terror as an excuse, the Tunisian government was able to procure his return having stated their claim on him to the Turkish authorities who arrested him. Ben Hassine's wife, Souad Zeroual, explained how her husband was initially arrested and eventually sent back to Tunisia:

The main reason for every Muslim being arrested in the world is terrorism. He was arrested in Turkey first, in February 2003, for about one month in Turkey. He was tortured a lot in Turkey, it took about one month for them to find out his nationality and then they sent him back to Tunisia. When they found out he'd been charged in Tunisia they sent him back in March 2003. When they sent him back to Tunisia, it was a big day in their government because he was the number one wanted person at the time.

[They claimed he was] involved in the international terrorist groups, Al Qaeda and the Taliban. I read on the internet about his case, they said they arrested him because he was the leader of these groups in Afghanistan and Europe. On top of that they mentioned something about the money, saying that he was getting money from drugs.

That's what they do, the Tunisian government, of course it was because he was religious, he was a very practising brother. Even in this country they know he's a good person in his religion, he used to live in London. He came in 1994 and left in 2000, and went to Afghanistan when Taliban was there. He wasn't feeling safe with this government in this country [UK], he wanted to go and live there with me and his children to teach them Quran, Islam and to be safe. But then the Taliban regime changed in 2001, when everybody left Afghanistan. My husband left here because he told me that they'll never give us residence or visa in this country.

He proposed Yemen, Sudan or Afghanistan, three of them they don't ask for visa, they're easy to go there, that's why he chose these three countries, there's more Islam there, practising and they're safe, it's easy life and not expensive, that's why he chose to go there. He chose Afghanistan, he went four months before me, he managed the papers and everything and then we followed him after that. We didn't stay there for more than one year. I stayed there for less than one year. I left Afghanistan before September 11th and I came back to London with the same passport that I went with.

[We don't actually know how long he will be detained for] that's the problem, even his solicitor doesn't know exactly. The solicitor sometimes say 46, sometimes 68, we're not sure how many years.

There is legal recourse there, the solicitors go to the court but they are not allowed to take any paperwork out of the court because it's not a civilian court it's a military court.

He chose the lawyer himself, but in Tunisia this kind of trial you get too many solicitors that want to get involved, maybe 30 or 40 solicitors. But no one can do anything, because the judge himself says it's not him whose giving the charge, it's from the president. The court is not independent. The solicitors said they find no proof that he was a criminal, this was from the president.

[With Sayfallah there has been] no communication at all, he's not allowed to write or receive letters, he's not allowed to see his family more than twenty minutes, most of the time 2/3/4 minutes, as soon as he starts talking about his situation in the prison, he's taken away, straight away. Now he can't see his family directly behind glass, they can't see him directly.

Of course, they said to him that he'll have special treatment from them, he's not allowed to talk to the people outside in the prison, and he's not allowed to pass on his information about his situation in the prison. I think they want to kill him slowly, he's been arrested in 2003, it's been nearly four or five years and his situation is getting worse and worse every day.[27]

Detention such as that of Ben Hassine is commonplace within the Arab world. Incommunicado detention without charge has always been practised, however just as worrying is the abuse of the law in order to secure convictions. The Bush administration sought to bypass the US Constitution by detaining 'enemy combatants' in Guantánamo Bay under military law—this process has however long been practised in the Middle East as Tunisia and other such countries have sought to use the military in order to secure convictions. In a post-9/11 world, the fear of terrorism has given a veneer of legitimacy to such practices while international condemnation has been placed on hold due to the general lowering of standards.

It is an unfortunate consequence that the families of suspects are arrested at the same time. For years, the authorities in the Middle East have made it a policy to detain women and children where they feel information can be gleaned from them. In May 2003, Umm Anas, a Swedish citizen, moved to Syria with her husband and children so that the children could be brought up to learn Arabic. Living in Damascus they were one day subjected to a raid by the police which would have devastating consequences for them in the years to come:

My husband and I were in Syria because we wanted to give our children an Arabic and Islamic upbringing. We had heard that Syria was rather cheap to live in and you could get a resident permit to stay. So we thought we should go there and check—he went there first, I went there after. He got us a house.

[Our house] was in Damascus, and it was an apartment. We went and we stayed there for one-and-a-half-months. [My husband] had some contact with some man on the phone—he went out to see another house, because we wanted to change, and he didn't come home. I was waiting and he didn't come, and then there was a knock on the door. There was a man there asking for…I don't know what he was asking because my son opened first.

I told [my son] Anas to say that my husband was not there and that they should come back after—I didn't know who they were. And they were discussing for one minute, and then they got in and it was like fifteen men coming into the house. I was in the kitchen and asked Anas to get my clothes, and then they came in and said they are police and they asked me to come and they directly asked for my mobile phone and my passport—both our passports—my husband and mine. I had time to phone my husband when I was in the kitchen, when I understood they were police, and I phoned quickly. He answered that phone. He was talking in a different way, and I understood that he had been arrested, because somebody was telling him to speak in Arabic. He just told me to put on my Hijab—that's all he said to me. That was the last time I spoke to him since four years now.

[The next day in the apartment] I said I have to go and find my son—I don't know where he is. And while I was staying in the taxi that the policemen had ordered for us to use, [the policeman] went inside the Mosque to look for Anas. The taxi driver said that you have to be very careful, because the police are very dangerous for you—he wants to put you in jail, he said. He took my name, and after that I heard he had gone to the Swedish embassy, but he had some number incorrect so they didn't understand who I was. But he was very nice. Anyway, I stayed in the apartment for two months. After a few weeks, the embassy came.

[The authorities came to me one day and] said we're going to send you now to Sweden. They just asked me to arrange my things, and they came and they took me to the immigration centre, and they delivered us to another facility in another part of the country. The immigration just took me in, and were talking to me, and we were there for hours—in a very small room, with a lot of men smoking, for several hours. And then I asked them we have to go and eat, we have to go and sleep, we have to go somewhere—you can't leave us here. And then I heard talking on the phone, and they mentioned the name 'Dolna' on the phone. And then they said ok, we will go somewhere where you can wash yourself, sleep and get some food. And they brought us to a prison—I didn't understand it was a prison at first—it looked like a police station. And suddenly they just opened my things—they went through them, and they looked in everything. I was very upset and I said what are you doing? And he said you are in a prison now in Arabic, and my son understood and he started to cry—he didn't understand why we had to go to prison. And then I had to choose what kind of things I wanted to take with me into the prison…and we went in there.

It was a big open space with small rooms around, like cells. [My children and I] we went in there—they locked [us up] and said you are going to this place. And in this cell—it was a big cell—there were many women—I think maybe twenty women in this big one. And there were many cells, I think…

...they didn't tell me [why they were holding me]. They said before that...they told me that they had to wait for the next plane or something like that. Before we left the apartment, I said but we have to check my ticket first—that there is a flight before I go. But they just gave me to the other authorities, so they have to put me somewhere whilst waiting for the aeroplane. That's how I understood it, but I was not sure about that—I was hoping it was like the reason for them to put me in jail—just to wait for the aeroplane. I didn't know...I felt completely cut off from every way of communicating with the outside world. But a few days after, they called my name. They said I was going to fly, but I went to another prison actually, and stayed for one night more.

I don't remember outside—it was a big house, like a multiple floor building, and we went down in the basement. There was an office and a big corridor with many cells. And they were very dirty—their toilet was very terrible, and there were no beds, so we had to sleep on the floor on blankets. There were four beds, but they were already occupied, so there were maybe five women sleeping on the floor...my children. And they left the light on, so there was a very strong light all night. But in the morning they came and got me back to the immigration centre, and I met the embassy people.

The day when I went from the first prison to the immigration centre, I met them for the first time after the week in the prison there. And I said to them that I don't want to go to another prison and can't you put me in a hotel and put a guard outside, but of course that's not possible. They put me there, and we went back to the immigration centre after that night, and they brought me to the airport. And when I was at the gate (just waiting to board) they gave me back my passport.

[When I returned] there was one Danish and one Swedish police officer waiting for me. They didn't say that at first—there was a uniformed officer waiting by the gate, and he told me to come because they wanted to check my passport. And then we went through the whole airport, and then two policemen—one woman, one man—came into the room, and said that we heard you were here and we want to discuss some things with you- they said they just "happened" to be there.

They were asking those kinds of questions about the World Trade Centre—they wanted to know about my opinion. And they wanted to know about my husband of course, they asked about him, if I had been to Sweden—these things. And then I got so tired—they didn't want to let me go, so I said could you please just let me go and come and talk to me another time. So they said ok, then they let me go out.[28]

3

THE RULE OF LAW

"We have waged a deliberate campaign of arrest and detention to remove sus-pected terrorists who violate the law from our streets. Currently, we have brought criminal charges against 110 individuals, of whom 60 are in federal custody. The INS has detained 563 individuals on immigration violations... Since September 11, the Customs Service and Border Patrol have been at their highest state of alert...My message to America this morning, then, is this: if you fit this definition of a terrorist, fear the United States, for you will lose your liberty...We have engaged in a deliberate campaign of arrest and deten-tion of lawbreakers. All persons being detained have the right to contact their lawyers and their families. Out of respect for their privacy, and concern for saving lives, we will not publicize the names of those detained."[1]

John Ashcroft—US Attorney General

The international community has long agreed on the guiding principles regarding the detention of suspects; these principles have been enshrined in articles 9 and 10 of the Universal Declaration of Human Rights (UDHR):

"No one shall be subjected to arbitrary arrest, detention or exile."[2]

"Everyone is entitled in full equality to a fair and public hearing by an inde-pendent and impartial tribunal, in the determination of his rights and obliga-tions and of any criminal charge against him."[3]

States have implemented these provisions in a variety of different legislative ways—however, the meaning of the above text always remains the same in a bid to ensure that all suspects receive a fair trial. The International Covenant on Civil and Political Rights, the Euro-pean Convention on Human Rights (ECHR) and the United Kingdom

Human Rights Act 1998 all incorporate these provisions in their respective documents.

The debates surrounding national security have become a prime influence over the way in which legislative and judicial authorities administer justice to suspected terrorists. Policies have been put into place that go well beyond recognised systems of justice, with the stated aim of promoting social cohesion and the protection of life.

Western democracies have long attempted to protect due process and the right to a fair trial without succumbing to the excesses of national security arguments. Despite this, Spain, with its history of conflict and terrorism, has for a long time implemented policies which go against widely accepted definitions of a fair trial.[4] In their attempt to tackle ETA, the Spanish already had in place counter-terrorism legislation which was later employed to deal with suspected Muslim terrorists. Similarly Britain has its own history with the Irish 'Troubles', which saw the introduction of reactionary legislation. Echoing policies of detention implemented during its colonial history and in mainland Britain during the 1980s, the British government has again brought in a raft of legislation which seeks to place national security before the right to a fair trial.[5] These legal measures differ very little from the illegal practices of the developing world.

After the bombings of 7 July 2005 the United Kingdom entered the War on Terror in a way that was previously unimagined. But even before these bombings, the British government had chosen to join the US-led 'war' through counter-terrorism legislation enacted prior even to the World Trade Centre bombings.

Although indefinite detention without charge was eventually quashed by the House of Lords after a number of legal challenges, the policy remained by other means. The British government introduced the longest period of pre-charge detention of all the western democracies. Initially the period of detention allowed to the police was seven days but this was quickly increased to fourteen. What then took place was the most significant rebellion against the Blair government, by members of his own party, as it attempted to introduce ninety-day pre-charge detention.[6] After much political wrangling, the government narrowly persuaded Parliament to pass twenty-eight day detention without charge. As part of the Terrorism Bill 2008, the Brown government attempted to increase this to forty-two days, but this was eventually abandoned due to lack of support.

At the height of the IRA campaign in Britain—which included mortar bomb strikes on Downing Street on 7 February 1991, rockets being shot into the MI5 building and a series of bombings spanning three decades—pre-trial detention never exceeded seven days. As late as 19 July 2001, when the MI6 building was attacked by a rocket launcher, those suspected of the attack were the IRA, yet there was no call to hold suspected terrorists for longer periods.[7] This increase has only been requested in the climate of fear of the post-9/11 world when the public has been more willing to suspend its civil liberties in the name of security.[8]

To counter the danger of being unable to detain terrorism suspects in prison without stringent judicial scrutiny, the British government brought in control orders—a system of confining an individual to his or her home for periods of the day and taking away nearly all forms of communication. In order to circumvent the need to charge the suspected terrorists, the home secretary has been given powers to issue control orders with immediate effect. A detainee can only challenge such an order through a very long process which allows the government to use secret evidence. The entire system has been established to take judicial scrutiny away from the courts and place strong counter-terrorism measures in the hands of the executive.

The British government has sought to bypass due process simply by using arguments surrounding security. Such fear-driven policies have had the negative impact of driving further wedges between government and the community it inevitably targets.[9] Britain is not alone though in its use of detention without charge and secret evidence. Canada has also used its legal system to detain individuals without the requirement of charging them.

Canadian security certificates have been in operation in Canada since before 9/11, however the early forms had a reasonable level of judicial scrutiny. These security certificates only apply to foreign nationals and allow the Canadian authorities to detain an individual without charge while refusing them access to evidence being produced against them if that evidence is in the interests of national security.[10] The system of security certificates in Canada is almost identical to Britain's system of control orders and deportations for suspected terrorists. The level of duplication suggests a strong complicity between the two governments in the way in which they are choosing to remove due process from those detained.

The US government has made it one of its primary concerns to establish the 'rule of law' around the world by exporting democracy—however the two are not necessarily synonymous. While the US claims to export democracy and uphold the 'rule of law', it is simultaneously dismantling its own system of checks and balances, and undermining the very principles it purports to wish to export.

Detention policies have become extremely problematic for the Muslim community in the US; they feel that the laws have been made in order to secure convictions. Of particular note within the arsenal of counter-terrorism legislation that the US has employed, is the Uniting and Strengthening America by Providing Appropriate Tools Required to Intercept and Obstruct Terrorism Act, otherwise known as the PATRIOT Act. With revenge being called for in the aftermath of 9/11, legal changes perverted the very foundations of the American Constitution.

Criticisms of the PATRIOT Act have centred on a few key points which are crucial to the concept of the rule of law within the US. Foremost, the act allows the security services in the US an enormous amount of power without any true accountability. Furthermore, the provisions deny the right of US citizens to freedom of speech, movement and even thought.[11] In terms of actual detention policies, the Act reduces the evidentiary standard required in order to detain an individual where there is a 'probable' level of justification for the arrest being made. In the current circumstances, when many Muslims are critical of government foreign policy, this lower evidentiary standard could even be applied to political dissent. The lower legal standard and vague definitions relating to terrorism result in a situation where many individuals are vulnerable to grievous miscarriages of justice.

The rule of law is a concept that has not been defined by any particular formulation, and yet it finds currency amongst international statesmen who wish to make public declarations about its importance to the world as a whole. Legal philosophers of the past have described the rule of law in the same terms as those that relate to due process, fair trials and transparency in the administration of justice. The US, UK, Spain and Canada are just some of the countries that have established systems which go well beyond such terms. The testimonies of those affected reveal how seemingly legal mechanisms are in fact covers for processes which are, by their very nature, unethical.

Detention without charge

The domestic legislation of western democracies has attacked the principle of the presumption of innocence in a number of ways. The terrorist threat has produced a climate of fear which in turn has enabled legislation that removes the requirement of charging suspects with alleged crimes. This lowering standard of due process has caused a ripple effect around the world, with countries using various detention policies in order to put into place counter-terrorism measures.

Although the phenomenon has taken on a form that is unprecedented in the western world, the policies of detention without charge have existed in various permutations in the past. Previously Britain implemented internment policies that lead to the mass arrest and detention of Irish Republicans without any charges being laid against them. Similarly, the Spanish have long used these policies in order to deal with the threat of Basque separatists and ETA. With the alleged ongoing threat of ETA to Spain, the Spanish authorities have made little changes to a system of anti-terrorism legislation that already reduces the opportunity for a fair trial.

After the Madrid bombings in March 2003, Muslim detainees became a serious target as the intelligence services attempted to root out the cause of the train disaster. Although initially ETA was blamed for the attacks, the accusations quickly turned to Al Qaeda and as a result the Muslim community of Spain came under heavy scrutiny.

On 10 January 2006, the Spanish Civil Guard made sweeping arrests in the Spanish town of Vilanova i la Geltru. The arrests consisted of North African Muslims who were part of the same community and attended the same mosque. Amongst those arrested was Mohammed Mrabet Fahsi, a British resident of Moroccan origin. Fahsi was well known in the community and was the president of the cultural association that ran the local mosque. On the day of the arrest, it was the Muslim festival of *Eid al-Adha* and before he was able to perform the prayers and other community work, he was detained along with other men. Eid was effectively cancelled for the entire community. His wife Khadija Podd was in London at the time of his arrest and described his incarceration:

In Spain when you are arrested for alleged terrorist activities you are held in what is known as incommunicado detention. In our case that meant they were blindfolded and had their ears blocked. They were taken from Barcelona to the headquarters of the Civil Guard but they were not held in the normal building, they were held in what was literally an underground cellar at the back of the building. They were each in a very small cell. They each thought initially that they had been the only ones arrested. They didn't realise that others had been arrested until they heard the shouting and screams caused by the torture. They each realised however that the others had been arrested. As they were blindfolded the entire time, they did not see where they were or who their captors were. They were not allowed to sleep or sit down during the days they were kept in these conditions, they had to spend most of their time standing up and facing the walls with their arms raised above them. They were also told to do press ups and when they could not continue to do so, they were beaten. They were beaten anyway, forced to renounce their religion, forced to insult the Prophet, forced to insult Allah, they were drugged with hallucinogenic drugs, they were not allowed to wash themselves at all and they didn't see or hear anyone else except when they heard the screams of torture.

One of the other things that they used was fear, they threatened to rape their wives, rape their children. In my case, they told Mohammed that the children and I would be deported to Morocco along with his parents, we would be kidnapped and held somewhere in the Sahara where no one would know where we were.

...Spain is a country that has in its legal system incommunicado detention and the possibility of being held without charge for up to four years and then to have all the evidence kept in secret for a long time. All this means that no defence can be seriously mounted to the detention. I don't see what the great difference is between Spain and Guantánamo Bay.

He was taken to the High Court in Madrid where they were placed in front of an investigative judge who would be different to the trial judge who is hearing the case now. What is really quite shameful is that these men were led in front of a judge in this condition, as I understand they could hardly walk let alone anything else, and yet he was content to accept them in this condition. They were still in a state of incommunicado detention, so even though a lawyer was brought to them, they were not allowed to communicate with him—the client makes a statement without having been advised by a lawyer at all, and of course this leads to self-incrimination.

After the self-incrimination, the incommunicado detention is lifted and at that point the client can speak to the lawyer. After that they were taken to some holding cells and prisons in Madrid which are used before the detainee is moved to his place of stay.

When the incommunicado detention was lifted he was able to communicate with his lawyer and myself however for the first year he was held in an isolation regime so the communication was extremely restricted. He was moved to a prison in Leon after a month which is where he still is—this made communication with his lawyer very very difficult as it is in the north west of Spain. His lawyer was not allowed to call him and he was allowed to call out for five minutes five times a week—so if he missed his lawyer during his slot, then he would lose that opportunity to speak to him. As the lawyer was a state appointed lawyer working for a pittance, he could not visit Mohammed as it was a plane journey away. So communication was allowed, but on a restricted level to the extent that it was almost non-existent.

In Spain they have a system of accusations which I guess are tantamount to informal charges—that is the best way of describing it. The prisoner can either be released while these charges are investigated or be held on remand which is what happened to my husband.

The informal charge is that he belonged to or collaborated with a known terrorist organisation which in this case was allegedly the Moroccan Combatants Islamic Group.

Until the secret summary was lifted in September last year it was very difficult to know the charges, which is why I continued with the State appointed lawyer, for all he could do was to every now and then mount an appeal against Mohammed's detention. Now things have changed—they have released the information from the investigative judge Balthazar Garzon which is his opinion and also a kind of summary of all the documents, police reports and evidence into one. There were lots and lots of arrests that night in Spain from all over the country and they bundled them all them together so it was the opinion of Garzon that all 22 should be processed at the same time.

What normally happens is that the Minister responsible for prosecutions would then press charges and it gives what it believes should be the sentence. Our case has differed in the sense that they still have not pressed charges and Garzon has last month issued a declaration that he wants more evidence, so he has actually asked for more evidence, that is how we stand at the moment. No charges have been formalised and they are still asking for evidence.[12]

Legal mechanisms for detention without charge and incommunicado detention have become institutionalised in Spain and, as a result, for those Muslims who are now the subject of scrutiny, these systems are already in place. Fahsi's situation is all the more problematic due to his lack of status in Spain. As has been seen with the PENTTBOM detainees in the US, most often foreign nationals are detained quickly due to their lack of rights and the ability of governments to be able to hold them over immigration offences.

As explored in the first chapter, the United Kingdom also consciously targeted foreign nationals as part of its counter-terrorism policies. With indefinite detention without charge having been enacted by the Anti-Terrorism, Crime and Security Act 2001, foreign nationals were particularly targeted as they could be held in a state of 'internment' by the government without the requirement for any charges or evidence. By late 2001, the government had begun to arrest people based on the weakest of evidence. One of the first men to be detained under the ATCSA 2001 was an Algerian asylum seeker, Detainee G, who cannot be named for legal reasons:

When I came...why we chose the UK...we saw that there was a nice picture-we heard it's a country of law, there are many people who fled their country and came to the UK. We have that nice picture, because everybody was talking about UK—that they respect human rights, they respect their law, you can ask for asylum there, and no-one can touch you, no-one can do nothing wrong to you. That's why I chose to come to Britain—this was in August 1995.

When I remember the story of how they arrest us—it's humiliation. It gave me the opposite picture—of what I was thinking of Britain. Because when they came- I remember, at 5 or 6 o'clock in the morning...the only thing they told me, they give me a piece of paper signed by the Home Office (Blunkett at that time), saying that you are under suspicion of being a terrorist and we have to arrest you. And I didn't know what was in the paper—I asked them can they tell what the purpose of arresting me is, or where they want to take me. They said it's a secret- we can't tell you anything. I told them Ok, can you give me a chance to call my solicitor- they told me no—I had no right to talk to my solicitor, no right to talk to my wife—the only thing I could do was take some clothes and other short-term things like that. They searched me and they took me straight away. They didn't even let me talk to my wife, and at that time I didn't know where I was going completely—to the police station, to prison, to Algeria—nothing at all. So they put me in the police van and took me away. This is the story.

...straight away they took us to the prison—it was Belmarsh—the secure unit inside Belmarsh. Belmarsh is a prison, and there is a prison inside the prison which is called the secure unit. So we were detained in that place. The problem is there was no charge. At the time they arrested us, we didn't know about this law, but afterwards- after a few months—we started to know—it is legislation, passed quickly by the House of Parliament because of 11 September—they passed it quickly in March. And this legislation is to do with foreigners—if you are a foreigner they can arrest and detain you indefinitely. Yes, so if you are suspicious, they can detain you indefinitely—no trial, no charge, you cannot see the evidence against you, your solicitor cannot see the...It's completely, you know, you just die...

[The entire time we were detained they did not question us once, for three-and-a-half years they did not question us] Even for me it was very shocking, very surprising—for me, for my family—for the community even. All the community, because I live in East London, and most of the people who live in East London are Muslims (Alhamdulilaah). When they heard that I was arrested, and they heard that there was such a law, they were all shocked—they were all worrying about themselves, about their children... So this legislation divides the community, and it shows the people that it's to do with Muslims. It's just to do with Muslims, because all the people that were arrested are Muslims.[13]

Detention without charge has deep psychological effects for those who are put through it. Many of those detained suffer terribly from not knowing the reason for their detention or the possible outcome. Detainee G suffered severe physiological and psychological problems during his detention:

At that time, because I suffer from polio, I developed mental and physical problems; I lost weight—when they arrested me I was 60kg—during prison I was 40kg. I had no appetite to eat, my mental problems got worse, and they were obliged to take me to have healthcare. They took me to healthcare and I spent nearly one year there.

In Belmarsh—it's not really healthcare—I call it "Hell care", because they put you in a cell for 24 hours…Yes there are many nurses and doctors there, but there are no kinds of activities or education or social association—they just put you in "Hell care", lock you up in a cell for 24 hours. It was for me worse in the "Hell care" than in the blocks. So I stayed there because of my mental and physical problems. My solicitor Ms Gareth Peirce put a bail application, and the judge granted me (his name was Mr Conan) bail, and then it was rejected by the Home Office. My family was happy that I was going to be released that day—I don't remember the month, but it was in 2004. So they appealed the decision of the judge and they went to the High Court. They stayed another three months, and the High Court Judge returned the Home Office to the SIAC (Special Immigration Appeals Commission) again—they told them that this case shouldn't be heard here—it should be heard in the SIAC. So I have the feeling that they are just playing games and gaining time. So after four or five months, the case returned again to the SIAC, and the same judge granted me bail.[14]

Along with Detainee G, many other foreign nationals were detained and have been held in various forms of detention without charge over the last seven years. They include Jordanians, Tunisians, Algerians, Moroccans and Kenyans but none have been so deeply affected as Mahmoud Abu Rideh. A veteran of Israeli jails, he was tortured by the Israelis for many months before his release and subsequent escape to Britain to claim asylum:

After 9/11 about 5am in the morning, I find some people in my house, coming, MI5, Scotland Yard, Immigration, too many people, police…they broke the door. And they just take me straight from my house to Belmarsh, single cell… no court, no lawyer, they didn't take my fingerprints still till now, they didn't take my DNA. Nothing, still till now. They take me at 5am in single cell to

Belmarsh High Security, and Belmarsh, it's a unit... no, I didn't go to the police station. This is the law, Anti-Terrorism Act 2001, you don't have charge, no trial, and you stay indefinitely in prison.

And my family didn't know where is me for maybe two months. My wife, she lived in New Malden, she phoned Kingston Police Station. They said I don't know where's this man. I don't know him. She tried phoning too many... Scotland Yard... too many...

This time you go Belmarsh, and you go in the prison, and you have in Belmarsh, a unit, a prison within a prison, Cat AA.

These people were racist, and you have racists and discrimination against Muslims. Terrorist everywhere, he thinks I am a terrorist, the officer. He just treats Muslims like this, and he's happy. These people are very bad people... And it's very, very bad, you work here, all the people who work in Belmarsh, he been in army. I see too many in the ward there. He been in army, twenty years, fifteen years, in Middle East and different places, Africa, everywhere—he been in the army. After he finish with the army, he come and work in Belmarsh. Like I see in Abu Ghraib, and Guantánamo, too many prisons, secret prisons in the world everywhere, I see the same. They treat you the same.[15]

Abu Rideh's physiological and psychological condition deteriorated rapidly during his detention in Belmarsh—to such an extent that he was moved to Broadmoor Hospital as a result of his going on hunger strike:

...it was not my decision. At this time, I go hunger strike, I did not eat anything for four months. I lose... Why? For detention without charge, for racism, for discrimination in Belmarsh, too many reasons, why I go hunger strike.

The officer told me many times. He told me I'll kill you one day, you go back your country, and this is the officer he told me this, and too many problems. Like, one day, I filled the form for my family to visit me and asked me the officer for your children's names. I put my Khalid, my son, Imad, Alaa, my daughter's name, Hani, Israa. Why don't you put Bin Laden with you? Don't ask me this, I don't know Bin Laden, I don't know where is Bin Laden. He said, just put Bin Laden.

No, the room is open. The room is open; he can easily come in my room. And he attacked too many, not just me, he attacked too many people, every day. These people, the European Human Rights Commissioner, he see this, he crying. He told to me, I find all of your complaints are true. I see in my face evidence. And this day he moved me to another ward, quiet, more quiet, but still the problems the same.

I stayed there three years. And very bad; maybe you have more association, more exercise, more something, but you stay with very bad people, very, very dangerous people.[16]

Abu Rideh has consistently disproved any accusations that have been levelled against him. As with the other foreign nationals who were detained indefinitely without charge, he has overcome various legal hurdles in order to fight his detention, and every single time the government's case has fallen. Unfortunately for Abu Rideh and the others, the government has just as consistently put together new measures in order to detain these men. Having been told by the House of Lords that the authorities cannot detain foreigners without charge, the government put together the Special Immigration Appeals Commissions and gave power to the home secretary to make orders for deportation for anyone considered a threat to national security. In the chapter Foreign Exchange, the effect of these deportation orders will be examined in more detail.

Control orders

As discussed earlier in the chapter, one of the new strategies implemented by the British government after its failure to legalise indefinite detention without charge was the use of control orders. A control order is essentially a formal order made by the home secretary to curtail an individual's liberty for the stated purpose of "protecting members of the public from a risk of terrorism". The order can be made whether the alleged terrorist activity is domestic or international, and is generally termed a non-derogating control order. In practice, this means an individual, whether a UK national or non-UK national, can be subjected to house arrest without any charges having been brought against them.

Control orders were legislated in Britain by the Prevention of Terrorism Act 2005. The urgency of the proposal was due to the House of Lord, ruling against the legality of the detention powers previously in place, under Part IV of the Anti-terrorism Crime and Security Act 2001.[17] As an immediate result, ten detainees whose release from HMP Belmarsh had been mandated by the ruling were immediately held under control orders on their release. It was the incidents of 7 July 2005 that led to the re-arrest of many of these men under immigration measures, until they were once again released under stringent control orders in 2008. One of those not re-arrested was Mouloud Sihali. He explains how the new measures became applicable to them once they were acquitted of any crimes in a jury trial:

After the 7th July bombings—the famous speech of Tony Blair declared that "the rules of the game have changed"—it is like the whole thing for him is a game for which he can change the rules as he pleases. I found this very funny, for a man to play with the lives of others as if it were a game, it is a very funny statement from such a big politician—a game!

When the rules of the game changed, they picked up the first batch of people who were all Algerians—they were on control orders. They were picked up on 15 August 2005 and this was issued by [then home secretary] Charles Clarke back then.

The control orders lowered the evidentiary standard required to keep them in detention. Some of the foreign nationals who were kept in indefinite detention without charge, and those who were accused of the ricin plot, were rearrested using these measures. Detainee W, an Algerian who was held as part of the ricin plot, was kept under such circumstances:

I was released in 2005 when I was free for a few months when in September 2005 the immigration police rearrested me for immigration offences. Maybe 25/30 policemen came to arrest me at 5am when I was leaving for morning prayers. They said they were taking me for immigration offences to Belmarsh prison for one day when I was taken to Long Lartin prison. I was in Long Lartin for four months at which point I was given bail.

They give me a small area with three hours freedom during which time I have to sign in at the police station every day. All it takes is for a police officer to sign me off quickly to say that I have been—but often they will keep me waiting for almost an hour just to make life difficult. I am not allowed to use the telephone or internet or fax machine—it is extremely limited.

[With regard to the new allegations] They go back to the ricin! They are still using it. They say that in the flat with the ricin there were blank papers that had his finger prints on it as well as a bottle of acetone. If my fingerprints were indeed there on that paper, then it was from the mosque as the paper had come from the mosque and acetone is used for the printer. They said I must have been in the flat and yet I did not even know this flat existed. They did nothing to prove I was in the flat—they did not even bother to use DNA evidence to try and place me there! The other thing they say against me is that Bourgass (the man convicted of being a public nuisance) had a bus ticket that had my phone number on it—I have never spoken to Bourgass on the phone and he has never called me. The police have done nothing to find out who could have written that number.

[After I was placed on the bail order I was affected terribly by the conditions placed on me.] I am not too bad now—but before I couldn't even walk properly. I used to shuffle around murmuring to myself and looking behind me all the time, I was in a really terrible place.

I am only allowed three hours where it is insisted that I sign on between 1-2pm. They have literally taken 55 minutes before for me to be signed off. If

I go and ask sometimes they are nice but most of the time they ignore me and tell me to wait. It takes all of ten seconds to sign. There is always pressure whether I will be late to get to the police station or whether I will make it back home in time due to my tag. I have to press a black box when I leave and return. People cannot visit me unless they are cleared—it took eight months for that to happen. When I have a medical appointment, in order to be cleared I have to tell the authorities which road I am going to walk down, how long I will be in that road, which road I am going to turn into, how long I will be in that road and so on. It is horrible what they are doing.

I love nature, animals, birds and so on. I would love to be working because my greatest concern is that of my mother who is alone since my father died. It is ludicrous to say that I am a national security threat—what is there to stop me from meeting someone bad within the space of the three hours I have free? Nothing at all—so they cannot really be serious that I am a threat because they know that I am not.[18]

Control order restrictions can be placed on travel, association and employment as well as allowing for unlimited police access to the detainee's life. The detainee can have their passport confiscated, specific twenty-four hour bans placed on their movement, curfews enforced both locally and internationally and requirements for them to be at a specific place at particular times of the day. Those detained and their families living with them cannot have access to visitors unless first vetted by the Home Office; this usually includes anyone over the age of ten. The restrictions to association are further enforced by banning access to the internet, phones and other communication devices.[19] It is with these detainees that the police have their most unfettered access, they are allowed to search the home of a detainee an unlimited number of times and have unlimited rights to remove property for testing.

Any breach of control order obligations can be punished by up to five years in prison, and/or an unlimited fine. This means that any suspect frustrated at being subject to such interference, despite having not been charged with any offence, and who intentionally or unintentionally breaches the conditions of their control order, will face criminal charges.

Those being held under control or bail orders have now risen close to fifty. The facts and figures however completely hide the true human cost of this policy. Although most that have been detained are foreign nationals, a few British citizens have also had control orders placed on them—and of those, six have fled due to the pressure of such a regime. Cerie Bullivant is one of the detainees who chose to abscond from his control order.

Bullivant was on his way to Syria when he was detained at the airport by the British authorities before being able to board his flight. The friends he was travelling with were placed under control orders immediately, however it was some time before he was placed under a similar order. His original trip to Syria was to study Arabic and to take part in aid work for orphans in the country. At that time, the British security services told him it was best that he did not go due to their fear that he would be detained by the Syrians on his arrival in their country.

Still eager to travel to the Muslim world in order to take part in aid activity, Bullivant made a plan with friends to go to Bangladesh thinking that it was far from anywhere to do with terrorism or the War on Terror. On his arrival at the airport he was detained again by the security services who told him that they felt he was going to Bangladesh in order to make his way across to Waziristan to fight with rebel forces in Pakistan. On returning home again for the second time, Bullivant was placed under a control order:

Control orders—I guess the reason that they are such a good tool for the government is that when you see the restrictions on paper, it doesn't sound like much at all, but the way they use the powers it gives them it means that they take away every single part of your life one piece at a time. For example, it is just my mum and I—I couldn't tell her about the order but when she did find out, the police would often search the house from top to bottom; at times the police would tell her blatant untruths about me about so-called evidence they had. One time they raided my house alleging that I had been trying to acquire false documentation, they said they found my pictures at a passport forging factory that they had broken down. Praise be to God my solicitors forced them to accept that I had never tried to obtain false documentation and that I had never had any involvement or plans to do that. They were lying to her in order to drive a wedge between us in the hope she may give up some information.

To be honest, I couldn't see any future here with the control orders and with the life I was being forced to live under the control orders. In the case in the Old Bailey, one of the liaison officers said that he felt that it would have been good for me to get out and go and get a job doing something else as the control order completely dominated my life. The irony is that I could not get a job without Home Office permission and I would have to find an employer who would not mind the Home Office calling him and asking if he knew I was a terrorist. With the security vetting it made it altogether impossible to get work. Even the police officers recognised that this was my life and that it controlled and dominated everything and it was those pressures and that stress that led me to leave; in that contextual moment when a door opened up and there seemed to be an opportunity to escape, I took it. It was not the best decision of my life, but it was a decision taken in the moment and it has to be considered within the context that it was taken.

About five weeks after I absconded I decided to return. Basically I had an anonymity order so we were not expecting a big press reaction to our disappearance. The government however lifted the anonymity order without consulting our solicitors or giving them any chance to argue our case and within a day we were the most wanted men in Britain. We were the lead item on both the 6 and 10 o'clock news and on the front page of every national newspaper. I could see on the news that the press were camped outside my mum's front door step and to be honest, two things occurred to me; I was very concerned with my mum's health and how she would be coping without me and also I realised that by absconding I was not solving the problem, only running away from it—it was a false euphoria, a false dawn. I came to the decision that I had to come back.

By now the precedent had already been set. The police had given up being nice a long time ago, especially SO15—they were just rude with me all the time, couple of them were ok. When I came back it was exactly what I expected—long sessions of interviews. Praise be to God that my solicitor helped me prepare a statement after which time I was sent to prison. Initially I was sent to Wandsworth after which time I was sent to Belmarsh.

I had my trial. Not based on whether or not I was a terrorist. The trial was for absconding. The jury were asked to assess whether my absconding had been legitimate with a reasonable excuse or a criminal one. They were told that they had to accept that I was a terrorist because the control order itself was not in question or allowed to be questioned. They had to accept that the control order was meant to be there and that it was correct for being there. I was going into a court room already branded a terrorist and not being allowed to defend that accusation. It is from God that we won an impossible case. I had previously spoken to my solicitor and asked him what our chances were, and he said that it was one of those impossible cases that we might just win. By the will of Allah we won.

I was up for seven counts including not living at the address I was supposed to be living. During that time I had been living with my mum because she was ill, so it was a criminal charge in front of the court that I had been taking care of my mother. Praise be to God I was found not guilty of all the charges.[20]

Other countries have also implemented this tool in their domestic detentions, as with the former Guantánamo detainee David Hicks in Australia. In Canada, Sophie Lamarche, the wife of Mohammed Harakat, has been campaigning for the release of her husband since December 2002. As with Britain's detention of foreign nationals, Harakat was detained along with other foreigners who did not have complete refugee status. After years of trying to get her husband released from the security certificate he has now been given bail under a control order with harsh conditions—including the wearing of an electronic tag—which affect the whole family. Lamarche explained how life is with Mohammed since his return home:

...first he wears the GPS [global positioning system] around his ankle with a monitor that is on the fridge, but when he is out he has it on his belt, 24-hour supervision, that is either [by] myself, my mother or a member of our community, which is a senior Anglican preacher who is with him right now, so if he steps out, I step out, and if he steps in, I step in. The boundary is the house, and the yard, he had a curfew on our property which was 8am to 11pm. We used to have a 9pm curfew, we used to barbecue and have to bring everything back inside, we couldn't enjoy barbecues at all, and when doing a barbecue, say if I forgot the salt, step in step in, step out step out, he is never unsupervised, not one minute. There are two surveillance cameras in the house, one at the front and one at the back, mail is monitored and opened by the CBSA, there is a little sticker, the phone is tapped, he can only use the mainline from home, he can't call from anywhere else, no payphones, no cell phones, there's no cell phone in the house, no blackberry, no portable computer, nothing with an internet chipping, including our superstation, we had to get rid of our superstation. My computer at home is under lock, every person who enters our residence has to be approved at least 48 hours in advance, and they have to have a criminal background check, including my niece, my 75 year old grandmother, every single person entering my house has to have a criminal background check, many of them got denied, because of their involvement in activism, because they had been charged with some stupid things, but even though they haven't been charged, they are on the list, and some people get shocked when they find out those results, they have no charge, but when they come down, they get denied.

Our outings are all prepared 48 hours in advance, so if you run out of milk. You have to prepare for you next outing, every place your going to outside has to be pre approved, so if you feel like going for a coffee at this location, and you put it down and it's too hot, you can't go. We have boundaries within the city, my sister was living just off the edge of our boundary, she bought a house just on the other side of the street, in a new area, we had to go down to court to fight to add that new boundary, so that my husband would be able to help with the move, because we all helped my sister move, just literally on the other side of the street we had to go to federal court, and it took us about a month to be able to go to my sister's. Other than the cameras, like I said he is never left alone, there is no spontaneity in our lives, because everything is approved in advance, so because of his curfew and limitations, he can't go near the airport, bus station, train station, car rental company, he can't have any weapons, including a nail gun, including a water gun, officers follow us on outings, immigration officers in Canada now own guns, so we get followed around with bullet proof vests, guns, and the car runs for 4 hours, there is a 3 minute deadline for the initiating of the car, people complain about the number of cars there, people call the cops on our officers because they leave the car on for 4 hours non-stop in front of the house watching us in front of the house, if we were to stop at someone's house which is pre-approved, pre-location, pre-everything, they're there waiting in the car. I mean we went to the mosque last week, they sent 5 officers with guns, and their car looks like a cop car, because there is a siren in the back, so the community has noticed a change, so no privacy whatsoever, they can enter the residence whenever they want, my computer is under lock, he has no access directly or indirectly.[21]

The United States of America

On 6 May 2004, Brandon Mayfield was arrested by the FBI under the PATRIOT Act for allegedly being involved in the Madrid train bombings. The FBI had misread his fingerprints. His defence team persuaded the judge in his trial to state that key pillars of the act are unconstitutional, particularly the use of secret searches and bugging in order to gather criminal evidence. The case also proved that the US government was making use of the so-called 'Foreign Intelligence Surveillance Court' to bypass the constitution. The court existed and operated beyond the knowledge of the general public and made decisions secretly.[22]

The US administration's attack on human rights and civil liberties has been conducted through various means. The PATRIOT Act is one such mechanism. By introducing the term 'enemy combatant' the US opened a Pandora's Box of legal incredulity that has manifested itself in many different ways.[23] The treatment of detainees at Guantánamo Bay is one example of the result of the legal innovation 'enemy combatant', something that will be discussed in a later chapter. However, those US citizens detained as 'enemy combatants' were treated differently from their foreign counterparts—they were taken to US soil and not put through the process of Guantánamo. Only four US citizens were given the designation of 'enemy combatant': Yaser Hamdi, Jose Padilla, Ali Al Marri and John Walker Lindh.

As a young man John Walker Lindh had converted to Islam and very quickly began to travel around much of the Muslim world. Eventually he travelled to Afghanistan where he decided to join the Afghan forces' fight against the Northern Alliance. At the time Lindh was under the impression that the US still supported the Taliban's efforts due to the legacy from the 1970s and 1980s. He was still present in Afghanistan when the US decided to attack with the help of their new allies.[24]

Lindh was captured in 2001 by US troops after he had been caught by soldiers of the Northern Alliance, under the command of the warlord General Rashid Dostum. He was treated badly by the Northern Alliance troops who had already earned a reputation for killing hundreds of Taliban suspects placed under their control. Eventually, after a chance encounter with the media, he was brought before the public eye in a dishevelled state and placed in US custody. Despite being injured during the course of his arrest and detention, the US did nothing to heal his wounds, and rather he was stripped naked and placed on a metal shipping container until his transfer to a US rendition ship.

Before his return to the US, Lindh had already become Enemy Number One with the American public. Without charge or trial, he had been convicted by the media, with many quarters calling for the death penalty. His father, Frank Lindh, explained how the US government collaborated with the media in order to demonise him:

To understand John's case, first you have to understand that it was the subject of extraordinary media attention in the United States and I guess throughout the world. His image was put on the first page of every newspaper in the United States and many of the leading news magazines. It was also covered extensively on television networks and so forth. And all the coverage of his case was extremely biased and emphasized—or alleged—that John was a terrorist and that John somehow had been involved in the 9/11 attacks. And this was not just the media. The very highest officials of the United States government made comments to that affect in the media: the president, the vice president, the secretary of defense Donald Rumsfeld, the secretary of state Colin Powell, and many United States senators and others went on television and said all these things about John: that he was a terrorist, that he conspired to kill thousands of Americans and so forth—all very inflammatory and prejudicial statements that were made by high government officials against this young man.

So when John was brought back to the United States, they deliberately brought him back to Virginia near the Pentagon, where the Pentagon had been bombed in the 9/11 attacks. They brought him to a court there where he was almost certain not to obtain a fair trial. The jury pool was so prejudiced against John because they had come to believe that he was involved in the 9/11 attacks. At the time there were polls that had been done in the media that showed that something like seventy percent of the people in the United States thought that John Lindh should be put to death. Even among liberals and other political moderates there were a huge number of people that thought that John, at a minimum, should be sentenced to life in prison. It was very clear from these polls, from these data, that it was not possible for John at the time to obtain a fair trial anywhere in the United States, but especially in Northern Virginia just adjacent to the Pentagon.[25]

When USA v Lindh was brought before the Virginia Federal Court, the judgement clearly reflected the fear and anger typical of the US at the time. Clearly misreading one of the Geneva Conventions in order to secure a conviction, the judgement in the case stated:

...It is Lindh who bears the burden of establishing the affirmative defense that he is entitled to lawful combatant immunity, i.e. that the Taliban satisfies the four criteria required for lawful combatant status outlined by the [Third Geneva Convention]. On this point, Lindh has not carried his burden...it appears that the Taliban lacked the command structure necessary to fulfil the first criterion, as it is manifest that the Taliban had no internal system of military command or discipline...[26]

Despite the government's reworking of the Geneva Conventions and the rules relating to participation in foreign forces such as that of the Taliban, the government was forced to drop all charges against him in relation to terrorism. Frank Lindh explained how the government came to accept the plea:

He was really just fortunate, I think, in that atmosphere, to be able to extract a plea bargain from the American Government by which all the terrorism related charges were dropped by the government. In return, John was forced to accept the twenty-year prison sentence, a very long and very harsh prison sentence for only one actual conviction. The only crime, so to speak, he was convicted of was that he was alleged to have violated the trade sanctions imposed by the American Government against the Taliban Government of Afghanistan by his volunteering for the service in the Afghan army. So, as a result of violating these trade sanctions, John received a twenty-year prison sentence.

I think it's clear however, if I can add, that the twenty-year sentence is really a proxy for the fact that the government was forced to drop all the terrorism related charges after having gotten the population worked up and convinced that John was a terrorist and was involved in terrorism. There was this sort of vindication thing where people felt that John had to receive a very lengthy prison sentence regardless of the facts, simply to satisfy that vengeance that the government had stirred up against him.[27]

Lindh was detained abroad and convicted in the US, however not all the terrorism cases in the US shared these characteristics, because the administration became very keen to prove the threat of home grown terrorism. The Virginia Jihad Network, as it was called by the US media, was a case that involved eleven men from the Washington area who were detained in 2003. The main allegation against the men who were involved in the trial revolved around claims that they were training to join Lakshar-e-Taiba, an insurgent group in Pakistan fighting for Kashmiri self-determination. The entire case against the men was based on circumstantial evidence and the testimonies of witnesses with questionable characters. One of the central pieces of evidence was that the men had used the game 'paintball' in order to train for jihad—that somehow firing paint bullets was actual training to fight in Kashmir.[28]

Of the eleven men who were originally arrested, six pleaded guilty. Three of the remaining five were convicted and the other two acquitted. Of the two eventually acquitted, one was Sabri ben Kahla, a US citizen who was born and raised in the country. Kahla was known to be well-mannered and studious. Having graduated from George Mason University, he decided to enrol at the Islamic University in the city of Madinah where he went to study Islamic Law. When Kahla was arrested in 2003 with his ten co-defendants, it was in relation to a trip that he had made to Pakistan in 1999. Unlike the others, he was detained by Saudi intelligence with the coordination of the FBI. He was held incommunicado in Saudi Arabia for a period of a month, but it was not until his return to the US that he found out it had been at the request of the FBI. His brother Souhail ben Kahla explained the circumstances of Sabri's detention:

He was abducted in the middle of the night, in fact the night before his wedding. They basically took him at gunpoint and did not inform him who they were. The only way we found out about it was because his fiancée said that he did not turn up to get married. He was transported by the FBI in a pod; they placed goggles on him and took him back to the US where he was placed in a federal prison in Virginia.

The original allegations against Sabri were that he was part of the Virginia paintball group, the eleven. They alleged that he was training through paintballing. His case however was eventually severed from the other defendants due to the fact that it was revealed that he had only played paintball once while he was on a break from school. Those original charges were dropped, however they brought new charges very quickly of providing material support to the Taliban and also for firing a weapon. The new charges stemmed from his trip to Pakistan where he had travelled for three weeks. It was during this time that they said that he had received training, fought with the Taliban and also returned to school.

The trial he had was a one day trial, it was very clear that there was no evidence against him, the only thing that they claimed was that he entered into one part of Pakistan and left from another. There was no physical evidence whatsoever, what they did do instead was to bring in a terrorism expert to testify about the global jihad movement in general, without any relation to Sabri. He was speaking about jihad and they used images trying to scare the court.

Sabri was found not guilty of all charges in the original case. He was immediately released.[29]

Sabri ben Kahla immediately began putting his life back together. Several months later though, he was requested to attend some debriefings with the FBI and he agreed readily to do so. They asked him the same questions that they had asked before and he replied with the same answers. He had not wanted to attend but they threatened that unless he talked informally with them he would be called before a grand jury. Despite their promises, Kahla was brought before two grand juries anyway, where he was questioned in exactly the same way regarding his trip to Pakistan, the very things he had been acquitted of.

During this period he had begun to attend Johns Hopkins University in order to continue his education further. Because of his Arabic, he was chosen to lead a trip to Kuwait but was stopped at the airport by FBI agents who would not let him get on the flight. The class he was taking protested about his treatment but he told them to go on without him—it turned out that Kahla had been placed on a no-fly list. Unable to obtain a conviction against Kahla for terrorism related offences, Souhail explains how the US prosecutor went after his brother again:

The prosecutor told us that he was bringing charges against Sabri for perjury and obstruction of justice. At this point he was not detained as during the original trial he was facing forty years and he had not attempted to flee at all, so they allowed him to remain with us. They brought this new case in front of a new judge. We went to trial with this case and it was about three or four days long. It was the same trial as last time with the same allegations and the same terrorism expert, however this time instead of going in front of a judge, we were going in front of a jury. The terrorism expert went on for a full day regarding terrorism around the world, and not one bit of the testimony had anything to do with Sabri, it was all about what is going on in other parts of the world. It was about camps, Chechnya, the Taliban, bin Laden, every terrorist organisation you can think of. It was supposed to be a perjury trial, about whether or not he had lied, yet none of the evidence against him related to this. Even the questions that were being asked of Sabri were problematic, he was asked to recall specific phone calls he had made five years earlier in Pakistan, something that would be impossible for most people to do.

The jury found Sabri guilty on basically all counts, the judge did throw out count number two related to the firing of an RPG and even referenced to the jury that they may have been influenced by talks of jihad by the expert witness.

The case was a whole new attempt to try and bring up the old case. The prosecutor lost and they were bitter. They were not going to stop until they got Sabri on something, it didn't matter what it was. They had the jurors they wanted and hit them with the terrorism expert who scared them completely, the first day of testimony was anti-Islamic rhetoric. They found him guilty on fear alone rather than any facts. Sabri was sentenced to ten years, for charges related to perjury, it should only be one to two years. They applied a terrorism enhancement to Sabri's case despite the fact that the judge explicitly stated this was not a terrorism case.[30]

There often exist peculiarities in the way in which cases of suspected terrorism are tried in the US. Disproportionate sentencing for cases of alleged terrorism has become a common feature in the US judicial process. As explained by Souhail ben Kahla, in many cases, the prosecution's evidence is often limited with cases being built around the wider contexts of what is taking place. Furthermore, people with connections to suspects under investigation by the US have been dragged through the courts by the most simple of associations.

Uzair Paracha is the son of Saifullah Paracha who is currently detained in Guantánamo Bay. Born and raised in Pakistan, Uzair was a typical boy raised in a middle class family in Karachi with very little interest in organised religion. According to his siblings, out of all of them, Uzair had a particular love for all things American and would spend much of his time listening to American music, movies and wearing their clothes. Deciding to join the family property business, Uzair moved to New York in order to advertise apartment blocks the family had built in Karachi. On 20 March 2003, Uzair was requested by five FBI agents to go with them at the end of work hours. According to his business partner, it seemed it would only be for a short while.

Uzair was put through a strict interrogation regime by the FBI who questioned him for three days straight without giving him access to a lawyer, his family or allowing him to sleep. By the end of the third day, Uzair Paracha told the FBI everything that they wanted to hear, but had lied thinking that they would simply deport him and it would be the end of his suffering. He was eventually convicted of lying to the FBI despite the conditions that he had been interrogated under.

Facing the difficulty of trying to work for the release of her husband and son while running the family business and bringing up three children, Farhat Paracha spoke of her son's sentencing:

Uzair was offered plea bargaining up until the trial took place, up to ten days before the start of the trial. He was given an option, but then Uzair still stood by what he said the first time and he wanted to speak out, he wanted to tell the judge and the jury his own version. He was so sure of his innocence, that he refused the plea bargaining knowing that he could get up to seventy-five years; he very well knew what could happen. The jury was more than likely to be biased as this was taking place in New York City and the court was very close to the Twin Towers. He had already been found guilty at a previous trial the day before thanksgiving. This was a sentencing hearing and he was given thirty years which was the absolute minimum sentence they were giving. This surprised him, as the day after he sent me a letter where he told me about his shock that they would have given it to him. He still has the same stance he always had.

I think he had been given a very unfair trial, and this is what his lawyer told him as well. The lawyer wanted him to plea bargain, but Uzair refused as he did not want to be known as a criminal. He took the stand, he was very respectful, I was told this by Mr GT Hunt who is my husband's lawyer and he attended the trial, he told me that Uzair spoke very well. The court was read out the statements of Majid Khan and Ammar Al-Baluchi, both of which exonerated Uzair, even though they were being held by the Americans at the time. In spite of this, the jury in five hours decided that he was guilty of all five counts.

He stated that he had no ill intentions, and that he lied to the FBI because they strip searched him three times during those days when they questioned him. He was twenty-three at the time, he was not allowed to sleep and he couldn't eat, he was scared. He was a privileged Pakistani boy and all this scared him. He said that whenever he told the truth, they would keep on telling him that he was lying and they would not believe him. Two FBI agents, one of which was a female, strip searched him, which in itself was a humiliating experience for him.

He said that he kept telling the truth, but as they wouldn't believe him, he told them what they wanted to hear. He thought the most they would do would be to deport him. However things got worse and he was soon thrown into a cell with a Qur'an. That was how it all started. Uzair kept on pleading not guilty despite all the pleas made to him by his lawyer and by myself, he kept on insisting upon his innocence.

What distressed me greatly, and I heard this from those at the trial, that before every morning the court would be shown a repeated video of the twin towers falling down. That is what it kept on coming back to; that Uzair had some affiliation to Al Qaeda, even though he had nothing to do with them. I'm sure he did not even know what Al Qaeda was; he is so poor in his general knowledge. I once asked him who Milosevic was, and he just said 'who?' I told him it was a shame he didn't know. He read a lot, but only books by John Grisham and other fiction, he was not interested in reality. He had other interests, he had his friends who visit me now after years, they have started visiting again.

I fail to accept that he is guilty; I don't understand why the Americans do not see it. It is all bias, it is all government policy, it is all the media which is giving such a negative portrayal of people. Somehow I have become anti-American now to tell you the truth, because I feel that the Americans have become too self-centred and they think that if they are safe, then that is what matters, no one else. The US is the world, and the rest are inferior sub-humans whose lives don't matter, whose health does not matter, whose families do not matter. They are hardly bothered, they are too self-engrossed. On the other hand, there are a few Americans that are helping us...westerners, and I cannot say...but I am sure that ninety-eight percent are not concerned, they are least bothered, they don't have enough knowledge as they watch channels like Fox News and CNN. CNN is totally anti-Muslim, they try to give a fair impression, but they are not.[31]

The most prominent difficulty for suspected terrorists in the US is the impossibility of getting a fair trial. In a country with a history of disproportionate sentencing, prejudiced juries, and, in the case of African-Americans,[32] outright fear, today's treatment of Muslim terrorism suspects can be seen as part of a historical tendency. The cases of Paracha, ben Kahla and Lindh are illustrative of a general trend in the US towards abuse of the rule of law in order to secure convictions.

4

FOREIGN EXCHANGE

"... diplomatic assurances are an inadequate no-guarantee for returns to countries where torture is 'endemic', or a 'recalcitrant and enduring problem.'"[1]

Chahal v United Kingdom

Nationality plays an integral role in the legal debates surrounding counter-terrorism. Since 9/11 various strategies have been implemented based on the nationality of the detainee. Different standards of human rights protection are applied to those with citizenship and those without.

After the Allied invasion of Afghanistan, a small number of American citizens were detained by the US authorities and, despite allegations that they were enemy combatants they were not sent to Guantánamo Bay, purely because of their nationality.

For the hundreds of other foreign nationals detained in Afghanistan, the lack of US citizenship granted them no such privileged treatment, and they soon found themselves illegally incarcerated beyond recognised systems of law. Due to the legal limbo, and under domestic pressure to have them charged or released, states began to request the return of their nationals. The British government was forced to make representations for the eventual return of UK citizens held at the base—it was their British citizenship that ultimately protected them.[2] Moazzam Begg, one of the British nationals, had been one of six men designated for trial by Military Commissions and, according to Lieutenant Commander Charles D Swift, "The plan was to begin Commissions with guilty pleas. Two weeks after the President's finding, a request to detail Military Counsel to Moazzam Begg of Great Britain and

David Hicks of Australia, believed to be likely candidates, was made."[3] Despite the insistence by the US government that Begg was a dangerous terrorist, he was still released from Guantánamo Bay, along with other British nationals, after the request by the British government.

Despite every single citizen from western democracies—except Omar Khadr—now having been returned from Guantánamo Bay to their countries of nationality; there still remain at the base around 200 detainees who have no reasonable chance of representation due to poor relations between the US and their nations. This has been especially difficult for those who fled from their countries of origin in order to escape persecution. The British residents (as opposed to fully-blown citizens) who were held at the base found it considerably more difficult to have representations made on their behalf by the British government due to their citizenship status. According to the then Foreign Secretary Jack Straw, "We can represent British citizens…[but] we cannot represent those who choose not to seek British citizenship and make their own choices presumably because they want to maintain the citizenship of their birth."[4] Although those detained did not have British citizenship, some had been in Britain as long as 14 years and for a multitude of reasons were unable to procure citizenship status.

The nationality of detainees, and the status of their residence within adopted countries, very much affects their ability to access the law. Measures introduced in the name of counter-terrorism involve the removal of citizenship in order to remove the protections that a state must give its citizens. It is commonly understood by all countries that foreign nationals have far fewer rights than do their own citizens as can be evidenced through domestic legislation. As a consequence many countries remove citizenship in order to justify policies which would otherwise be completely illegal. This chapter looks at the processes that have been used to remove the citizenship of individuals and the implications of such policies.

The policy to remove citizenship is very much affected by the desire of states to *refoule* certain immigrants to their countries of origin. In the current climate of fear, governments have become worried about the presence of foreign nationals who have escaped religious persecution in their native lands or come to their countries in order to settle. *Refoulement* is completely illegal under international law, and yet governments are now finding increasingly convoluted ways of returning to their countries of origin those they profile as a threat.

Whether the foreign national is an asylum seeker, or a foreign resident who has had their citizenship removed, the process of returning them is always the same. Countries invariably rely on Memoranda of Understanding in order to justify their policies, by claiming these as evidence that an individual will not be tortured or detained illegally on his or her return to the country of their birth. These Memoranda have been widely criticised by lawyers, NGOs and political figures as being worthless in terms of their legal enforceability and for not giving any protection to those being deported.

While deportations are taking place through mechanisms which may be considered beyond the law, the use of extradition has also been tainted by the War on Terror. The ratification of extradition treaties between states has been on the increase as governments attempt to have suspects tried in foreign jurisdictions, even where that jurisdiction is not appropriate. This section will focus particularly on the British Extradition Act 2003 which has removed the need for a prima facie case prior to the extradition and relies solely on allegations.

Citizens no more

Bosnia and Herzegovina (BiH) declared independence from Yugoslavia on 1 March 1992 during a period of mass secession in the region. The Serbian army, first as the Yugloslav National Army (JNA) and then as the Army of the Serbian Republic (VRS), began a program of ethnic cleansing in BiH against the Bosniak (Bosnian Muslim) population.[5]

With the indirect backing of the Clinton administration in the US, a route was opened for the Bosniaks to receive arms and help from states such as Iran, Pakistan, Saudi Arabia, Malaysia, Sudan and other predominantly Muslim countries.[6] Along with arms, many foreign nationals entered the Balkans to help the Bosnian army repel the Serb invasion; anywhere between 1,000 and 4,000 foreigners entered Bosnia during the conflict. Many of the organisations which arrived came from the Muslim world and established themselves with the help of foreign governments.

In 1995, Presidents Izetbegovic, Tudjman, Milosevic and Clinton agreed the Dayton Peace Accords. One of its provisions was the removal of all foreign fighters from Bosnia and Herzegovina (BiH) with the aim of keeping stability in the region.[7] The provision in the accords relating to the removal of foreigners states:

In particular, all foreign forces, including individual advisors, freedom fighters, trainers, volunteers, and personnel from neighbouring and other states, shall be withdrawn from the territory of Bosnia and Herzegovina...[8]

By the end of 1995, ninety percent of all foreign fighters had been removed from Bosnia via Zagreb Airport (in Croatia) in compliance with the agreement. Despite the large numbers of those who left the region, several remained who had married Bosnian women or had earned the right to citizenship by fighting in the conflict.

But the War on Terror brought in new counter-terrorism measures that targeted these naturalised Bosnian citizens. On 14 November 2001, the interior minister, Tomislav Limov, issued an order for the revocation of citizenship from 108 foreigners who had become naturalised Bosnians. Previously two commissions had been conducted in 1996 and 2001 in order to assess the status of these naturalised Bosnians and on both occasions it was held that there was nothing irregular with their status and that they should continue to keep their citizenship. The November 2001 decision was made without any consultation or commission approving the new measures.[9] Official statements came from the government cancelling the citizenships and claiming this was due to clerical errors at the time the citizenships were processed.

According to Abdelilah Daudi Karrache, one of the naturalised Bosnians facing deportation:

In 1995-1996 they gave us citizenships through Acts but at the same time they did not put these in the institutional archives but are now saying these citizenships are fiction and do not really exist! All the foreigners got their passports and ID cards and even travelled on the documents given from the government—so how can they not be real?[10]

Among the first to be targeted under this new policy were the Bosnian Algerians wanted by the US and who were eventually rendered to Guantánamo Bay. Facing the difficulty of having to process them through the legal system before handing them over to the US, the Bosnian government initiated the removal of their citizenship in the hope that as foreigners it would be easier to remove them.

On 13 December 2001 a number of the naturalised Bosnians who had their citizenship revoked began legal action to overturn the interior minister's decision. By 4 December 2003 the Supreme Court in Sarajevo finally concluded that the revocations had been illegal and that the citizenships of those naturalised Bosnians must stand, especially in light of the two previous commissions. Sabiha Delic, the wife of Mustafa Ait Idir, explained how the process was used:

In December 2001, this was the first time they tried to deport him. They cancelled the citizenship of my husband, they did so in order to make it easy to deport him. I pressed charges, and the decision of the Supreme Court, they decided the cancelling of the citizenship was illegal. At the moment he is still a citizen of Bosnia.[11]

In response, the BiH Interior Ministry attempted to claim that those people that were being deported and extradited were part of a global terrorist organisation. Despite the ruling of the Supreme Court, all those foreign fighters and aid workers who settled in BiH with Bosnian families once again came under the purview of the BiH government. Abu Hamza Emad Alhusin, a naturalised Bosnian facing deportation to his country of origin Syria, explains:

Some of those people from the list were extradited to France because France had asked for them. They called them the French Group. They tried to connect those people with some group in France by calling them terrorists.

After that the Ministry Council changed the law for citizenship three times to make a decision of taking citizenship very easy. One of the men, Hisham, in the French group was in prison for four-and-a-half years after the end of the judgement against him. France did not deport him to Morocco due to issues of human rights, but they deported him to Bosnia and they asked the Bosnian government to give guarantees that they would not send him to Morocco. The Bosnians guaranteed this, but after a few months broke the guarantee and sent him there.[12]

Then in March 2006, despite the decision of the Supreme Court of Bosnia and the two previous commissions, a third state commission was asked to review the citizenships acquired in BiH between 6 April 1992 and 1 January 2006.

Immense pressure was being placed on the Bosnian government to deport these people regardless of the legal implications of their removal. According to Abu Hamza:

I was told by our contact within the government that the Americans had given the Bosnian government fifteen names of foreign fighters and humanitarian workers and emphatically stated that their citizenships would be taken under any conditions. They said to our contact that they would break every law and human right if need be in order to take away these citizenships because that would be the price of Bosnia getting into the European Union.[13]

The commission was structured in order for there to be two Bosnian Muslims, two Bosnian Serbs, two Bosnian Croats and three foreigners from the international community. The specific goal of this commission was to look at those individuals within Bosnia who had descent from Africa or Asia. They began by asking all foreign persons to bring their papers. The process of the commission was heavily flawed as those being brought before the commission were told they would have no right to complain and that any decision taken would be final. The appeals process would only be permitted after the deportation had taken place, and no other appeal mechanism would be permitted.

The manner in which the commission was constituted caused grave difficulties to the naturalised Bosnians. As part of the evidentiary standard required for each defendant to make their case of citizenship, the commission requests many original documents from their countries of origin. Even in circumstances where no such papers exist, original documents are still demanded. This condition often cannot be fulfilled and is thus used as a means to build a case for the revocation of citizenship.

Abu Hamza Emad Alhusin is now campaigning against his deportation. A Bosnian national of Syrian origin, he came to the Federal Republic of Yugoslavia in 1983 in order to study medicine. For many years he studied in Croatia, until 1992 when he moved to Bosnia at the start of the war. During the conflict Alhusin became an aid worker and started coordinating the efforts between humanitarian organisations coming in and out of the country. In 1993 he married a Bosnian national and by 1994 they had their first child and he received his citizenship. Since then Alhusin has not left the boundaries of BiH other than to go on pilgrimage to Makkah. Speaking of his citizen revocation and deportation, he explained:

In 2005 I heard that they were going to put together a commission in order to review our citizenships. One day I received a call that I had to bring my Bosnian passport and they forbade me from leaving Bosnia until they asked me questions. If I moved anywhere, I would have to immediately give them my new address.

I was the second one who received the decision by the commission of taking away my citizenship. They have charged me now by saying that I was lying to the government when I was taking citizenship. That was because someone who made this decision by giving this citizenship, he made a mistake and gave it to the whole group before Bosnia was an internationally recognised country. Someone jumped the gun and put us all in a bad situation unfortunately. They are trying to get rid of me on a technicality.

Now it appears that I have two citizenships, one before Bosnia was made in 1992 and the second in 1994. The person who made it in 1992 did not give us any papers but in the government papers there is a paper that shows that we have citizenship before 1992.

Now the commission is charging me that I was lying in 1994 as I had received citizenship in 1992 which was incorrect anyway. Due to that, they are saying that the citizenship of 1994 is deleted. They are saying that in the law if you lie about your personal information, then they can remove your citizenship.

After that I claimed to the court and tried to take the decision from 1992 and I went to all the ministries that could be connected to the case and no one can give me any decision. All of them admitted that there is no case of 1992 only 1994. When I claimed to the court, as we know the court has to be correct and neutral, and in this case they have to see my arguments and the other sides and then make their decision—they put away all my arguments and the courts find out three other new reasons why to take away my citizenship. That means the court has simply taken the commission's word.[14]

Another student who came to study in Yugoslavia arrived in Bosnia in 1979. Fadhil Al Hammadani arrived in Zenica to study engineering but also to study the Bosnian language. Originally Al Hammadani is from Iraq and came to Eastern Europe due to the standard of education that was being offered. Breaking his studies with work in order to delay having to return to Iraq, he eventually married a Bosnian national in 1987 and continued to live in Yugoslavia. Seeing the affects of the war, he decided to join the Bosnian forces in order to repel the Serbs:

When the war started, I only had one exam to finish but then the war started. I joined the army in 1993 and fought until the end of the war in 1995.

I was given Bosnian citizenship in 1995 before the Dayton Accords in February 1995.

In February 1995 I had three children and all of the information when I applied for nationality was complete. In 2001 when they gave me my decision to cancel my citizenship I had four children and one on the way.

I have been told that I am an unwelcome person in Bosnia.

In 2006 we all got a call about the new commission to revise citizenships. I went to the commission and gave documents and statements to the Commission. When I gave the documents they gave me a receipt of them for 29 June 2006. 29 August 2006 I received the decision for the cancellation of my citizenship and they said three reasons why they removed it:

1. The citizenship of 1992—the one I knew nothing about—which there is even no proof over. This is not possible as I knew nothing of this and they do not have anything in archives.

2. According to Dayton I was supposed to leave as a foreigner. I got citizenship before Dayton.

3. That I did not come to the commission in 2006—which is a lie because I was there and had attended.

By the law the commission is supposed to give all my information to the court—all of my documents, but they did not do so. The court did not know I was in the army and because of that the court said that I must go back to the commission from the beginning.

In the decision of 29 August I do not have the right to appeal but I have the right to prosecute them. If I have the right to appeal then I would be safe. But as I do not have the right of appeal, so in this case there is no guarantee that I will not be captured and extradited.

When they extradite me to Iraq, they will do so as a terrorist, not like a man without papers, but as a terrorist. I will more than likely go missing as soon as I land there.[15]

The fear of being returned to their countries of origin is caused by the threat of what will take place once they return. With the stigma that is attached to the presence of foreigners fighting in Bosnia through suspected links to Al Qaeda, those being returned to countries which practise torture are in serious risk of being abused. For those who openly admit to having fought, the situation becomes even worse. Abdelilah Daudi Karrache, a Bosnian national of Moroccan origin arrived in 1992 in order to fight in the war. Having been particularly recognised for his bravery during the conflict, Karrache was awarded the fleur-de-lis by the Bosnian government:

Since the end of the war all I have done is to live peacefully with my family working in the marketplace.

The commission asked me to give them a statement on 26 February 2006 about gaining nationality in 1992—but I didn't even know I had been given this citizenship. We had just been given papers being told we had nationalities, but the formal processes had not been finished. I wasn't even aware that I had been given nationality in this informal manner. The mistake was of the administration—not ours!

When I applied in 1995 for citizenship, the minister of the interior told us that first they must cancel our first citizenships of 1992 and only then could they start the process again for formal citizenship in the correct manner. They gave me citizenship in 1995 but they never cancelled the one from 1992.

I then made a request according to this conclusion that I put my name in the Book of Birth so that I can get the rest of my documents—but they failed to do this. After I applied for the new ID at a high security level, I received this. It is ridiculous I received this ID and cannot get more simple documents.

What we found out later was that they had proceeded with my 1992 citizenship and stopped my 1996 one as there were problems with the 1992 one—it is clear that the administration knew that they would be able to revoke my 1992 citizenship at any time due to the procedural problems attached.

On 30 January 2007 they cancelled all my citizenships since 1992, this was by the Commission. The reason for this was that they gave citizenship in 1996 and by this time I was supposed to be out of Bosnia according to the Dayton Accords.

I did everything I could to stay here properly and through the process—but all they want to do is to get rid of me using whatever means they can. My wife and children are Bosnian and they still want to get rid of me.

Due to the mistake on my permanent residence I am in complete legal limbo—I don't know how to get any kind of stay in this country.

Because I voluntarily fought out of Morocco without asking permission—this is an offence over there. This is illegal there. They would probably send me to prison, there is a ninety percent chance they will send me to prison for what I have done.[16]

The policy of removing citizenship is not limited to Bosnia. The British government has also brought in measures to remove the citizenship of those it deems a threat to the British public. These laws were brought in to deal with the controversial Muslim cleric, Abu Hamza Al Masri, who was convicted under incitement of hatred laws. Currently Al Masri faces extradition to the US, however he has already been through the process of having his British citizenship revoked. The consequence of this revocation is that he will be left with only his Egyptian citizenship and, if and when he is released, will face deportation there:

The home secretary is attempting to take my British citizenship away from me however the case is still pending in the court and I am fighting that my nationality is being taken away. I do not have any legal status at the moment until the outcome of the court case which will determine whether or not I am a British national. My family in the UK are British citizens they are not residents.

These laws have been tailored especially for me and even before these laws came into force the immigration and nationality act and the confiscation acts came into force in order to serve to affect me personally. How can I receive justice when people are only interested in one thing which is a permanent lock up to set me up as an example of what happens to a person who will not toe the line to keep me quiet.[17]

The policy of sending an individual back to their country of origin when there is the prospect of torture or ill treatment is entirely against international law. Critics claim that governments in Europe have implemented such policies in order to remove any suspected threats from the European continent. By removing citizenship ties, the legal obligations on those countries diminishes and thus any action taken seems less unlawful, and is harder to challenge in the courts.

Deportation

With the treatment of citizens and foreigners being different under the domestic laws of all states, the War on Terror has particularly affected foreign nationals as the most weakly protected category of detainees. Although foreigners are generally weakly protected due to their lack of complete national status, principles of international law and especially international refugee law help to provide overarching protections. The principle of non-*refoulement* is considered to be *jus cogens* (compelling law)—meaning that it is one of the principles of customary international law which is applicable to all nations regardless of their ratification of the principle. The rule has been enshrined in the 1951 Geneva Convention Relating to the Status of Refugees and also the 1967 Additional Protocol.

Although states are aware of their international obligations, they have sought new ways to remove individuals from their countries. With the failure of indefinite detention without charge (see Chapter 3—The Rule of Law) the British government brought in measures to detain foreign nationals, except this time with the aim of having them deported. After the attacks of 7 July 2005, the home secretary was given specific powers to be able to deport or remove the citizenship of anyone not considered to be 'conducive' to the public good, with appeals only allowed through the Special Immigration Appeals Commission (SIAC). By making the issue one of immigration, the British government was able to manoeuvre the detainees into a completely different legal position.[18] The nationalities most affected by the policies of the government include Libyans, Algerians, Tunisians and Jordanians.

Despite the orders from the home secretary being in direct contravention of the rule of *non-refoulement*, the British government sought to side-step the legal issues by signing Memoranda of Understanding with the countries[19] to which they seek deportation. These memoranda have been dubbed worthless due to their lack of enforceability in the international arena. Kal Raustiala, visiting professor at Columbia University School of Law, makes reference to the architecture of these agreements as being 'soft law'—a form of law which is without substance. He writes, "...I argue that the notion of 'soft law' agreements is incoherent. Under the prevailing approach, pledges are being smuggled into the international lawyer's repertoire by dubbing them soft law."[20]

By signing agreements with countries that practise torture, the British government has found a way to deport foreign nationals with the pretence of legitimacy.

Since 2005 the government has particularly targeted Libyan nationals as one category of detainee they wish to deport. Having signed a Memorandum of Understanding with the Gaddafi regime many of these Libyans suddenly faced the very real threat of torture in their country of origin. The British courts eventually stopped the deportations, defying the orders of the government. One of the detainees who faced this deportation is Faraj Hassan Faraj, who opposed the Libyan government as a student. He explained the significance of the memoranda to the situation of the Libyans and all those affected:

For this country to sign this Memorandum of Understanding with Libya that I would not be harmed means Libya practises torture against its people otherwise why would a memorandum be needed? By seeking this so called "Memorandum of Understanding" the UK acknowledges that Libya does carry out torture. You can go and search yourself in the Human Rights.org website and read about the prisoners in Libya. More than 12,000 Muslim brothers were shot in the Prison of Abu-Salem in Tripoli by the members of the very same regime that signed this memorandum! And they wanted me to be in the same prison where the blood of those innocent Muslims is still not dry yet. The British government simply forgot who Gaddafi is; the British government simply forgot the killing of more than 258 people in the bombing of Pan-Am Flight 103 over Lockerbie in Scotland; the British government simply forgot about Gaddafi's reputation, which is well known to everyone in this country.

What I am trying to say is this so-called "memorandum" was being dealt by a very big mafia in Libya, by people who themselves should be in prison for the crimes they have committed against humanity, By signing this so called "Memorandum of Understanding" the UK government was willing to sign our life away to these people who would not even ensure the rights of animals let alone human beings. It makes a mockery of the so-called civilised democracy and human rights the UK professes to uphold and uses as an excuse to invade countries like Iraq and Afghanistan claiming to be bringing democracy and human rights to these countries and removing dictatorship, when the UK itself deals with these very dictators as and when it suits it. The irony is how the UK government is courting Libya now and in particular Gaddafi when only less then twenty years ago Libya was denounced by the West as the country which harboured terrorists and Gaddafi was reviled as an enemy of the West in the same way Osama Bin Laden is today. Most recently Tony Blair himself visited Libya and announced Gaddafi as the West's ally against terrorism and resumed diplomatic relations with Libya!

The double standards and the blatant hypocrisy of the UK government towards countries which torture is clear for everyone to see and the UK government wonders why Muslims feel angry?[21]

Detainee DD left Libya due to his opposition to the Gaddafi regime and came to Britain to seek asylum. Although he had only been involved in non-violent political opposition, the Libyan government sentenced DD in his absence to execution by hanging. Despite clarifying that the execution order was still in place, the British government still made an order for his deportation (see pages 34–35 for his deposition):[22]

Of the scores of Libyans who challenged deportation, only Hassan and DD remain under control orders—the rest have been cleared[23] through a special court known as the Special Immigration Appeals Commission (SIAC)—this appellant process however is not without its own problems. Created by the Special Immigration Appeals Commission Act 1997, SIAC aims to resolve appeal cases in which the British Home Secretary has made an order to deport or exclude someone from Britain on grounds of national security or the public interest.

The government has worked hard to centralise as many powers as possible to enable decision-making outside the legal process. Although SIAC may appear to have legal safeguards, these are superficial in nature, and the system in fact is non-transparent in the way it is implemented. According to the rules of the commission, the SIAC hearings take place in an open court, which the public and press are free to attend. However, there is a provision which allows the court to hear evidence in closed sessions. These closed sessions cannot be attended by the public or media. Many of the cases brought before SIAC involve individuals suspected of terrorism or of 'not being conducive to the public good'. In these cases, the judge will choose to maintain the secrecy of government evidence, and will opt to hear the case in a closed court.

The use of secret evidence in the closed session is not only hidden from the public—it is also kept secret from the appellant or his representative for alleged reasons of national security or public interest.

When such a circumstance occurs, the judge will appoint a special advocate to represent the interests of the appellant.[24] The special advocate cannot disclose the secret evidence to the appellant, and is not able to take instruction from the appellant or his representative. The implications of this process on the application of due process and justice are great—appellants before the SIAC proceedings are incapable of answering the evidence against them if they are prevented from seeing the evidence itself.

Considering the use of secret evidence and special advocates, the Special Immigration Appeals Commission has much in common with the Combatant Status Review Tribunals (CSRT) that are used at Guantánamo Bay. The Guantánamo review tribunals deny detainees access to the classified evidence against them. Further those detainees are required to be represented by a court-appointed advocate who is usually from the military.

The SIAC process is extremely slow and detainees subjected to its appeal mechanisms are in legal limbo while they await their turn in front of the court. For the Algerians who were subjected to the process of detention without charge in 2003, then again subjected to deportation orders in 2005, the uncertainty of the position became particularly unbearable. At one stage a small number of Algerians chose return to Algeria rather than be subjected to any further legal manipulation by the British government. Detainees such as Benaissa Taleb, Mustafa Melki and Omar Dijid opted for voluntary deportation and the certainty of unlawful detention in Algeria with a known sentence, rather than the continuation of their unknown status in Britain.[25] For other Algerians still fighting their deportation orders, the decision to be returned to Algeria is not an option. Detainee G suffered from polio at the age of two and since then has been wheelchair bound. He came to Britain to study, having fled Algeria after protesting against the regime as a student. Since first detaining him in December 2001, the British government has attempted to detain him again, using various measures culminating with the decision to deport him once a Memorandum of Understanding is agreed with Algeria:

They said because they have a memorandum—these Arab regimes yesterday were dictatorships, anti-democratic—like Jordan, like Palestine, like Egypt, like Tunisia, like Algeria, like Libya, but overnight they became ok. These governments get a piece of paper that it is ok for them (the detainees) to come and we will treat them well, and they will be very welcome. But they didn't get a memorandum from Algeria. Even despite that they want to deport us.

My fear is great...I am facing death—if I go to Algeria I will die and make trouble to myself and my family. When we were in Long Lartin Prison (in northern Britain) under deportation, there were guys who couldn't stand being in prison, because of their families and things like that, and they were obliged to sign and go. They gave them the guarantee that they would be safe in Algeria, but when they went to Algeria it is completely the opposite. One of them I remember, I cannot use names, but he is now facing eight years in prison Algeria, and one of them three years. So for me they can kill me now or I can kill myself—that is better for me than to go to Algeria. It is impossible for me to go to Algeria.

SIAC is a slow court—we have been under this deportation for nearly two years, but nothing has happened—we are still waiting for SIAC, we are still waiting for the Appeal Court, and nothing happened.[26]

Unlike Detainee G, Detainee Z came to Britain in order to complete his Masters in Civil Engineering but in the summer of 1991 was convinced by his family to remain due to political turmoil in Algeria. One of the many detainees arrested after 7 July 2005, he was placed on a deportation order to Algeria with an appeal allowed only through the SIAC:

SIAC actually itself is a 'kangaroo court', it's a show, so when they try and abuse the power and try to give you an injustice they put you on SIAC. SIAC has nothing to do with the law or justice or whatever, because it's based only on one person. I don't how he's been selected, the judge, he makes the decision, it's vetted, and most of the arguments are in secret, even your solicitor can't tell you what it is and whatever has been said is done in secret it's kangaroo. You see the judge, I think the previous judge is very well known that he's got fascist views, because we know some of his neighbours and he said, 'we know this guy and he's a fascist', and we know he's a fascist basically this judge, because what happened, when they tried to secure the memorandum in Algeria, because when they arrest us on the condition that they won't send us until they get this memorandum. So, they arrest before getting, signing the memorandum with this country, but they didn't manage to get this memorandum with Algeria. Algeria, they refused to sign it. So, when we went to the court in 2006 to say there's no memorandum 'Why are you holding these people?' So, they were waiting for the ruling of the judge, even the 'Home Office' they know that they cannot deport us for this memorandum and so they issued an order to the prison to tell these people to pack their stuff. They sent even a van to pick us up; I mean I think they were planning to put us on a 'control order'. So, even the 'Home Office' who is the man responsible for our detention, he was convinced that this was it for the case, but the surprise was that the judge said 'Yes, we can deport them without this memorandum, just on their word, because he made the ruling without having any sort of background about my country, not at all, he wrote some piece of few paper about the reconciliation in Algeria and he said 'o.k. we don't need this memorandum, that's it, we deport them under this reconciliation. He makes his own mind, like he became the Home Office.[27]

The British government is not alone in its use of deportation orders to countries which practise torture. Other countries have incorporated similar provisions into their legal systems, in an effort to remove those deemed to be a threat. In 2005, Denmark brought in the Alien (Consolidation) Act which in Part VIIa, Clause 45b allows for the minister of refugee, immigration and internal affairs to make a judgement on whether or not a foreigner is a danger to national security based on evidence that does not have to be shown to the individual facing deportation. Mohamed Hamid, an Iraqi citizen who was tortured in Syria after being wrongfully detained, was subjected to this law when he returned to Denmark. Hamid's wife, Umm Hadigah, a Danish citizen, explained his situation:

Immediately in the airport when he arrived in Copenhagen they arrested him, and then he got one phone call to call and say that he'd arrived in Denmark, and that the police have arrested him. They arrested him because they said they took his residency in Syria—they took his residency away from him, and in the airport when he arrived in Denmark they said you don't have residency.

It's called 45b it's a new law after the terror attacks in America. It has only been used twice this year, and it says that anyone whom the intelligence service says is a danger to the Danish authorities or country we can arrest him and keep him in prison without a trial. He doesn't need to go in front of a judge and have his case tried. That is how the new law is, and then if he is not a Danish citizen they can take his residency and tell him to leave the country without coming in front of a judge.

Now he has been in Danish prison for seven months—I don't think there's a minimum or maximum, at the moment his case is being tried at the refugee ministry and whatever their decision will be it will be definite, because we already write many letters to them. We explained to them the situation and they wrote back that they will take the letters into consideration when making a decision—but they still have not made a decision. My husband has a lawyer already and even the lawyer he says that it is very unusual that you cannot have your case tried in front of a judge.

I am very concerned because my husband is originally Chukmanee, and they lived in Northern Iraq. In Northern Iraq there are many Kurdish people and the Chukmanee people are very very disliked by the Kurdish. My husband's brother was arrested four years ago and still now we have not heard from the Kurdish military. They just took him and the situation right now it is that my husband's family they have been told by the Kurdish military to leave the city or else they will be arrested and not only their family but all the Chuckmanee families have been told because of their nationality to leave the city.[28]

Canada has greatly influenced the resurgence of *refoulement* evident in western countries striving to counter terrorism. All of these countries attempt to hide their breaches of international law behind the assurances they ascertain from the deportees' countries of origin. Mohammed Harakat has faced deportation to Algeria since 2002 after the Canadian authorities detained him as a suspected terrorist. Married to his Catholic wife, Sophie Lamarche, he was very far from being involved in any form of organised religion before being sent to prison. Lamarche has become a well known activist in Canada and explained how the law has been used in order to detain her husband and attempt to send him to his native Algeria:

At first we didn't even know what he was detained for, there was no charge, he was the only inmate that our detention centre held without charge, and it took me 48hrs to see him; within that period they weren't sure if they were going to deport him or whatever, and then the charge report came out about 70hrs later. There was no evidence to support his arrest, every sentence started with "we assume, we believe, we suspect ... that he has been in the past, present or future linked to terrorism" but they had no evidence whatsoever.

... in Canada, they say if you have citizenship, you have every right, but as an immigrant, you have less rights, and if you have refugee status, then you have less rights than an immigrant, and if you have non-status, you have no rights at all. You're basically considered crap if you don't have status.

We had over 30 group organisations that testified in front of a senate committee, including my husband, that was a big moment, to have my husband, testifying himself in front of a senate committee in Ottawa, there were senators and MPs of Canada, and he addressed the House of Commons himself, and that was a historical moment, that my husband did, in front of senators, he begged for the abolition of this law. We've done things that you couldn't believe, but a guy who has spent two-and-a-half years in prison, appealing by himself in front of a senate committee, surrounded by officers and testify himself, and within two days, the new law passed, they just passed the new law, because there was a one year deadline and the certificate got reissued.[29]

The principle of non-*refoulement* has been compromised by general acceptance that foreign nationals have no real legal protection. In their bid to deport suspected terrorists, many governments have chosen to change their existing immigration legislation in order to manipulate internationally accepted standards of due process. In Bosnia, Britain, Canada and Denmark the same logic has been used to change legislation to circumvent the rules against refoulement, and the current climate of fear means there is little popular resistance to these changes. Foreign nationals are useful scapegoats, and due to their lack of protection are easier to remove than home-grown suspects.

Extradition

Extradition refers to the formal legal process by which an individual is delivered from the country where he or she is located to another country to face prosecution, or, if already convicted, to serve a sentence. The participants in extradition are therefore the two countries and the individual who is the subject of the proceedings. There is no other legal means of transferring a detainee from one country to another.

Although there are no concrete international rules to regulate the formal process of extradition, there are many treaties, both bi- and multi-lateral, which establish a formal legal framework for the process. According to Professor Ian Brownlie, "...states have to depend on the co-operation of the other states in order to obtain surrender of suspected criminals or convicted criminals who are, or have fled, abroad. Where this co-operation rests on a procedure of request and consent, regulated by certain general principles, the form of international judicial assistance is called extradition."[30]

Article 38 of the Statute of the International Court of Justice states the 'general principles' of international law can cover any lacunae in international law. Ultimately the practice of extradition is internationally recognised to be part of due legal process.

Various courts around the world have upheld the principle that an individual cannot be subjected to transfer to another country without a recognised form of due process. In the South African case State v Ebrahim, the Supreme Court held that the conviction of a South African citizen should be set aside because he was kidnapped from Swaziland by South African agents. According to the court, "The individual must be protected against illegal detention and abduction, the bounds of jurisdiction must not be exceeded, sovereignty must be respected, the legal process must be fair to those affected and abuse of law must be avoided in order to protect and promote the integrity of the administration of justice. This applies equally to the state. When the state is a party to a dispute, as for example in criminal cases, it must come to court with 'clean hands'. When the state itself is involved in an abduction across international borders, as in the present case, its hands are not clean...It follows that, according to our common law, the trial court had no jurisdiction to hear the case against the appellant. Consequently his conviction and sentence cannot stand."[31]

This judgement is backed by other cases. In the British case R v Horseferry Road Magistrates' Court, ex parte Bennett, the House of Lords firmly stated that if Bennett had been forcibly transferred from South Africa to Britain then that was a violation of international law and the rule of law. In the judgement, Lord Bridge stated, "To hold that the court may turn a blind eye to executive lawlessness beyond the frontiers of its own jurisdiction is, to my mind, an insular and unacceptable view."[32]

The use of extradition as a means of legal transfer between countries has been abused in the name of counter-terrorism. Understood safeguards in the process of extradition have been removed to expedite any requested transfers which in turn have led to abuses of human rights and the 'rule of law'. France and Spain have led requests for extraditions from Britain for suspected terrorists. Spain's historical use of counter-terrorism measures against Basque terrorists led to its extradition request for Iñigo Castillo Macazaga. Accused of involvement in ETA's bombing of a military barracks, Macazaga contested his involvement in the British courts. He was cleared of all charges by the High Court after it was revealed that the Spanish government had falsified evidence. After voluntarily agreeing to a lesser public order offence he returned to Spain, where he was immediately re-charged with the same falsified information that was thrown out by the British courts.

Despite the treatment of Macazaga, the British government detained Farid Hilali on a European arrest warrant. The subject of rendition flights, Hilali was tortured in Morocco and the United Arab Emirates before being released and making his way back to Britain. In September 2003 he was detained for extradition when Spain claimed that he was involved with the 9/11 attacks on the US. As with Macazaga, the Spanish government produced questionable evidence which was rejected by the British courts. On the agreement that Spain would not bring false charges against Hilali, he was extradited by Britain only to be charged by the Spanish government with these very same crimes.

But the removal of foreigners suspected of terrorism has become a priority for Britain and it resorts to numerous means to rid itself of any possible threats to the public, whatever the cost to the rule of law.

Before the attacks on the World Trade Center, the use of extradition was subject to the protections of due process. Adel Abdel Bary and Khalid Al-Fawwaz were detained in September 1998 in Britain after the US embassy bombings in East Africa. Al-Fawwaz, a Saudi reformist seeking change in the Saudi regime, and Bary, a lawyer who partook in non-violent protests against human rights abuses in Egypt, sought asylum in Britain fearing for their lives. The fact that a prima facie case must be proved by the government before their extradition can be approved has resulted in their continued detention in Britain. For over a decade the UK government has searched for ways to circumvent this bar to their removal. They have still never been charged with a crime despite the length of their detention and these extradition proceedings.

A new trend has emerged; one where manipulation of the essence of law is used to circumvent international understandings of what is considered due process. The fast-tracking of the US-UK Extradition Treaty and its subsequent ratification through the Extradition Act 2003 provides the strongest example of how the formal process of extradition is being used as a form of legal rendition.[33] Playing on the general anxiety over the threat of international terrorism, the former home secretary David Blunkett managed to push the act through parliament without any scrutiny or debate.

The most controversial issue to arise from the act is the abolition of the requirement for a prima facie case in requests from the United States for extradition from Britain. In other words, the accused does not have the right to challenge evidence provided by the US in a British court of law.

To give an example: if the US sought the extradition of suspect 'A' to stand trial for a murder committed at a particular time, the extradition could be approved once the US provided documentation with allegations that it appeared that suspect 'A' could have committed a murder. Suspect 'A' does not have the right to challenge this 'evidence' before a British judge, even if suspect 'A' can himself provide clear evidence that he was not present in the city of the murder when it occurred.

Although the legislation was aimed at dealing with suspected terrorists, the legislators never envisaged that others might be affected by it. But others, most notably the Nat West Three (all bankers), have faced extradition to the US, sending tremors through the entire business community.

There are currently four Muslim detainees facing extradition to the US under the Extradition Act 2003. Haroon Rashid Aswat, Abu Hamza al-Masri, Syed Talha Ahsan and Babar Ahmad face the prospect of life sentences and the death penalty. Although differing in the facts of the cases, the four men face the same fight against their extradition.

Babar Ahmad has been detained for over two years facing extradition, after allegations made against him by the US. Ahmad was arrested on 2 December 2003 in London by the officers from the Metropolitan Police Counter-Terrorism Command under the Terrorism Act 2000. The provisions related to his detention referred to the commission, preparation or instigation of an act or acts of terrorism. By 8 December 2003, he was released without charge after the police and the Crown Prosecution Service recognised that there was insufficient evidence to charge him with a criminal offence. Ahmad had never committed a crime in Britain relating to terrorism and had not broken any laws within the jurisdiction of the country. On 5 August 2005 things changed for him dramatically, as he explained:

The second time I was arrested (5 August 2004) on my way home from work in London by officers from the Metropolitan Police Extradition Unit in conjunction with Counter-Terrorism Command officers. This time I was arrested on the orders of the United States Government who were seeking my extradition to the US under the Extradition Act 2003.

By law, the police have to tell you why you are being held, ie suspicion of terrorism, extradition, threat to national security, etc. However, this is just standard rhetoric. During my first arrest in December 2003, I was never really told what crime I was supposed to have committed. As for my second August 2004 extradition arrest, I was given some 'details' two months later.

I am currently in prison detained subject to an extradition request from the US under the 'Extradition Act 2003 Category 2' legislation. I am held under the provisions of the controversial, one-sided UK–US Extradition Treaty of 2003, in which the US does not have to provide any prima facie evidence when seeking the extradition of anyone from the UK. In layman's terms, this means that the US does not have to prove to a British court that there is actually a case against you before having you extradited.

I have been held in high-security prisons for nearly four years without charge now. I am Britain's longest detained-without-charge British detainee, held as part of the War of Terror. There are foreign nationals that have been detained longer than me, but I am the longest held British citizen.

I have been notified by the Crown Prosecution Service and UK Attorney General several times in writing that I have not been charged because there is insufficient evidence to charge me with any criminal offence.

'They' continue to detain me because, even though I have lived all my life in the UK, I am supposed to have committed a crime within the global jurisdiction of the US. Since the UK is the closest ally of the US, the UK will detain and extradite anyone to the US upon request. That is why I am still in prison.

The US has alleged that I was involved in supporting websites publicising the cause of Chechen rebels fighting Russian troops in Chechnya in the 1990s. This is the main allegation, with dozens of other allegations to make it look serious. According to the US, supporting Chechen rebels fighting Russian soldiers is terrorism, punishable by the death penalty or life in prison without parole. Ironically, the European Court of Human Rights has ruled that Russian soldiers have been killing defenceless Chechen civilians in Chechnya.

If I am extradited to the US, there is a real risk that I could be tried by the new military courts being set up to try Guantánamo detainees on the US mainland. The alternative scenario is that I can expect to spend the rest of my life in a 'Supermax' US prison in total solitary confinement. This is not an exaggerated scenario. There are several people that have been extradited to the US who are now serving life sentences in Supermax prisons in solitary confinement.[34]

Those facing extradition to the US are not able to see or challenge the evidence against them. The UK–US Extradition Treaty 2003 is a 'rubber-stamp' policy whereby the US merely has to state their accusations without producing evidence. British courts only consider issues relating to potential abuse of human rights faced by the defendant being extradited rather than the validity of the allegations. Despite weighted international evidence to the contrary, Britain has so far failed to recognise the real risk of human rights abuses these men face if sent to the US.

GUANTÁNAMO BAY

"...I was deeply troubled by the fact that to ensure that Mr Hamdan would plead guilty as planned, the Chief Prosecutor's request came with a critical condition that the Defense Counsel was for the limited purpose of "negotiating a guilty plea" to an unspecified offense and that Mr Hamdan's access to counsel was conditioned on his willingness to negotiate such a plea."[1]

Charles D Swift—US Navy Lieutenant Commander

The origins of the facility at Guantánamo Bay can be traced back to the Spanish-American War of 1898. On 23 February 1903, the first president of Cuba, Tomas Estrada Palma, an American citizen, agreed a perpetual lease with the US for the area around Guantánamo Bay following victory against the Spanish. The Cuban-American Treaty allowed for Cuba to have sovereign control of Cuba, however the US was granted full jurisdiction and control of the naval base.

The area become home to the US Naval Station Guantánamo Bay which covers an area of approximately forty-five square miles. It is commonly abbreviated as GTMO or 'Gitmo'. Under the agreement, the terms of the lease can only be broken with the consent of both parties. Until that time the US pays a sum of $4,085 a year to the Cuban government. Fidel Castro, the former president of Cuba, rejected all but the first cheque in protest at the US presence.[2]

Following Operation Enduring Freedom, detainees began to be rounded up in prisons in Afghanistan. The Bush Administration decided not to grant prisoner-of-war protection to any of the suspects caught by the US forces. This meant that the detainees were not protected by the Geneva Conventions, and resulted in a number of cases of human rights abuses, including the Dasht-i-Leili massacre where Taliban prisoners were shot and suffocated to death in metal truck containers while being transferred from Kunduz to Sheberghan prisons.[3]

In the wake of Operation Enduring Freedom suspected Taliban troops and Al Qaeda members, whether captured on the battlefield or not, were labelled 'unlawful combatants' rather than prisoners-of-war. This has since been used to justify unlawful detention practices which violate the most basic concepts of the American Constitution and the international rule of law.[4]

Before being sent to Guantánamo Bay, the detainees were taken to either Bagram or Kandahar Airbases where they were processed. Both of these makeshift detention facilities were used to filter those detainees who would subsequently be sent to Cuba. What is surprising are the number of detainees sent to Guantánamo who clearly had nothing to do with the conflict and were rather picked up from parts of the world thousands of miles away.

The detention centre in Bagram has often been included amongst the worst torture facilities by those who were held there. The deaths of Habibullah and Dilawar at the hands of US Army soldiers resulted in the charging of twenty-seven officers.[5] Although these were just two examples of actual murders that took place, there are reports of a pattern of widespread abuse from all who gave testimonies of their time there.

In January 2002 the international media began to report the first instances of the transfer of Taliban and Al Qaeda fighters to Camp X-Ray in Guantánamo Bay. Initially there were 110 prisoners in Cuba. These were all classified as 'illegal combatants' rather than 'prisoners-of-war'. The US administration argued that it was not obliged to implement the Geneva Conventions or US constitutional obligations because Guantánamo Bay is not located on mainland US soil.[6]

On 29 April 2002, all the prisoners were transferred from Camp X-Ray to Camp Delta. Camp Delta was constructed between February and April 2002 specifically to hold detainees still being filtered through from Afghanistan and other parts of the world. Camp Delta itself comprises the detention camps I, II, III, IV, V, VI and Camp Echo. These form the permanent 612 cell detention facility that houses most of the detainees. Camp V is notorious for being the worst in its treatment of detainees. Camp Echo, also part of Camp Delta, is a detention centre where prisoners who were due to face the military commissions were held in isolation for years on end.

Although there have been public lists produced by the Americans relating to those held in the detention facility, it is commonly believed there exist many 'ghost detainees' who are held without any public acknowledgment. The International Committee of the Red Cross are quite simply not given access to certain areas of the facility, thus making it easy to internally transfer those they want to remain hidden.

As the number of detainees held at Guantánamo Bay increased, so did international anxiety about the legal basis for their detention and the apparent lack of respect for rights or due process. The Executive Order of 13 November 2001 and President Bush's order of 7 February 2002 set the framework of the detainees' status as 'unlawful combatants' and of the judicial system they were to be subjected to.[7]

The November 2001 Executive Order authorised the detention of persons outside as well as within the US and established the ground rules for the conduct of military proceedings. These rules gave the US president a central role. According to the order, the prosecutor and adjudicating panels were to be military officers accountable only to the president. Consequently, it was the president alone who bore responsibility for the final review of all verdicts given.

Further, the order stated that there was no appeal to any civilian court, nor were the defendants to have right of access to the courts of any country or to any international tribunals, including human rights courts. Also, they would not be able to choose their own counsel and all communication between defendants and their advisers was heavily restricted. The military commissions were to be conducted in secret and the prosecution would be allowed to rely on secret evidence and secret witnesses.[8]

The British law lord, Lord Steyn, has described these military commissions as kangaroo courts "which make a mockery of justice"[9] with their corrupt, hasty and biased proceedings and harsh punishments, while Lord Hope, another member of Britain's highest court, has publicly denounced the situation as a monstrous failure of justice and Guantánamo as a legal black hole.

What is more, well before any proceedings had been initiated against the detainees, the US administration prejudiced the trials by deciding in advance that the Guantánamo detainees were guilty: the president called the detainees "bad people" while secretary of state Donald Rumsfeld described them as "hard-core, well-trained terrorists". Although the order to establish military commissions to try detained non-Americans suspected of violating the rules governing the conduct of warfare was given on 13 November 2001, the first preliminary hearings were not held until August 2004.[10]

The US administration claimed that detainees held at Guantánamo Bay had no access to the fundamental rights set out in the US Constitution because the facility was not on American soil. However, the case of Rasul v Bush before the US Supreme Court changed this, as the court declared that the detainees "have been imprisoned in territory over which the United States exercises exclusive jurisdiction and control."[11]

Later in 2004, in the case of Hamdi v Rumsfeld, the US Supreme Court recognised the right of the US government to detain 'unlawful combatants', but the case was also important because of the ruling that detainees must be given the chance to challenge their detention before an impartial judge.

In November 2004, the first trial before a military commission (of Salim Hamdan) was halted by a federal judge in Washington, DC, who ruled that the proceedings lacked the basic elements of a fair trial and violated the Geneva Conventions. Following this decision the Bush administration began using Combatant Status Review Tribunals (CSRTs) to determine the status of detainees. Doing so addressed the obligation to determine the status of the prisoners established by Geneva Convention III, Article 5. These hearings were conducted based on the assertion by the United States that detainees were not eligible for the status of prisoner of war.

The CSRTs functioned from 8 July 2004 to 29 March 2005 to define the status of the detainees. Ninety-three percent of the then 554 detainees were classified as unlawful enemy combatants. The Court of Appeals reinstated the tribunals in July 2005.

It has been suggested that the tribunals are inherently even more flawed than the initial military commissions. At times the proceedings of CSRTs have been rudimentary at best, affording the detainees few basic protections. Many detainees lacked counsel, and the CSRT only informed detainees of general charges against them, while classifying the details on which the CSRT based their decisions. What is more, detainees had no right to present witnesses or to cross-examine government witnesses.[12] Indeed, it is hard to argue that the procedures of CSRTs would qualify as status determination under the Third Geneva Convention.

On 29 June 2006, in the case of Hamdan v Rumsfeld, the US Supreme Court held that trying detainees under the Guantánamo military commission was illegal and broke both the Geneva Conventions and the Uniform Code of Military Justice, and that as a consequence of this violation they lacked the power to proceed. Judge Robertson held that it was impossible for a CSRT to be considered a competent tribunal as it failed to meet the requirements of Article 5 of the Third Geneva Convention.[13]

The Bush Administration pushed for acceptance of the commissions in Congress. Eventually, the proposed bill to "legalise" military commissions passed through the Senate and the House of Representatives. The bill was signed into law by President Bush on 17 October 2006 and became known as the Military Commissions Act 2006. The act's stated purpose is "to authorize trial by military commission for violations of the law of war, and for other purposes" The wording of the text was left purposefully vague in order to bring under its remit any act which the US may deem related to international terrorism.

The act has come under the severe scrutiny of international human rights organisations and lawyers. Amongst the restrictions impeding the progress of free and fair trials, military commissions differ from regular trials in the following ways:

- The prosecution is authorised to make use of secret evidence that the suspect is unable to obtain;
- Evidence obtained through "coercive interrogation techniques" is considered valid. These coercive techniques have already been admitted by the CIA to include 'waterboarding' (simulated drowning) and beatings. Testimonies of detainees have painted a far more sinister picture of the techniques used;
- The Appointing Officer in charge of the commission is authorised to shut down any commission without offering any justification or explanation;
- The suspects are only allowed attorneys entitled to a secret security clearance, and not a representative of their own choosing;
- Charges brought by a commission which are dismissed do not entitle the suspect to be released from detention. Release will only be granted when the US military deem the individual to be no longer a threat to US interests, and even then it will depend on whether or not US foreign policy allows for the individual to be returned to their

home country. For example, US foreign policy on China does not allow them to return the ethnic Uighurs,[14] despite their having been cleared of any wrongdoing.

On 12 June 2008, the courts dealt a major blow to the US administration over the continued detention of foreign nationals at Guantánamo Bay and elsewhere. In the case of Al Odah v United States the Supreme Court ruled that all foreign nationals detained at Guantánamo Bay have the right to pursue habeas corpus challenges to their detention. Although the decision was strong in one sense, it did not go as far as actually challenging the nature of the detentions themselves at Guantánamo. The judgement did not cover the issue of whether or not the detainees should be released or indeed whether or not the president had the authority to detain them.

Facing public humiliation, the Bush administration fought back with the trial of Salim Hamdan, a man accused of being Osama bin Laden's driver. The US government attempted to lend legitimacy to the system they had created by securing their first conviction with a military commission. On 6 August 2008, Salim Hamdan was convicted of his role as a 'small player' within the Al Qaeda structure. The decision of the commission was heavily criticised by many within the international community. Zachary Katzenelson, legal director and attorney for thirty-two Guantánamo detainees, said of the conviction:

Fighting terrorism is a deadly serious game, but the show trial of Salim Hamdan looks like amateur hour. We heard during the closing arguments that Salim Hamdan gave the US information about where Osama bin Laden was—and the US botched the job. At the last minute of the trial, prosecutors realized they hadn't proven some of the charges, so asked the judge to rewrite the law. And throughout, evidence gained from coercion—evidence that would never be allowed in a civilian or regular military court—was allowed to form the very heart of the prosecution's case. These trials need to be professional, clear and open. Instead, we've got a shambles that brings us no closer to justice.

These trials are not just about a few men and what they may have done—they are about the message the United States is sending to the world. And that message right now is flat wrong: convictions by any means necessary. The US needs to show it stands for openness and fairness—the very values we are fighting for. Instead, we get verdicts rammed down the gullet of justice. That's not going to bring anyone to our side.[15]

The prospect of change at Guantánamo Bay was never considered until the presidential campaign of Barack Hussein Obama. Having promised to close the base down, President Obama silenced critics days into his tenure when on 22 January 2009, he signed an executive order for the base to shut within one year.[16] The move was quickly praised by NGOs who pushed for details of how the base would be closed. President Obama will face difficult questions ahead, from the repatriation of detainees that no country wants, to establishing which system of law is best applied to men who have been detained for seven years without charge or trial.

Whatever the future of the base, Guantánamo Bay exists as a legal black hole. Even without references to the treatment of detainees at the base and the abuse they have been subjected to, the picture of detentions is bleak; particularly when scrutinised through the lens of the rule of law. And Guantánamo's existence does not simply impact upon the detainees present in its cells. Its very existence has become associated with US abuses in the War on Terror and the very symbol of human rights violations in detention.

This chapter seeks to provide the views of those on the frontlines of dealing with Guantánamo Bay. The detainees, their families and their lawyers have all come to know the Guantánamo system and to understand its implications in the worldwide context. US actions at the base have taken on a greater significance in terms of the entire War on Terror and the concurrent battle of ideas that is taking place.

Guantánamo's lawyers

Guantánamo Bay changed the landscape of military justice through the introduction of military commissions. The US government planned on proceeding quickly with military commissions in order to try the detainees. These initial commissions removed the right of the defendant to appoint independent legal counsel and so military lawyers were drafted in to represent the detainees.

Among the first military lawyers to be brought in as counsel for the detainees was Lieutenant Commander Charles D Swift, a judge, attorney and naval officer in the Judge Advocate General's Court in the United States Navy. Swift expected the system of justice in Guantánamo to be very much akin to the system he was already familiar with after seventeen years of service; he was soon to realise otherwise. Having been brought to the base but denied the right to see any clients, the lieutenant commander began in-depth study of the history of the United States military justice and of previous commissions that had been convened. He soon realised there were inherent differences between the military commissions in Guantánamo Bay and those of the past:

Unlike other military commissions in the past, these aren't per se military, they are only military in the sense that they are being staffed by military officers but they were not created by military officers. The military commission instead of being run by the military is being run by the Department of Defense which is the civilian portion of the US military. The order was written by the president, who also created them. The next set of orders has been written by the secretary of defense and his general counsel, and the person who is in charge of administering them is a civilian appointed by the secretary of defense. So they are basically civilian controlled instruments. Historically, military commissions were about like trying like, i.e. one military tried the other military. That in fact helped with their fairness. When you are in the military and you are trying someone on the other side, you realise what goes around comes around and you can hardly complain when the same thing is done to you or your fellow soldiers or sailors because it is about the understanding we have in our relations. The same understanding did not play into this system. So this was one of the fundamental differences this had from past military commissions.[17]

The concept of fair trials has been lost in the process of military commissions in Guantánamo Bay. By using the term 'military' the US government has attempted to add a layer of acceptability to the process, however the international community has long recognised that the detainees are being held off the US mainland in order to remove their constitutional protections:

Why do I believe the detainees will not receive a fair trial? It comes down to several things. The first and most important is the system is set up to protect the government, not the individual. That is, in every single balance that has gone, absolute discretion is given to the government. It is better in this system to find an innocent man guilty than hurt the government. The US justice system is founded on the absolute opposite principle, that is, it is better to let ten guilty people go, than punish one innocent man. This system turns that on its head, and it is demonstrated repeatedly in the process ... The first thing the administration says is these people are 'unlawful combatants', that is why we can try them before military commissions. Well, another word for 'unlawful combatants' is criminal. So they are presumed guilty. Also instead of the individual having the right to defend himself, this system gives the individual no right to defend himself. They can be excluded from significant portions of their trial, they are not allowed to defend themselves against the evidence against them, the punishments are indeterminate ie they are whatever we feel like giving you, no set statutes on who deserves the death penalty or how long you would get—it is solely discretionary. All of these things violate international law and US statute. The system doesn't adhere to the basic ideas of either international or US justice so it is difficult to come up with the idea of how it could be a fair trial. This system is supposedly good enough for everyone except American citizens. If it's good enough for everyone else, why isn't it good enough for American citizens?[18]

Working towards trying to improve the situation of detainees in Guantánamo, Swift legally challenged the make-up of the panel presiding over the CSRTs. Taking a moral position, Swift was one of the few military lawyers to push hard for regular military justice to be applied rather than the new military commissions. Originally the commission rules dictated that there would be a five-member panel presiding over each case. With his challenge against the format of presiding judges, Lieutenant Commander Charles Swift inadvertently made the situation worse for the detainees:

Under commission rules, you must get two thirds of the panel to vote guilty. When there are 5, 4 must vote for guilty, or 2 must vote for not guilty. When there are 4, 3 votes for guilty, and 2 votes for acquittal. When they are 3, you need 2 for guilty and 2 for acquittal. So statistically, all I did is make my odds worse of getting an acquittal. At the time when I challenged them, I thought there would be 5 on the panel. The commission see it, as if it is bad for the accused then that's the way it is going to go. Every decision seems to come out with "what is best for the government, that is what will be decided".

The panel was flawed from the off set, this is not intended as a criticism of any of the officers on it. But, look at it from this standpoint—my wife is a professional pilot and I don't claim that just because I have seen her fly and heard about flight, it doesn't make me able to be a pilot. I don't have the training or experience to do that. And so we cannot look at the complicated subject of international law and claim that any officer can do that. Yet this panel is required to make some of the most difficult and unprecedented legal decisions in modern history, in a situation that even the administration refers to as unprecedented. They have no legal training with which to be able to do this, with the exception of one retired judge on the panel who is no longer licensed to actively practice US law in a Court Marshal.[19]

The military commissions were established as the primary tool to convict those the American administration felt were guilty of terrorism. The process was designed simply to obtain convictions. Alongside Lieutenant Commander Charles D Swift, there were other military attorneys who took an interest in ensuring that the detainees had access to all the procedures of a fair trial. Lieutenant Colonel Yvonne Bradley was appointed counsel for the British resident, Binyam

Mohammed Al Habashi, a man who was kidnapped in Pakistan, sold to the US, placed on a rendition flight to Morocco where he was tortured, sent back to Afghanistan and finally rendered to Guantánamo Bay. Al Habashi was one of the few detainees set to face charges under the original military commissions:

...under the old commission he was charged with, and when I say the old commission, the commission hearings that were going on until the Hamdan v Rumsfeld case which the Supreme Court ruled that the commissions were unconstitutional. But under the old system Mr Mohammed was charged with this complex conspiracy. He wasn't even charged with any substance offences, one large conspiracy of attending camps and of knowing almost anybody you can, a Who's Who of Al Qaeda individuals that he allegedly knew. Which I mean it was absolutely, if we weren't in a real life situation it would be almost hilarious. But it was one large complex, illogical conspiracy.[20]

For Lieutenant Colonel Yvonne Bradley, the difficulties of representing her client were accentuated by her status as a military lawyer. Regardless of her ethics—of being an individual who wishes to see all human beings receive a fair trial—her position within the US military has made any representation of Binyam extremely difficult:

It's frustrating because individuals really expect an attorney/client relationship. Given after four or five years of abuse by, at the hands of either military authorities and or law enforcement authorities of the United States, that I am supposed to go in and establish some kind of trust relationship with this, with my client, and to be able to represent him in any fashion is almost ridiculous. In the sense, there's so much to overcome and it's not going to be overcome within months or years given that he's still psychologically in prison, physically imprisoned. And there's no way to establish a trust. The system that they set up at Guantánamo doesn't allow it. It doesn't allow communication of attorney/client privilege. As far as letter writing, without my letters or anything that was sent being looked at, it doesn't allow telephone communication. It allows nothing that can establish attorney/client relationships. So I smile and I shake my head in desperation, because it's almost hard to describe what that relationship is because it's not designed or fostered to ever establish anything but the continual distrust that any individual would have given the abuse, given what this individual has, Mr Mohammed has gone through.

During the last set of commissions, before they were shut down by the US Supreme Court in the Hamdan case Binyam was asked to choose an attorney and he was pretty much being forced to choose me because he couldn't represent himself, and the rules state that he had to have American counsel, pretty much American military counsel. And Binyam put it very succinctly. He told the judge imagine you as an American over in Pakistan or Afghanistan and you get picked up by the Al Qaeda or the Taliban, and once you get picked up and arrested you are put away for a long period of time, not allowed to see anyone, tortured and abused. And then one day after three or four years someone with a turban and a beard came in and said I'm here to represent you, trust me. At what stage would you ever trust that person?[21]

The inherently flawed process of the original military commissions was recognised by the Supreme Court in the US, however this was as much to do with the commissions having been unilaterally formed by the president without any congressional approval as with any human rights abuses. The Bush administration sought to rectify this through the drafting of the Military Commissions Act (MCA) 2006. Requiring the acquiescence of Congress, the administration provided a framework that would allow them to legalise many aspects of the commission system that were considered unethical. Despite her status as a military lawyer, Bradley strongly contested the ethical nature of the MCA:

If anyone believes that individuals would be fairly treated and receive due process under the MCA they're under a great delusion. And as I say I can only compare it to the Japanese internment where we justified locking up people without due process. The MCA will deny people due process; will deny them a fair trial. It is designed for one goal and one goal only in my opinion, and that is to secure convictions. It's not there to decide innocence and guilt; it's designed for the government to ensure that these individuals are convicted without solid evidence and with the use of torture and things that would not be tolerated if we were looking at this from a very logical, fair and due process viewpoint.[22]

What worries Bradley and other lawyers about the MCA are the provisions which strip away the recognised due process as the US has always known it. Secret evidence, hearsay evidence, the inability to call witnesses and to cross-examine are just some of the consequences of the legislation which seeks to establish a war crimes tribunal. As a result the lawyers have spoken harshly of the provisions as Bradley explains:

That the use of coercion can be used against a person, that is against every constitutional principle I've ever been taught. Against every due process principle I've ever practised. That you can coerce someone or torture someone or abuse someone physically or psychologically and then allow those type of unreliable, false statements, confessions, admissions to be used against the individual, that's absolutely unacceptable in civilized societies. So that is one.

Secondly, it's allowing the use of hearsay. Not requiring the actual witness who made mention or statements against the individual to come into court room to testify and then not allowing the methods, the techniques that were used to obtain this statement or to obtain this evidence to be fully disclosed. And for the Government to hide behind this national security in classification to avoid the embarrassment of how they obtained this information.

Along with habeas corpus, I mean that act is so bad that I could probably go through a laundry list but the torture, the hearsay, the ipso facto, the making up of laws after the fact to make them offences, the habeas, it's not even, words really actually escape me of what I can really say about the MCA. It's not a fair piece of legislation at all. An embarrassment, that any country or any government or anyone would allow people to be processed under that and call it fair and full trials.[23]

Running concurrently with the difficulties of bringing legal challenges, the lawyers have faced an onslaught in the media, particularly within the first five years of Guantánamo's use as a prison for terror suspects. Public opinion in the US favoured the abandonment of due process in order to detain those who may have possibly been involved with terrorist attacks in the US. Clive Stafford Smith, a civilian lawyer for the Guantánamo Bay detainees, has been working towards due process despite these intense difficulties. Much of Stafford Smith's work has centred on changing public perceptions of the detainees in order to bring about a demand for their collective justice:

When we first brought litigation against the Bush administration two-and-a-half years ago [2002], I think it would be safe to say, ninety-nine percent of the Americans were against us. You have to remember that the presidency of the US is a powerful bull pulpit, and George Bush and his henchmen have been preaching about how wicked and evil everyone in Guantánamo Bay is for a long time. We don't have a pulpit of any kind to respond, and while we may have made some gains in terms of the notion that everyone should be accorded basic human rights, we have made very little headway on convincing Americans that a large proportion of those at Guantánamo are not guilty. It's hardly surprising. I am one of many lawyers who have been banging on for decades about how we are fallible, and how many people on Death Row are innocent. It is only recently, in the wake of many DNA exonerations, that people have just begun to listen, and the polls still put support for capital punishment at seventy-five percent of the population. It's a long battle.[24]

Stafford Smith has often commented on the politicised nature of the events surrounding the War on Terror, a view that has become more and more accepted around the world as US actions and interventions are exposed as having purposes beyond those initially stated. One of the main concepts he puts forward is that of the 'politics of fear'[25], a concept which he believes drives the War on Terror and helps perpetuate it:

The politics of hatred dictate what a government does when it is faced with immense problems—like crime, drugs or, in this case, attacks of the sort that happened on September 11. Such a government has a stark choice. On the one side, they could do something sensible about the problem, which may take years to resolve, and will definitely not be solved in time for the election cycle. On the other hand, the government can just tell the electorate to hate a small group of people to try and hope this distracts the public from what the real problem is. Internationally, terrorism, as we label it, is clearly a problem, although I would argue that it has been with us a long time, and the pretence that we are in a new age is very questionable. But no matter what your view, the solution to terrorism requires an analysis of the causes of it, and some effort to address the grievances of people around the world. That would take a long time—much longer than the American election cycle—and it would take a lot of work and resources. The Bush administration must face an election, and it is simply not willing to take the longer view. It is much easier to win an election by frightening and inspiring the electorate to fear and hate Muslims than it is to do something sensible about terrorism.

The politics of hatred is not unique to America—we do this in Britain as well. But hatred is a two-way street. So do the countries that we label the Third World. If America tells an Iraqi to aspire to fancy cars and McDonald's burgers, what is the Iraqi government to do? The per capita national income in Iraq is roughly one hundredth of the US. The government can either say that people can have the American lifestyle if we all work very hard and are patient for a couple of hundred years ... or the government can tell its people that the money-grubbing, oil-grabbing Americans are to blame for their misery. If there were true democracy in Iraq at the next election, there is no doubt who would win it, and it would not be someone who purported to admire America.[26]

Despite all the debates back and forth regarding due process and the true intentions behind the War on Terror, one of the main areas of concern for the international community is the repercussions of this war in terms of the way it is being fought. Like many other lawyers, Stafford Smith sees Guantánamo Bay as a symbol of what is wrong with the American counter-terrorism strategy, and further sees it as a weapon of propaganda in the hands of terrorists. He has proselytised that the War on Terror is nothing more than America's crusade against the Muslim world, a sentiment that is echoed strongly throughout the Middle East and Asia:

The short term impact has been an absolute catastrophe where we have damaged the international reputation of the US, we have damaged relations with everyone in the Muslim world, and we have inspired thousands of people to commit violent acts against the US and others. This is very sad and utterly pointless. The long term impact is very difficult to gauge and it will depend very much on all of us, whether we can repair the damage that Bush has caused. The first step to repairing that damage is to get a new president. America is very uncomfortable unless it has a black and white enemy. American needs clarity in its world. Everyone was happy when we had the Soviets and the Red Menace, opposed by America and everything good on the other. The US was uncomfortable after the Berlin wall fell because things were no longer black and white. There was the war on drugs and the war on poverty, but these were complex and did not have evil people who could hold their own as the bad guys in a James Bond film. Unfortunately, the War on Terror re-established America's black and white world, and refocused our fear and hatred. As long as America takes the idiotic and naive approach that it is taking in the War on Terror then an American passport is going to be an increasingly dangerous commodity.[27]

Guantánamo Bay has become a very strong icon in the War on Terror—its existence has had great ramifications for the way in which other countries view their counter-terrorism policies and the way in which they administer justice. For many lawyers, Guantánamo has led the world in a back-sliding of human rights and due process with right-wing commentators keen to seize on the example of the US. German lawyer, Bernard Docke, who represented the interests of former Guantánamo detainee Murat Kurnaz, has previously spoken about the 'Guantanamisation of German Immigration Policy':

Guantánamo has triggered discussions about the value of constitutional protections. There also is a debate about the rightfulness of torture in extreme cases, a separate enemy criminal law for alleged terror suspects as well as preventive security detention on simple grounds of suspicion. So far the constitutional state has prevailed and this is good.[28]

Constant references are made similar to the term 'Guantanamisation', making Guantánamo synonymous with injustice. The families of those detained for suspected terrorism in the United States refer to Indiana's Fairfax prison as being the mainland's Guantánamo, while Long Lartin prison in Britain is sometimes referred to as 'Lartanamo'. Guantánamo Bay has permeated the psyche of the international community.

Guantánamo's families

The families of those detained in Guantánamo Bay have been just as quick to understand the value of American justice as their detained loved ones. The difficulties they face range from psychological trauma to economic problems as they strive to cope in a situation where they are not being allowed any semblance of justice or recourse to the law. One pervading and recurrent sentiment common to all the families, however, is that they never expected a system like that in Guantánamo to be administered by the US.

An interesting consequence of the detentions in Guantánamo has been the activism of the families; they have been forced to enter into the public eye and fight through the media for their loved ones. With no way to challenge the unlawful detentions, families have often sought to gain public and political support through organising events and demonstrations. Some of the families have become figures of national pride as they speak out for justice for all those detained. Others however, are perpetually demonised for their link to a suspected terrorist or enemy combatant.

The wives of the Algerians taken from Bosnia were amongst the first to involve themselves with international campaigns to close Guantánamo in late 2001. Their husbands are still amongst the longest serving detainees, some of whom have still not been charged with any crime. Emina Lahmar, the wife of Saber Lahmar, constantly went to various courts and lawyers in order to find one source that could provide them with justice, but each time reached a dead-end:

One year ago [2006] the American lawyers said they saw secret documents in the Bosnian courts and the US and had been given access to American documents, but under one condition, that they could not say anything about the context of the documents. I asked one of the lawyers about whether or not there was any reason we should be worried about the contents, the lawyer said that there is no reason to keep them in Guantánamo.

Our lawyers pressed charges against Bosnia and Herzegovina (BiH) in the court in Brussels and one week ago we got information that the Brussels court will take this case in the court. Unfortunately the court, if their decision be positive for us in those charges, the court cannot enforce it to release them but still this decision can be very heavy. The court decided on material compensation, and immediately after the decision two days after, this decision will be imposed and because Bosnian officials know they will lose, already we got proposition from Bosnian government, that they will support our children every month.

In 2003 because of the decision of the HR Chamber in Bosnia, the government paid us compensation because they send them innocent to Guantánamo. There is nowhere anywhere anything on these Algerians. They were in every Bosnian institution, they were clean from charges, they have been found completely innocent. I have a document from the Supreme Court for releasing of my husband and below in capital letters it is written, "They have to be released now". This means that when prison guards have this paper, they must release them.[29]

The hardships faced by the women are not limited to the legal and political challenges on behalf of their husbands. The detention affects the entire family structure, particularly children. Released detainees have often spoken of letters received from their children, where the US military has blacked out nearly the entire letter out of fear that there is some secret message contained from Al Qaeda. The children become shadows of themselves and isolated from society. Some children are left in ignorance by mothers who are too afraid to taint their childhood with such information, other children have become political activists themselves, speaking on platforms around the world about the loss of their fathers. In Britain, Anas El Banna, the son of former Guantánamo detainee Jamil El Banna, has become a household name and been awarded prizes for the campaign he led for his father. In 2007, the *New Statesman* awarded him the NS Person of the Year Humanity Award for his role in campaigning for his father's release. But nothing can hide the underlying sadness that exists within these children. Nadja Disderavic, the wife of Boudella Haji, explains the impact of Guantánamo on her children:

My children are not children, they are grown up persons. Instead of cartoons and movies, they are watching news, and political stories. My son Abdul Aziz said to me, mum, why don't they take you to Guantánamo, because our Baba didn't do anything against anyone and you are fighting all the time. This means that he has now started to think about who is guilty and that his father is not, he is eleven years old. Once he said to me, I will go in front of the US Embassy and make some trouble, so they send me to Guantánamo to be with my Baba. All of my children are living in trauma, for example, when they have to buy something from the school, a book or anything, any need of the school, they don't tell me, because they are ashamed or afraid.

Once the teacher of my daughter Iman she called me and said that she did not have the necessary things for mathematics so she cannot concentrate on this subject. I was very concerned because I always buy for them whatever they need, I always ask from them why this is happening, and she told me, well I know that you will buy for me all that I need, but I do not want to make it hard for you to release our Baba. Then I opened all their school bags, then I found out that every one of them is missing some things for school and they told me that they agreed not to ask me anything in order to help me. That means that they are not like ordinary children who talk about playing and other children's stuff, but they are thinking about how to help me release their father.[30]

Understanding extra-judicial detention is something that seems to come unnervingly naturally to all these children. They are not only perceptive to their own plight, but to the plight of others around the world, whether it is in Guantánamo or elsewhere.

Saifullah Paracha, a Pakistani citizen and businessman, was requested by his American colleague to attend a business meeting in Bangkok. Flying from Karachi, Paracha disappeared at some point during the flight. The Thai authorities denied him ever having entered the country but there was no record of Paracha being in Pakistan and his name was present on the Pakistani Exit Central List. The next time the Paracha family heard of Saifullah's existence was when a letter from Bagram declared his detention there. After fifteen months at Bagram, where he suffered abuse at the hands of the US guards, he was rendered to Guantánamo Bay and placed in Camp V. Now in his early sixties, Paracha has suffered from two heart attacks as well as other medical ailments but has still not been charged with any crime. Saifullah Paracha's detention has had a great impact on his family, and particularly on the lives of his children. The youngest, Zahra Paracha, was ten at the time of his kidnapping. She spoke four years later about the impact of his incarceration on her life:

My friends are all occupied in stuff like 'does this shawl look good on me' and they model in front of the mirror for like hours and go like 'hi', try to pretend how to say hi to people and it's just materialistic and it's just ridiculous and they love shopping, I don't know why. Something is wrong with them, something seriously wrong with them, they should go to a psychiatrist and I'm looking at stuff like Lebanon and Israel war and I know if I ever mention it to them, they will have the dumbest look on this planet because they won't know a single thing I'm talking about. The first reaction will be 'will I still be able to go shopping' stuff like that and I know they can find their own spaces and I wouldn't blame them because they're not really that old, they are only fourteen and when I realise that I am only fourteen then I realise there is something wrong with me.

It was just really weird. I told my friend I am supposed to go to Islamabad, there's this workshop, I have to go to a press conference and she said 'what', I said 'yeah', 'you're crazy' and I said 'you're crazy'...in my head of course. Then she said 'how come you're going to such huge things and you're only fourteen' and I said, I thought in my head fourteen doesn't mean only fourteen, fourteen is an ideal age to start but according to her fourteen is shawls and shopping and stuff like that.[31]

Children younger than Zahra have equally strong views formed by the detentions of their fathers, but there are many children who have never met their fathers at all. Shaker Abdur Raheem Aamer was detained in Afghanistan after the US invasion. Aamer had been working for a charity when the conflict began and had made preparations for his family to leave the country. He was sent to Guantánamo at a time when his wife was expecting their fourth child—which means that he has never met his youngest. The US government has cleared Aamer for release, but the British and Saudi governments have made his return difficult. His eldest daughter, Johaina Aamer, remembers her father and understands the impact that his detention has had on them all:

My father Shaker Aamer is away since I was four years old and now I am eight. I have three younger brothers. I miss him a lot because he looked after me day and night whenever I fell ill. He would take us shopping, parks where I would feed the ducks etc. I enjoyed being with him he would always make me happy. I remember when he used to hold us in his arms, me and my two younger brothers altogether, we all had fun with him, now I miss him and I miss those days I spent with him. When I started my school I would cry every day because I wanted to go with him. My youngest brother Abdussalam is four and he has never seen my father but he does know that he is someone special because we always talk about him. If he sees some children calling their father Abi he thinks that he is our Abi as well.

Sometimes my mum cries for him. I feel like crying as well and sometimes we all cry with her, she says "I need your father to help me take care of you". I can't see my mum crying because I don't know what to do when she cries. My brother Abdullah once said in his tears don't worry mum maybe he was on his way and his car broke down that's why he is taking long, but now he understands it's not him who doesn't want to come, it's those cruel people who don't let him come. He feels really upset about it, he says don't they go back to their own families whenever they want to so why they keeping our Abi for so long.

Before I could not read my father's letters but since I learned to read and write I read my father's letters, it makes me extremely worried about his health. I wonder what they do to my father, I see the cages on TV which frightens me even more. I and my brothers don't understand why he is kept because they think he is dangerous, I think if he was he would have killed us first, but he is a loving and caring father, to me he is more important than the whole wide world. I dread how long he would be there for, being treated as an animal in a cage. The bad part I don't like is that we can't even go and see him, not even on Eid day. Here is another Eid without him, we go to the mosque. I see other happy children with their father and mother, my little brothers look at them and wonder, is this how Abi is.[32]

One family that has faced incredible turmoil during the War on Terror has been the Khadr family. During the 1980s, Egyptian-born Canadian Ahmed Said Khadr fought alongside Osama bin Laden against the Soviets in Afghanistan at a time when Muslims were travelling en masse to do so. Returning to Canada, Khadr joined the NGO Human Concern International which was funded by CIDA, an aid agency for the Canadian government. Khadr was helping with post-conflict reconstruction work in Afghanistan funnelling money from Canada through the NGO. In the mid-nineties Khadr made the decision to move his entire family to Afghanistan where he wished them to settle. The Khadr family became well known in Afghanistan for establishing institutions such as schools and hospitals, but particularly for their work in establishing schools for girls.

The attacks on 9/11 changed the lives of the Khadrs forever. During later fighting that took place, Ahmed Said Khadr was killed, his son Abdur Rahman Khadr was caught by the Northern Alliance and sold to the US, his other son Omar Khadr was shot by the US army three times before being detained, and his other two sons were eventually wounded and detained. Abdur Rahman and Omar were eventually sent to Guantánamo Bay, Omar was only fifteen at the time.

The experience of the two brothers in Guantánamo has been very different. Although both were asked to work on behalf of the US, only Abdur Rahman agreed, seeking a quick exit from the US naval base. He claims that he was requested by the CIA to work as a spy in Bosnia. Eventually he decided to renege on his agreement and asked his grandmother in Canada to go to the media exposing the conditions of his release from Guantánamo Bay. The Canadian Embassy in Sarajevo allowed Abdur Rahman entry and he was later returned to Canada to be reunited with his family.

Omar Khadr was one of the few children to be placed on rendition flights to Guantánamo Bay, where he has been detained for the last five years. In many ways he has come to symbolise everything that is wrong with the system in Guantánamo. One of the most challenging aspects of Omar's situation, however, has been his demonisation by the Canadian press. Despite having been moved to Afghanistan by his father, Omar remains a Canadian citizen and for his family seeking due process for him it has been as much about fighting for his rights in the media as it has been about finding him legal recourse. Determined to rid the public of any misperceptions about the family, the eldest sister,

Zaynab Khadr, published her private email address, requesting the Canadian people to write to her to debate what was happening to her family:

> It's been a very difficult three years when you feel that your whole life has been turned upside down in such a short time. Three years when you lose your home, your surroundings, your friends, your brother, your father, your life, your security in three years is quite bad. Then you end up in a land where you are not really wanted and they don't think like you, and you are condemned for your thoughts, not for your deeds and actions. Those years were very hard but hardening at the time, as children. There is not a house nor a family we know that has not had a death or a prisoner until now. Everyone is suffering and the Muslim Ummah is just watching. This is the saddest thing. That the Muslim Ummah is watching and it's not even condemning the actions.
>
> I thought that the people have this picture of us as these very arrogant, selfish, scary people who did not care for anyone. So giving my email address out would give everyone a chance to throw what they had at me and see what they could get out of it. I like to know the point of view of people and I like them to know my point of view in return. Sometimes you fear what you don't know and what you don't understand. I want people to know that we can be different but that does not make us bad. We can be different but we have to accept each other for our differences. This is what freedom is all about. As Canadians, even if as a non Muslim, if I can respect you for what you are and accept you even if I don't like it, you should have enough in you to respect and accept me as well. As for the responses, I got a lot of very bad responses but once in a while I would get something good. It was strange that some people would find it in their hearts to say, I know you are different and we may not agree on everything but you should know this is your country and we welcome you back.[33]

The notion that the War on Terror has become synonymous with a war against Islam is a feeling that pervades Muslim communities around the world. Having suffered at the hands of despotic regimes in Muslim countries, many Muslims fled to the western world in order to escape both religious and political persecution. For many, Guantánamo Bay and the treatment of the Muslim detainees there is reminiscent of practices in the Arab and Muslim world, and for those who have escaped such atrocities, the reality of Guantánamo becomes even more stark, and bitterly ironic.

In 1986, Omar Deghayes fled as a child with his family from Libya after the political assassination of his father for being a trade unionist under the Gaddafi regime. The family claimed asylum in Britain. Despite over a decade growing up in Britain, Deghayes never claimed

British citizenship due to the family's desire to maintain their claim on land they owned in Libya.

Deghayes decided that he wished to live in Afghanistan because it was a Muslim country, eventually moving out there and marrying an Afghan woman. At the outbreak of war after the attacks on the World Trade Center, he decided to move to Pakistan. Here he was kidnapped by the authorities and eventually sold to the Americans like so many others in his situation. Very soon, he found himself detained in Guantánamo Bay, far removed from any recognisably western notion of justice.

For the family, his detention became a repeat of everything they had been through two decades before in Libya, except now the abuse of the law was by the Americans and British. Amani Deghayes, his sister, became extremely active in lobbying for her brother's return; especially as this was the second time she would feel the insecurity of injustice:

I personally feel really depressed. I cannot believe this could all happen. All this that people take for granted—that we live in this country where there is rule of law, there are all these rights you're supposed to have, but at the same time, if the Government doesn't want to implement them, they don't have to. International law, it seems as if it only applies to some people, and not others.

Up to now it [the British government] has been very blasé. That is, 'we cannot do anything because he is not a British citizen, and it's up to the Libyan Government to act on your behalf.'

It's just ridiculous because he is a recognised refugee and they are supposed to be his surrogate state, which means they are supposed to protect him. I don't know how they can pretend that that is not an issue. Omar has never been back to Libya. Even if he wasn't a refugee, I think the situation would merit his becoming one, because in Libya, just the fact that he was in Camp X Ray is enough for him to be persecuted. His being religious is quite dangerous in Libya especially when you are active in the community like he was.

Until recently, they have shown little responsibility to their own British citizens, which is quite shocking. I don't want to be paranoid, but I think it's a racist thing. It seems that being Muslim or being religious is a terrible thing, and that if anyone is religiously active, it must mean they have links with terrorism and they hate the west and democracy. This is outrageous. There are a lot of people in this country who are held without trial, just because they suspect them of something, which makes you think that if they have evidence, why don't they bring them to trial. It's not considered acceptable for anyone else except Muslims.[34]

Guantánamo's victims

The most public detainees in the War on Terror have been those held in Guantánamo Bay. Innumerable books, research papers and articles have been written about them and the extra-legal phenomenon that is their prison. While the detention of those in Guantánamo is often considered to be terrible in the extreme, at times it pales in comparison with the experiences of other detainees worldwide, something that will be discussed in subsequent chapters.

After their long periods of detention at the US naval base, released detainees find problems on return to their host countries. Detainees such as Adel Hamad, Salim Mahmoud Adam, Hamad Ali and Sami El Hajj have received a welcome fit for heroes, whereas others, such as those returned to Britain, were arrested on arrival. For others living in countries with questionable detention policies, the situation is far worse.

Airat Vakhitov was one of a few Russian detainees sent to Guantánamo Bay. After three years' detention the Russian authorities deemed him to be a terrorist threat. Despite never having been charged with any crime by the US, and indeed purposely delaying his own return to Russia after refusing to sign a statement of guilt, he has been consistently harassed by the US. Vakhitov had never been in Afghanistan before his kidnapping and rendition by the US in Tajikestan. He was placed under Afghan custody at the time of the Taliban and was still in the country at the start of the conflict with the US. The Northern Alliance took control of the prison he was detained in and handed him over to the US who, after a period of detention in Afghanistan, placed him on a rendition flight to Guantánamo Bay. Despite his lack of connection to international terrorism, the mark of Guantánamo branded him and Russians took that as a sign of guilt:

The conditions in the Russian jail lack sanitary conditions. When I was held in the Afghan prisons, we were visited by the ICRC and they disinfected the place. There is no such thing in the Russian prisons. All possible kinds of insects and vermin, they're all there in the prison cells. We had fleas, the food was rotten cabbage which has been held somewhere in the basement for a few years or more. And when they placed this in the corridor, it still hadn't reached the cell, the reason was because we used to shout, 'we don't want to eat, take it back, take it back, we are on a hunger strike today.' There were some soups but they were always made with pork, so I couldn't eat it. I should express my gratitude to Fatima Tekayva (the mother of former Guantánamo detainee,

Rasul Kudayev) who visited all seven of us in this prison every fortnight, and she was passing food to us, and thanks to her, I didn't die of starvation. With regards to torture in the prison, it is normal practice to torture the prisoner in Russia. Of course it is prohibited by law, nevertheless the last time we were detained we were not tortured, but only because they didn't want to. If they wanted to, they would have tortured us. Somehow they lost interest in us. Now they are quite interested in Rasul, and that's why they are torturing him big time.

My recent arrest was directly connected to my statement I had made during the press conference that the corrupt special forces of Russia decided to act on the order from the Americans to arrest me. My friend and I, Rustam, were detained and I thought they were going to kill us. But I managed to make one call and I considered this call had saved my life. First of all I would like to express my gratitude to Allah for saving my life, secondly to Alexandria Zernova; thirdly towards the journalists who made the huge noise in the media about this, and then the Prosecutors Office where they took us, they literally had no choice but to save our lives and not kill us. They were asking for some sort of evidence on us, they had nothing on us and that's why they had to release us. Out of the seven Russian detainees who have been released, I am number six who has been accused of terrorist activities. The majority of us have been kidnapped three or four times like for example Rasul Kudayev, I have been kidnapped only once.[35]

It is often assumed that many of the detainees who have been released will be filled with hatred because of the abusive conditions to which they were subjected. However, despite their ill-treatment, their statements betray a surprising level of benevolence towards their captors and towards the people on whose behalf their captors acted. Vakhitov's statements convey the general feeling of disappointment and betrayal caused by his experiences at the hands of a country he felt would help to provide him with some semblance of justice. He comments that after his detention at the hands of the Northern Alliance, the news that the Americans were coming to speak with him came as a relief. But that was soon to change with his subsequent detention:

I think mostly, the whole world has to know what is happening in Guantánamo, especially the American people. I respect American people. I just consider that they don't know the truth. When they realise what their government is doing in their name, their government has betrayed democracy, then next time they wouldn't elect such presidents like George Bush.[36]

The complicity of nations allied to the US in the detention, rendition and torture of detainees in Guantánamo is now finding more prominence as those detainees bring legal challenges against their governments. The roles these governments play, although seemingly small in comparison to the program of detentions run by the US, are still significant in their disregard for due process or the rule of law.

On 21 August 2008, the High Court of the United Kingdom in the case of R (Binyam Mohamed) v Secretary of State for Foreign and Commonwealth Affairs ruled that the British government is duty bound to disclose evidence of any British resident detainee's detention, rendition and torture by the US. Lord Justice Thomas and Mr Justice Lloyd Jones agreed that British security services were complicit in the questioning of Binyam Mohamed Al Habashi during his torture in Morocco. Al Habashi was kidnapped in Pakistan and sold to the US, which subsequently sent him to be interrogated in Morocco and finally had him sent to Guantánamo Bay after a period of 'processing' in Afghanistan. The judges criticised the manner of his detention and were particularly scathing of the US Military Commissions procedure:

It might have been thought self-evident that the provisions of information as to the whereabouts of a person in custody would cause no particular difficulty, given that it is a basic and long established value in any democracy that the location of those in custody is made known to the detainee's family and those representing him … In these circumstances to leave the issue of disclosure to the processes of the Military Commission at some future time would be to deny [Mr Mohammed] a real chance of providing support to a limited part of his account and other essential assistance to his defence. To deny him this at this time would be to deny him the opportunity of timely justice in respect of the charges against him, a principle dating back to at least the time of the Magna Carta and which is so basic a part of our common law and of democratic values.[37]

Although the case only refers to Al Habashi's right to have information related to British complicity divulged to his legal team, it sets another precedent that recognises the extra-judicial mechanisms being implemented by governments around the world in their cooperation with the US. Another detainee to have allegedly suffered from a similar form of complicity by a western government is Murat Kurnaz, the German Guantánamo detainee. Following his five years of detention, Kurnaz released his memoirs in the form of a book explaining how he ended up in Guantánamo and his complete innocence despite his detention. One of the things that he has found most difficult to prove though, is the level to which the German security services were complicit in his detention, rendition and torture:

I don't know much about the terrorists but I see people supporting governments who're torturing people and killing people by torture. I've seen many people supporting those kinds of governments.

The German government closed that case many times. They don't want me to go to trial as they know they are going to lose; that is why they are trying their best not to go to trial.

They've stopped it many times and it's not happening, anything. They told me after I talked about it, the German government said in the news to the public, he is a liar. They said, Murat Kurnaz is a liar and there weren't any German soldiers in Kandahar. Afterwards, journalists got photographs of the German KSK soldiers during that time in Kandahar. Then they came back to the public, (saying) 'ok, he is not a liar but they didn't torture him. They (the KSK) used to be over there but they didn't torture him.'

They used to be over there but they didn't torture him. There was a truck that he's talking about. The journalist brought the photographs of Kandahar, of the same truck, in the same place. They said, okay, the truck was there but it was not there at that place, at that date. So they asked for witnesses from British ex-prisoners who came to Germany and said that they saw the truck over there. Then they said they found something else. They asked me to show (identify) the soldiers. They brought me like forty-eight pictures, forty-eight photographs, all very similar and new photographs of the KSK soldiers. And those two soldiers used to be between those forty-eight photographs. They asked me to show the right guy, right soldiers... it was five years after and I asked them for photographs from five years ago. They said they didn't have any photographs before five years. No actual photographs. All of them had the same clothes on. Many of them didn't used to join the KSK even ... I could recognise the guards, the soldiers. I showed them.

Yes. It was the right ones. He knows the guy. Between forty-eight photographs, after five years of torture, I could recognise them and I could show them. Ok they are the right ones, you are right. But I'm not authorised to go to court because they will lose. That is the democratic position.[38]

Victims of Guantánamo's detention policy are not limited to the detainees and their families. The impact of the prison camps has deeply affected the conscience of those who were involved in the process of detention. Since the transfer of detainees, slowly a number of former guards have stepped forward in order to apologise for their role in the detentions. At the age of seventeen Christopher Arendt joined the US Army National Guard because of the limited options that he faced in life. Three years later he was one of a number of soldiers given orders to go to Guantánamo Bay. In January 2004 he began his tour of Guantánamo, where he was given responsibility for feeding the detainees and ensuring that toilet paper was properly dispensed on the prison blocks.

Arendt's time with the prisoners was cut to two months, at which point he was placed at the detentions operations centre as the escort control. He had been moved from his former position because of his interaction with the prisoners, who he would speak with in order to keep some sense of his humanity. His dislike for the way in which the detainees at Guantánamo were treated caused his release from service. He has now become an outspoken critic of the unlawful detentions at the prison camps, choosing to contact former detainees in order to express his regret at having been involved:

I think that the first thing that needs to be said is that Guantánamo is a terrible public relations exercise for the US. Growing up in the US I was taught about the importance of our system of justice and Guantánamo has totally ruined my belief in the legal system and our protection of human rights. It has just destroyed a lot of things that I stood for growing up; thinking about what the military was going to be. My grandfather was very proud to be a World War II hero and much of that formed my own ideas about the military and its importance.

At Guantánamo it was very difficult to go through the daily motions of being there as guards. Checking in, getting on with the routines of the day and working behind the razor wire, it became harder to distinguish whether or not we were acting just like Nazis. What was happening there made me feel a little out of control due to the lack of reality of our situation, it was nothing like I thought. The result of our time there was that I now have a very uneasy relationship with politics and with people in authority.

Seeing 650 men being locked up in little tiny cages day after day and being treated poorly was only part of what is wrong with Guantánamo. Further than that you have the ERF teams who abuse the detainees and I videoed many of those raids on detainees myself. Knowing that there are many people like Moazzam Begg who were inside those cells who just did not belong there at all was probably the single most depressing thing for me though. It had a devastating effect on me. If it had been up to me, the entire situation would have been changed, but I was just a specialist and followed orders like everyone else through a long chain. I guess it would be fair to say that the whole of the system in Guantánamo was awful.

Sometimes I really wonder how much Guantánamo has impacted the rest of the world. I watched America go on before I left for Guantánamo and watched it again on my return and I wonder if people really are affected by this. In some ways Guantánamo has become part of the common language for a few but for many people there is no knowledge or understanding at all. I recently spoke with a few people who did not even know that we had detainees at the base. Based on what I see in the US, I don't know if the world is really affected by it at all. In many ways it does remind me of before World War II when people knew about the concentration camps and did nothing to stop what was going on.

I think that people don't give enough thought to what Guantánamo Bay means except for maybe a few passing minutes. It is a shame that Guantánamo exists in the way that it does, for even if the worldwide public is not paying attention, other governments are; and so what Guantánamo does is to give other governments the opportunity to treat prisoners however they like as the US is already doing it. I fear that governments will start to ignore human rights to a greater extent, and that eventually will be the legacy of Guantánamo.[39]

6

DARKNESS

"Since shortly after 9/11—when many Al Qaeda members fled Afghanistan and crossed the border into Pakistan—we have played multiple games of cat and mouse with them. The biggest of them all, Osama bin Laden, is still at large at the time of this writing but we have caught many, many others. Some are known to the world, some are not. We have captured 672 and handed over 369 to the United States. We have earned bounties totalling millions of dollars...[1]"

Pervez Musharraf—former President of Pakistan

Human rights organisations have worked extremely hard to help unravel the mystery that is Guantánamo Bay. After six years of the prison being in operation and with the release of almost seven hundred detainees, testimonies were taken from detainees to paint a picture of detention practices implemented by the US in Afghanistan and Guantánamo Bay. Over the course of the last few years, a picture has emerged that goes beyond what the US presented as detentions in line with the Geneva Conventions. An entire network of global detentions has been uncovered, where enforced disappearances, rendition, incommunicado detention, and torture were the order of the day. It would seem that Guantánamo Bay was the humane face the US administration felt it could show the world.

Enforced disappearances have always been condemned under international law; and finally in 2006 the United Nations General Assembly adopted the UN Convention Against Enforced Disappearance which provided an international legal instrument to govern the already accepted position. In the same month as the adoption of the convention, after months of research, Cageprisoners released their report,

137

Beyond the Law: The War on Terror's Secret Network of Detentions.
The report highlighted over one hundred confirmed or suspected detention facilities used as part of the global counter-terrorism strategy with at least seventy-two of those having some form of US involvement. Further details highlighted in the report included the fact that at least thirty-four countries were used as sites for the outsourcing of detention. Writing the foreword for the Report of the UN Special Rapporteur on torture, Manfred Nowak, commented:

The use of secret places of detention and the practice of enforced disappearances are among the worst human rights violations of our time. If such practices are applied in a widespread or systematic manner, they even constitute a crime against humanity according to the Rome Statute of the International Criminal Court. In order to eradicate such practices, the newly created Human Rights Council in June 2006 agreed on the text of a United Nations Convention on Enforced Disappearances ... It is ironic that in the very same year, Cageprisoners publishes a comprehensive report which reveals the systematic practice of enforced disappearances in a global network of secret places of detention.[2]

Although disappearances are the main element of the secret detention program, there are a number of methods employed in the War on Terror to keep detainees beyond the law. The disappearances can take place in a variety of contexts and using different techniques. These include the use of black sites, rendition, proxy detention, military detention facilities and also civilian buildings. All of these elements have been used by the US and her allies to keep individuals beyond the law.

Part of the program of secret detention used by the US included the now infamous 'High Value Detainee Program'. Although the US had declared the detention of key Al Qaeda suspects for the previous five years, no official position had been taken by the US authorities on the practice of secret detention. On 6 September 2006, the Office of the Director of National Intelligence published a summary of the 'High Value Terrorist Detainee Program' (HVD). The document stated:

Since 9/11, we have been engaged in a struggle against an elusive enemy; terrorists work in the shadows, relying on secrecy and the element of surprise to maximise the impact of attack. Timely and accurate intelligence is crucial to success in the War on Terrorism. One of the key tools in this war has been the information we have gleaned from the terrorists themselves. Detainees who have been in the inner circle of al-Qa'ida, occupying some of the most important positions in that organization, hold information that simply cannot be obtained from any other source.[3]

For the first time the program of secret detention was given an official face through this HVD categorisation, although the US only admitted that this process was being used in a limited capacity. The process of HVD detentions included the use of secret detention sites. The ones that are used by the CIA and run completely outside the law are termed 'black sites'. These CIA black sites have been reported in countries all over the world, from secret prisons such as the Bagram Theatre Detention Facility, to the use of prisons in Europe.

To this day, very little is known about the location of many of these black sites, but the work of human rights organisations has managed to reveal parts of the process. For the last few years the organisation Reprieve has worked tirelessly to extract information from the British government about the use of the British island of Diego Garcia as a possible black site. Between October 2003 and January 2008, the British government was provided with assurances by the US authorities that the US base on the island had not been used as part of the program of secret detention. Finally, in February 2008, British foreign secretary, David Miliband, was forced to admit that two US rendition flights carrying prisoners had passed through Diego Garcia in 2002, but he claimed that Britain had been assured by the US that this was only for refuelling.[4] At the end of July 2008, *TIME* magazine and BBC Newsnight reported that a senior American official admitted to a high-value prisoner being detained on the island, and the Spanish newspaper *El Pais* revealed that the Spanish citizen Mustafa Setmariam Nasar had also been detained there. According to the director of Reprieve, Clive Stafford Smith:

The United States must come clean about the existence of its secret prison on Diego Garcia—and the British government must ensure the US does so. In February 2008, General Michael Hayden, the Director of the CIA, stated categorically that Diego Garcia had never housed a secret prison. It now seems that simply isn't true. It is time for these evasions to come to an end, and for the full details of the CIA's secret prison system to be revealed.[5]

On 7 June 2007, after extended meetings, Amnesty International, Cageprisoners, the Center for Constitutional Rights, the Center for Human Rights and Global Justice, Human Rights Watch and Reprieve published *Off the Record: US Responsibility for Enforced Disappearances in the "War on Terror"*. For the first time all six organisations came together in order to publish the names of thirty-nine individuals who were allegedly being held by the US in their secret detention program. Although the work of the six organisations accounts for hundreds of other names being held in secret detention, the organisations came together to agree definitions which would account for these thirty-nine. The names on the list were split into the following categories:

CATEGORY 1: Individuals whose detention by the United States has been officially acknowledged and whose fate and whereabouts remain unknown.
CATEGORY 2: Individuals about whom there is strong evidence, including witness testimony, of secret detention by the United States and whose fate and whereabouts remain unknown.
CATEGORY 3: Individuals about whom there is some evidence of secret detention by the United States and whose fate and whereabouts remain unknown.[6]

It is suspected by the organisations that nearly all on the list were considered to be some kind of 'high-value' detainee, even if they were not officially stated to be within the HVD program. Many of those named within the report still have not surfaced despite quite clear declarations of their detentions. It is only sometimes through the testimonies of released detainees that indications are given as to their location. One such example is that of Hassan Ghul, who was detained in Iraq and then went missing in US military custody. According to UK detainee, Rangzieb Ahmed, the two men were kept in a secret detention facility in Pakistan—but Ghul's whereabouts still remain unknown.[7] The enforced disappearances that have taken place are contrary to the wealth of international legislation covering this area, however the US has attempted to circumvent such norms with pseudo-moral justifications.

The presidency of Barack Obama has in its earliest days seen an executive order to close CIA black sites[8]. This was an unanticipated step for human rights NGOs—a step that showed Obama's commitment to reversing the trend of detention policies during the Bush era. However further pressure has been put on the American president as the extent of abuses in prisons outside the black site system continues to be exposed. According to Karen Greenberg, many of the detention facilities around the world, including Guantánamo and Abu Ghraib, were merely distractions from other more serious facilities, such as Bagram Theater Detention Facility in Afghanistan.[9] The closure of the

CIA program, however noble, tackles only a small fraction of the issues that need to be dealt with.

Another aspect of the process of secret detention has been the extra-judicial transfer of individuals between territorial jurisdictions, what has commonly been referred to as 'rendition' or, for those in the US, 'extraordinary rendition'. In June 1995, President Clinton issued his Presidential Declaration Directive 39 which allowed for the forceful seizure of suspected terrorists in circumstances where a host country would not cooperate.[10] Although rendition existed as a legal mechanism in US law, it was generally accepted that this process was an exception and that in order to maintain friendly international relations and respect for international human rights, it was important to transfer individuals through the due processes of extradition or deportation.

The post-9/11 world encouraged the US administration to centralise more powers in the name of international peace and security. Although there was no accepted international norm allowing for renditions, the US secretary of state, Condoleezza Rice, explained the US position:

> For decades, the United States and other countries have used "renditions" to transport terrorist suspects from the country where they were captured to their home country or to other countries where they can be questioned, held, or brought to justice.[11]

With the start of Operation Enduring Freedom and the transfer of suspected terrorists around the world, rendition has become a common feature of the secret detention process. The most famous destination for those rendition flights was Guantánamo Bay, but there exists a vast network of destinations that have been used across Asia, the Middle East, Europe, Africa and the Americas.[12] However horrific the treatment of those in Guantánamo may have been, other sites exist with records on the abuse of prisoners that are even more horrific.

The system of transporting detainees to third-party countries for detention is known as 'proxy detention'. Thousands of suspected terrorists have been detained over the last seven years, many of whom have been sent to countries such as Syria, Jordan, Egypt, Morocco plus other unknown destinations outside US control. This has now become the most worrying aspect of the global network of detentions.

There are two main forms of proxy detention, the first being that western agencies are not only heavily involved with the interrogation process of a detainee, but also have some form of administrative responsibility in running the detention facility. An example of this form of proxy detention can be found at Kohat, were detainees allege to have been under the control of the US despite being in a Pakistani prison.[13] The prison was used as a filtration point by the US who sent detainees to other parts of the country or the world. Media accounts have also alleged that Al Jafr prison in Jordan was a facility which gave unfettered access to the CIA in order to house high-value detainees such as Khalid Sheikh Mohammed.[14]

But the involvement of western agencies in the process of proxy detention is not always active. The second form involves the passive contribution of external agencies to the interrogation of suspects. Many countries would rather wait for suspects to enter foreign countries and then request their detention, than play an active part in the rendition or torture of the suspect. An example of this form of detention can be found in the case of Farid Hilali, who alleges that the British were not only aware of his detention in Morocco, but also contributed to his interrogation:

...in fact they were asking these questions on behalf of the British Intelligence Service. How else could one explain why I was being questioned about people in the UK and my whereabouts in UK mosques, etc? I was never questioned about my activities in Morocco or who I knew in Morocco, the questions were always about the UK and people in the UK.[15]

The refusal of President Obama to end the use of rendition[16] as a counter-terrorism tool has proved to be extremely controversial—it has sent the message that although the US will not continue its policies of detention at Guantánamo Bay or use CIA black sites around the world—they will still allow detainees to be transferred through the proxy detention system to other jurisdictions. Despite the welcome given to his first executive orders, this position has negated hope for any meaningful change.

Ghosts

Two-thirds of the entire prisoner population in Guantánamo did not originate from the battlefields of Afghanistan, but rather from Pakistan. Pakistan was at the very centre of the War on Terror, as the former president Pervez Musharraf sought to ally himself with the US in global counter-terrorism efforts. The relationship the two countries had is best summed up by the quote at the start of this chapter—the Pakistanis sold foreigners and their own citizens in a bid to be seen as a country at the forefront of fighting terror, rather than as a potential target of US belligerence.

Prisons across Pakistan have been used in order to house detainees beyond reach of the law, with the security services constantly transferring detainees to prevent them from coming under the jurisdiction of a petition for habeas corpus. Detention sites have been located from the south in the provinces of Sindh, through Balochistan, Punjab, and up to Kashmir and the North-West Frontier Province.

Due to the number of agencies involved, both Pakistani and American, it is often unclear exactly who is detaining an individual. With the Pakistani Inter Services Intelligence, Intelligence Bureau, Federal Investigation Agency and Police collaborating with the CIA and FBI, families of detainees do not know which entity to petition in order to have their loved-ones released or charged. The protections given by habeas corpus have been completely diminished by regional constrictions to its application; detainees are moved too quickly for any petition to take effect.

Given Pakistan's terrible human rights record, a natural consequence of its collaboration in the War on Terror has been the use of enforced disappearance, torture and rendition. With detainees being held incommunicado, all manner of abuses and extra-judicial transfers have taken place.

The treatment of its own citizens has led to an unprecedented activism in Pakistan. The families of the disappeared have gathered together to make these detentions a central issue within the country's national debates. The sacking of the Chief Justice and the ensuing Black Tie Movement (a movement by Pakistan's lawyers and judicial figures to protest against this sacking) have all contributed towards considerable pressure to re-establish due process within the Pakistani legal system.[17]

One of the leaders of the movement, Amina Masood Janjua, has come to prominence through her lengthy campaigns against the government. Her role as a spokeswoman for the families of the disappeared has been by necessity, rather than desire. On 30 July 2005, her husband Masood Ahmad Janjua and his friend Faisal Faraz went missing on their way to an Islamic retreat. After their disappearance it soon became clear that the men had been detained en route to their destination.

Simple and religious men, Janjua and Faraz had decided to join an Islamic retreat in the north of Pakistan. Janjua was supposed to take a bus from Rawalpindi to Peshawar. He had purchased a ticket on the Daewoo bus service which has a policy of video recording all passengers before the departure of a bus from their terminals. Janjua was not seen on any of their footage from that day. His wife Amina explained how the family attempted to find any information concerning his whereabouts:

[The first we heard of his detention was] only indirectly. They never admitted it themselves to me. There was a colonel working in the college, who knew somebody who asked someone else and the other person asked somebody else. It was a very long process. Every single person tried to keep themselves safe not wanting to admit that they have any information. It came to us in the end that he was with an agency and that he would be released at some point.

It was about three months that we heard anything from the first time, and then we heard some things again after another few months. Constantly after a couple of months through our own efforts we were hearing things. We were not sitting still, through our own efforts we were trying to track his whereabouts, meeting so many different people. We went to meet the friends in Peshawar that he was supposed to be with and so many others. We called them here; we were investigating things all the time.

There was a call from the president's house that came from the military secretary to the president who contacted my father-in-law. He said that Masood was alive and that he will come back soon and that he was seen somewhere, their informers told them this after they rotated his photograph. We were told he would be coming home soon.

That [call] came because on Eid, my father-in-law went to an army get-together and there raised the issue of his son's disappearance. He had written a petition to find his son; he was senior to President Musharraf at one point. He went directly to the president who then said that he would find out. That was 11 January 2006, and the phone call came 31 May.

On 1 July 2006, someone spoke to us; he said he was from an agency at a junior level so he could not do much. He said that he could only give a brief description of what happened. He said that they were picked up in Rawalpindi and that they were kept in a cell 20 of I-9 district in Islamabad. He went on to say that your mobile, it is not safe, whatever you are talking about I can intercept—I heard you talking to Javed Ibrahim Paracha, you were talking to him and then told me the contents of that conversation. Maybe it was his duty to intercept my calls ... maybe.

We believed him because we were so hopeful when someone tells us something, or anything. We say that this person must be sincere. Both my father-in-law and I thought that he must be sincere and that obviously he wants to help us. He told us that we can contact Colonel Habibullah at cell 20 in I-9 and we can ask him why he was kept there. He told me that he would contact us after two days by which time I must have a new cell phone because even changing the SIM will not work. He told us to change the cell phone and the SIM, and that on that we would coordinate with him alone and no one else. That was the way he was guiding us. We had no choice, we had to believe him.

On the third day, he came to us again and said to us, ok give us the numbers that Masood was using. Which numbers was Masood calling to anywhere in the world, his friends, colleagues or wherever. We were so fooled, I don't know whether we should have given them or not, but we did. He said that as he was in that department, he would be able to help. He told us that by number maybe my husband was in Kashmir where they keep people for longer periods. There are two cells there, one is Shaukat Killa and one is Amoor Camp. He even gave the names of these places so we were convinced he was telling the truth. He told us that they were holding people there in these prisons, and that it was very possible Masood could be there. He said that over there people are detained for longer periods, those who are under investigation or are still in the process.[18]

Masood Janjua's friend Faisal Faraz, a graduate in Mechanical Engineering, was employed by the Wartsila Pakistan as a service engineer. When he failed to show up at a wedding after his retreat was supposed to have ended, his brother Sohail became worried and realised that something was wrong:

We were here, we didn't know he had disappeared; we knew he had gone to Tabligh [retreat] so we were waiting for him to return because he knew of the wedding. He didn't turn up on the wedding day. That was 26 August. On 26 August, no one in the family knew that he has already gone missing because we knew he was in Tabligh and he will come because sometimes they send you in farfetched areas where there is no contact, no telephone, nothing. So when he didn't come on the wedding, then I was really worried (as to where he is) so I started calling all of his friends.

… I got a number from another common friend of Faisal and Masood then I called up their home and talked with Amina; she said we cannot discuss anything on the phone, please come to our house. It was 28 August last year [2005]. So it was really scary when I went there; Masood's father, his brother, Masood's family they were all there and they told me that Faisal and Masood were going to the Peshawar and they had disappeared.

They had already started searching Masood and Faisal because Masood had said that both of them will be back after three days. They knew that Masood had told them three days so they had started looking for Masood and Faisal after eight or nine days. When I asked them what is the priority, the probability that what happened? Them being picked up by security agencies?

There was no indication from anyone. There was once a man who came to our house. It's quite strange in Pakistan, like people opening the door and simply walking in, especially you know if the ladies of the house are alone in the house.

So the person, my sister told me he simply walked in, opened the gate, walked in, tried to open the doors of the house then my sister confronted him. He was like trying to act stupid, trying to look a little clever and asked "where is Faisal? I've met him". We told him, he's missing for so many months. He told them that one of his nephews was Faisal's friend, he is also missing. We asked his number and he gave us the wrong number, which was totally rubbish. We tried calling him back, he said that he had met Faisal some months back, three months back but he was already missing for six months. He was the only shady character that came to our house. Nothing else.[19]

In July 2008, after three years of investigating the disappearances of Janjua and Faraz, Cageprisoners was able to confirm through a senior security official in Pakistan that the two men were being held by the Pakistanis at the behest of the CIA, and that the Pakistani authorities themselves had absolutely no interest in them. This latest development has raised very serious questions about the nature of the US operations in Pakistan and the extent to which they are behind the detentions that are taking place.

US involvement in the detention of individuals in Pakistan has been well documented, especially in relation to those being detained in Guantánamo Bay. In late 2006, Majid Khan was declared to have been moved by the US authorities to Guantánamo Bay, after a period of three years in secret detention under the HVD program. It was on 5 March 2003 that Khan, his brother, sister-in-law and their one-month-old baby were forcibly taken from the brother's home in Karachi and detained by the security services. Members of the family said that at the time of the arrest, US officials were present along with the Pakistani forces and that they seemed to be conducting the entire operation.

Khan had only been married to his wife Rabia Yaqoob for just over a year when he was detained. She describes her husband as being religious in his adherence to Islam, but not as someone who was by any means extreme in his views about the US. Yaqoob had been staying with her family when he was arrested because she was unwell while pregnant with their first child. Due to her fragile state, it was days before she was told that Khan had even been arrested. For the three years of his disappearance into US custody, Yaqoob's daughter Minal was growing up knowing that her father was made to disappear, only to resurface in Guantánamo Bay:

No one came to me personally to tell me what happened; the men came from the agencies to meet Majid's uncles and they were warned that they should not cause any fuss over his kidnapping, otherwise something bad would happen, so everyone got scared. When my brother-in-law was released, then they similarly warned him from raising any issue which once again renewed the fear of raising awareness about the illegal detention. We were all warned away from doing anything. My father-in-law had wanted to take a lawyer immediately and go to court, but due to the fear it didn't happen.

They didn't specify which branch of intelligence they are from; they simply said that they are from intelligence. Once or twice they have contacted me, but never since then. In a single sitting, they sat down with my brother and asked him many questions about Majid, what he was like, they said that don't worry, he is going to come back. They were all Pakistani people. I didn't really know what was going on so didn't ask too many questions.

Mashallah, that when Minal was born I knew things would be so much better. I thank God for that. However it hurt to know that Minal's father was not with me; that made it a little more difficult. It is so difficult especially when you have done so much planning for when the child to be born not to be able to share those moments with your husband. I thank God that he has sent me this little gift that I can play with and she constantly makes me happy.

At the age of one, we would show Minal pictures and explain to her that this is who your father is. Just to give her an idea that this is who he is. She has since then started speaking to the picture saying things like the picture will get angry if she does something wrong, she tries to put the picture to sleep, to feed it, she cleans it, and even just today she was wiping the nose of her father using a tissue. She asks the picture so many questions. Whenever she is eating, she will always offer the picture food first. Every night she has a daily routine of praying for her father before she goes to sleep. She specifically asks God to bring home her father and also to bring home all the uncles that have been taken away from their families.[20]

Often those detained by the US, and specifically the CIA, have been termed 'ghost detainees'.[21]. Those held beyond the law quite literally become ghosts to those that they love—they are still in this world, but strangely outside it. Detainees such as Majid Khan have been subjected to the whole process of ghost detention which includes kidnapping, enforced disappearance, torture and rendition. Due to rules on classification of material in Guantánamo, Khan's complete story has still not been released, so it is impossible to say which other countries participated in his detention process, but the outsourcing of detentions to third-party countries has often been used.

Detainees such as Binyam Mohammed Al Habashi and Mamdouh Habib have been taken to countries such as Morocco and Egypt in order to be interrogated as part of the US policy of proxy detention. Often detainees are subjected to treatment in these countries that would not be possible elsewhere. Among the first detainees to be outsourced by the US in Pakistan was Abou Elkassim Britel, an Italian citizen, who was detained on 10 March 2002. His detention by the Pakistani authorities resulted in his transfer to US officials. Until this time, Britel had not been given any access to a lawyer or to the Italian consulate. His wife, Anna Lucia Phigizzini, explains his rendition from Pakistan to Morocco by the US:

24 May 2002. He was taken to the airport by car, travelling handcuffed and with a hood on his head. After about half-an-hour waiting, someone grabbed him abruptly, having come onto him very quietly. He seized his neck with powerful strength, so much so that Kassim thought he was going to die. He was taken to a place that turned out to be a bathroom. Everything happened very fast. Brandishing a knife, they cut his clothes and took them all off. He was then able to see four or five men all dressed in black, with only the eyes showing, all around him.

They searched him all over, also in the intimate parts, took a picture and quickly put his clothes back on cutting most of his t-shirt off. They put a sort of nappy on him and blindfolded him again. They made him wear what felt like metallic underpants to which they attached chains connected to his handcuffs and to his legs.

They took him to the aeroplane and forced him to lie down on his back; another passenger got on the plane after him. He was forbidden from moving from that position and every movement was punished by being hit, maybe with a stick, maybe with a shoe ... he could not tell. Not having realised he had a nappy on, he held his bladder the whole journey with tremendous discomfort. His back was in great pain, when he asked to be allowed to turn they covered his mouth with tape.

While the plane was landing, they managed to swap his metal handcuffs with some plastic ones. After hearing the Moroccan dialect he understood where he had arrived. Some Temara policemen were waiting for him and transported him to the town. The route of this plane was recorded among the documents of the TDIP (European commission for CIA flights): the Gulfstream N379P, known as the "Guantánamo Express", which flew on the 24/25 May 2002 from Islamabad to Rabat, took off the same day in the direction of Porto and landed in Washington on 26 May.[22]

Black sites, although the most talked about form of CIA detention in the War on Terror, are still the least well known. The US has tried very hard to keep details of the black sites secret from the public by manipulating legislation to keep the information classified. Because the detainees are hooded, they are often unaware of where in the world they have been taken and can only hazard guesses based on knowledge of the languages, dialects and customs of those that detain them.

With the enforcement of global counter-terrorism measures, the US has often relied on the participation of local authorities to detain possible suspects as part of their program of secret detention. Although Pakistan is notorious for its involvement, other countries have also played their part in detaining those within their borders. On 21 June 2003, Khalif Abdi Hussein, a teacher at Blantyre Islamic Centre in Malawi, was detained by the Malawi police along with four other men. The men were detained in the middle of the night on the pretence of immigration issues. They were taken to Lilongwe prison blindfolded and handcuffed. Despite being told they had been detained for immigration reasons, the men soon found themselves on a rendition flight at the international airport:

When we got to Lilongwe they took us just next to the international airport in a very small plane. They did not ask us any questions—we had not been interrogated by anyone up until this time. For the first time we recognised one another—up until now we did not know that we friends had been arrested—we were all friends. We stayed there one night.

On the Monday they took us from Lilongwe to Harare, Zimbabwe on Air Malawi. They chained two of us together on this empty plane. I have travelled on this plane before so I recognised it as we were not blindfolded.

When we were in the air—we knew that we were on our way away from Malawi—I knew how far Blantyre was from Lilongwe—but our journey was too far. The air trip was one hour. When we arrived we saw Harare International Airport.

When we arrived in Harare they separated us—the Zimbabwean authorities were obviously working with the Malawi authorities. When we arrived there they put me in prison like a common criminal—in a very small cell. They kept an OB (observation book). They asked for my name, when I gave it they wrote something down that was altogether different. I told him that my name was Khalifa, but he wrote a different name which I couldn't even recognise. They did not want me to exist.[23]

Conditions in the cell were extremely dark and uncomfortable. Hussein was left to sleep on a cold hard concrete floor, resulting in extreme pain throughout his body. He was soon taken to another location and given a different name—a tactic he felt had been employed to ensure that there was no way for him to be traced. Much of the questioning that took place regarded Al Qaeda, jihad and Osama bin Laden. Hussein did not suspect any foreign involvement until the time of his release after one month in detention. He was once again blindfolded and taken to Harare International Airport with the other men:

There were two or three people with the one who put me on the plane. It was a very small plane—it had five or six seats only. When I sat on the seat, I realised that all of us were there, and only Fahad was not there. They eventually brought him as well and they chained us all up by the feet. There were two whites on the plane and two Africans. The pilot was white.

From there we didn't know where we were, but in fact we thought they would be taking us to Guantánamo Bay. We could not see one another and we did not try to speak to one another. I only saw Fahad who was sitting in front of me.

From Harare we stopped somewhere but I didn't know where we were, but Sheikh Issa, after he was telling me that he heard the pilot that we stopped off in Entebbe to refuel. We were crying for water because it was such a long journey, but we were told there was none. We then continued on our flight, but we were not sure for certain.

We eventually landed in Khartoum, Sudan, but we didn't know that. We had been on the plane for about six hours. They started removing us and took us off the plane. We saw one another and they started giving us water and food which we took. Sheikh Issa said that he thought this place must be Khartoum as we could see a mosque that only was built in Sudan.[24]

Khalif Abdi Hussein said that he felt the men that were on the plane with him were Americans. Although he could not hear them, he was informed later that the ones responsible for his rendition were indeed American officials.

Detention by proxy

Despite international statements between countries regarding their hostilities to one another, behind the scenes in the world of the security services, a completely different level of cooperation exists. In his State of the Union address on 29 January 2002, President George W Bush described Iran, Iraq and North Korea as being part of the 'Axis of Evil', "States like these, and their terrorist allies, constitute an axis of evil, arming to threaten the peace of the world." Although the US president did not specifically mention any other countries in that speech, on 6 May 2002, the US Ambassador to the United Nations, John R Bolton included Libya, Syria and Cuba as countries that should be considered part of the 'Axis of Evil'.

The reality is that some of the countries mentioned as part of the axis, particularly Syria, Libya and Iraq, have been instrumental in the unlawful detentions, renditions and torture of suspected terrorists around the world. The security services of these countries have worked closely with western allies in order to detain individuals and interrogate them using methods generally considered completely inhumane.

The most famous example of the cooperation that exists between these countries within the context of the War on Terror is the case of Maher Arar. While on a connecting flight through the US in New York, Arar was detained by the authorities for allegedly being on an Al Qaeda watch list. Despite being a Canadian citizen and having been given access to Canadian consular officials in the US, he was placed on a rendition flight to Jordan en route to Syria. It was in Syria that he was taken to the now infamous Fara' Falastin prison where he was to face torture.[25]

Arar's case is one that clearly demonstrates the use of proxy detention. In this case the party detaining simply handed over the suspect to a third-party for detention and interrogation. Although the US sent Arar to Syria, the recent Arar Inquiry forced the Canadian authorities to pay him damages for the role they played in his continued detention in Syria. This form of proxy detention has often been used—where a home country will allow a suspect to be detained by a third party, and then capitalise on it by having him interrogated outside the law. Canada in particular has been involved in such practices, with examples including the detentions of Muayyad Nureddin, Abdullah Almalki and Ahmad Abou El Maati. These Canadian men were already in Syria when they were detained by the Syrian authorities, however, the questions they were being asked during their interrogations made it perfectly clear to them that it was the Canadians who were interested in their answers.

Detained in the same Fara' Falastin prison as the four Canadian men, Adam Brown was refused access to both the British Embassy and Consulate. Brown believed that the British authorities were very much aware of his presence in the prison and may even have colluded with the Syrians:

...I didn't have knowledge of anything I didn't even know what was happening on the outside world I didn't even know where my wife was. So there was nothing like that, I was not spoken to by anyone from foreign intelligence services and there were no questions asked that would hint to that. But there was something that they said that made me think that there was no way they could have known that; when the final interrogator wanted me to fingerprint some paperwork that he did. It was quite embarrassing because I was with some other guys from different countries he said "O you're not actually married are you? You live with your wife like friends" and I was like "excuse me I'm married to my wife, I was just married in a mosque I've not been married in a court, I just got married in a mosque", when he said this I thought that they must have interrogated my wife by now and I was quite sad because I didn't know what state she was in. There was no way that they could have known that other than from my wife because I didn't tell anyone the whole time I was in Syria I was never asked for a marriage certificate or ever been asked for any sort of proof for my marriage and everyone knew she was my wife, I'd never stated anything other than that so I was certain they had spoken to my wife. When I came out and came back to UK, I said to her, were you ever asked for a marriage certificate or anything regarding our marriage, and she was never asked by anyone anything about that so there was no way they could have known that other than from me or my wife or from the authorities here, so that they could check on their system and see that these two have never been married under British law, and there is no way they could have known that other than from them.[26]

Having already been detained by the authorities in the United Arab Emirates, Alam Ghafoor found himself an unfortunate suspect of the London bombings days after they occurred. Ghafoor was convinced that if he had the opportunity to speak to someone from the British Embassy, then his name would be cleared quickly and he would be released. Although he did not believe it at the time, it soon became clear to him that the British had requested his detention:

When I asked to speak to the British Embassy, the interrogator said to me, "Where do you think you are? This is not a police station, you are with the secret service, and we have total control of everything that happens to you. You have been taken from this restaurant, no one will speak, no one will say what has happened to you, no one will know that you are gone, nobody knows about this building, you will probably die here, we will kill you, chop you into bits and feed you to the dogs. There won't be any trace of you, the best thing for you, is that maybe if you give some information which is helpful, give us the names, how you built the bombs, the whole operation, maybe you will get ten or twenty years here, but we will be your family from now on."

I said to them, "That if you are saying that I am a liar, and that British intelligence told you to pick me up, why don't you hand me over to the British along with the polygraph results. They may be able to get the information and see the truth of things". They said, "No no no, you are our Muslim brother, we do not want them to take you away, they will torture you, they will kill you, you are our Muslim brother, and if you give us the information, we will make sure that you will walk out of here safely to your family". I said to them, "That I have no problem with trusting you, thank you for giving me your support, but I am quite happy for you to hand me over to the British. Let them shoot me if they have to, don't worry about that, just hand me over". He said, "No no no, they are very evil, we can't do that, they will hurt you". I said, "I am not worried about that, I can deal with them and know that I can clear my name within thirty minutes of them having me". I said to them, "Please check, I don't have a police record, I drove through a red light, but that is it".

After a few days I was allowed a shower again and they gave me a shave after which I was handed my original clothes. At that point, Rehana Hafiz from the British Embassy met us in another office, and she told me that they were trying to get me out possibly today or tomorrow. I broke down, I thought I was going to die and rot there, I told her that they had tortured, humiliated and degraded us. Thankfully soon enough we found our way home. One thing that does stick out, is when I told them that I was a British citizen, they said, "Who do you think you are? You are not Tony Blair, they know you are here, and no one cares." All through the questioning I would ask, "Why am I here?" They said, "Because British intelligence told us to pick you up".[27]

The types of questions that were asked of Ghafoor and Brown, like many others, betray the complicity of their home countries. Detainees such as Binyam Mohammed Al Habashi also went through a similar process where he only realised the level to which the British authorities were complicit in his detention and torture in Morocco because of the questions that were being asked of him. In an attempt to escape any liability for these unlawful detentions and even torture, many western governments have used the lack of judicial safeguards in countries abroad to have their own nationals interrogated.

Abou Elkassim Britel was detained by the Pakistanis, handed over to the US and then sent to Morocco in order to be interrogated. Despite the clear proxy detention of Britel by the US in a third-party country, other aspects of his case indicate that the Italian authorities were also very much complicit in his detention. His wife is certain that the Italians agreed to keep his arrest and interrogation secret.

For those who ended up in Guantánamo Bay, a common feature of their initial detentions, wherever in the world they took place, was the presence of security service agents from their home countries. Martin Mubanga, a British citizen, was visited by UK officials during his initial detention in Zambia, but despite knowing of his detention there, they still allowed him to be sent to Guantánamo Bay. Similar treatment was also given to other British citizens detained before being rendered. Although not necessarily responsible for the initial detention, the security services, and, according to the testimonies of detainees, particularly MI5, attempted to use the unlawful detention of these suspects as a means to interrogate them without any formal arrest or charge.

Detained without any charge or trial, Rangzieb Ahmed, also a British citizen, was secretly held by the Pakistani authorities who claimed that he knew members of Al Qaeda. Although the Pakistanis were behind his arrest, other agencies were given access to interrogate him. Ahmed did not receive a single visit from British consular officials. The British authorities continued to question him even after he had demonstrated that he had been tortured:

At this location I received a visit from British officials, following which I was taken back to the interrogation centre. These two males introduced themselves as being from Britain and that they worked for the British government; they clarified that they were not from the consulate but they did not say if they were intelligence officers. They did give their names but I cannot remember them.

They asked me questions lasting approximately forty minutes. During this period I was shackled and handcuffed (to the front) throughout. They saw my hood in the room.

They asked me questions relating to what I was doing in Pakistan, why I had come, my movements and my connections to Pakistan. They said that I was picked up in Haripur and they asked me about links to Al Qaeda. They also said that they believed that I was in Waziristan and asked about Hamza Rabia. I denied being at this location or having any links to Al Qaeda or Hamza Rabia. They did not ask about any other names or any others [I told them that I was in Pakistan for earthquake relief work].

They were both taking notes on small reporter pads. I recall they also showed me approximately twenty surveillance photographs, one by one, of Asian and black males, some of whom had beards most did not. These photographs were taken out from an envelope by the mixed race male. These are the only documentation they had during this meeting. I did not recognise any of these individuals. They did not tell me anything about the individuals in the photos. They just asked me if I recognised them. These two males saw me in handcuffs and shackles. I told them that I had been tortured. This was clearly visible due to sleep depravation and my three fingers being bandaged on my left hand. They could see that 1 was uncomfortable and I was unable to sit due to the beatings I had received on my buttocks.

They asked me how I was being treated and I told them that I was being tortured. They did not note this down. I recall that they also asked me about the UK, in particular if I know anything about funding terrorist activities and Al Qaeda in the UK[28]

MI5's involvement with the detention of British citizens abroad has been on the increase since the start of the War on Terror—this role was previously played by MI6. The British security services are now present at many different detentions around the world, often asking the same questions of all those who are detained. Interest in Britain's domestic affairs often plays a large part of the interrogations, as well as requests for the suspects to work with the security services.

Among those who fled from Somalia to Kenya was Mohammed Ezzouek. He had been trying to study his religion and the Arabic language in Somalia before war broke out with Ethiopia. He left immediately with other foreign nationals as they attempted to make their way towards Nairobi. However, they were subsequently arrested by the Kenyan Anti-Terrorism Police Unit and secretly held at prisons in Nairobi. During his detention, Ezzouek was visited by MI5 who were not only interested in his activities in the Horn of Africa, but also at home in Britain:

This time the woman [MI5 agent] did most of the talking. She asked me to go through my entire story again. She asked me questions about my religion, my beliefs, whether I had given my allegiance to any group. She asked me if any of my friends were extremists. I told her no and she said that she did not believe what I was telling her. I told her that she would have to accept it as it is the truth. She said to me that I and Hamza Chentouf had made up a story.

The woman agent asked me what I thought about 9/11 and 7/7. I replied that both of those events were wrong as innocent people had been killed. She replied sarcastically and then she said that she did not believe me.

The woman agent told me that her stay in Nairobi was limited and that she would soon have to return to the UK. She told me that she was the only person who could help me, but that I would have to cooperate with her. She told me that if I told her what she wanted to hear, I would be on the first plane back to the UK, but if I didn't come up with the information she wanted, I would stay here forever. I told her that I would like to come home but that I could not give what she wanted.

Francis [one of the agents] asked me if I had heard about all the people being sent to Somalia, and if I knew about Guantánamo Bay.

[On a third questioning by MI5] Francis sat down with me at the coffee table. She had a notepad and a folder. She asked me if I had thought more about what she had said to me. She said that I was not cooperating with her. She talked about my family and asked me what I wanted to do when I went home. When I answered her she replied that it would be difficult for me to do these things from a cell.

She asked me if I would ever tell anyone about her when I went back to the UK. When she said this she sat back with her arms crossed in front of her. I thought she sounded frightened when she said that.

Francis then asked me if I would come and work for her. I replied that if I heard anything that would harm anyone then I would tell her anyway. Francis asked me for more names and addresses of people that I knew. I told her that I could not remember any more.

Francis asked me about which mosques I visited and which tapes I listened to. She then said to me that this was the last time I would ever see her.[29]

The global system of proxy detention requires the collusion of the security services of many countries to operate beyond the law. Due to deeply entrenched norms relating to due process and the rule against torture, the western world is outsourcing detention and torture to countries across the Muslim and Arab world. There is a line that western security services cannot cross, and the process of proxy detention has been implemented to save them from having to hold individuals incommunicado themselves. In this way they aim to avoid the responsibility of being directly involved with any abuse, but, as the chapter Torture and Abuse shows, their position often amounts to the same thing.

African rendition

The US led War on Terror finally found its first major duplication in the Horn of Africa during the Ethiopian-Somali conflict in 2007. Many aspects of those detentions that took place in Pakistan, Afghanistan and indeed around the world by various US agencies and their allies began to be mimicked in Kenya, Somalia and Ethiopia. As discussed in the Chapter 2, Guilty, the Kenyan Anti-Terrorism Police Unit made sweeping detentions across the country in an attempt to pick up suspected Al Qaeda terrorists fleeing Somalia.

When Millie Mithounie Gako, a Christian grandmother unlawfully arrested for being a suspected terrorist, was released, she took up the case of her friend Kamilya Mohammed Tuweni, who had been placed in secret detention by the Kenyan authorities. After realising that she had been unlawfully detained, the Kenyan authorities took her to the border with Tanzania in order to claim that she was Tanzanian and that she was pretending to be from the UAE. At the border with Tanzania, Tuweni was met by immigration officers:

One of the Tanzanian men said that I should be set free. The Tanzanian man told me that I should sue the Kenyan security, he told me, "You entered in a legal way." The Kenyan security promised that I would be returned. They said to the Tanzanians that they would give me back my passport and ticket and they would make sure that I returned safely. After that we left and were back in Nairobi. We stopped at a first police station which was in a village. We stopped there and the security men were leaving me here. I became frightened and I asked them to take me back to the same cell I was in before saying that at least I knew the people there. They said they were leaving me here as this was the closest police station to the airport and that they would return with my passport and ticket.[30]

Tuweni was detained again in Kenya as the authorities decided what to do with her. They had already realised their mistake in detaining her, and were now forced to cover their own tracks. Although she was told that she would be sent to Nairobi and then sent home, she knew they were lying. On 28 January 2007, Tuweni was taken to an airport and placed on a flight with other people who she did not know:

The plane landed and the cars went to where the plane landed one by one. There were people inside the cars. It was very dark and very cold.

I said to the security, "I am not leaving this car without my passport, if you give me my passport in my hand then I will go wherever you tell me." Before I left the car, I was holding onto the door… I said I would not leave until I got my passport. I wouldn't let go of the door. One officer kicked me from behind and I fell out of the car and then they beat me with black sticks. They threw my passport at me. I took it and I put it in my trousers.

When we reached the plane I was sprayed with something, I do not know what it was. The security men that I saw there were masked. They then tied my hands behind my back and covered my eyes. They put me on the plane. Until then, I didn't know where I was being taken.

When we arrived after the plane journey, they took me down from the plane, they untied my blindfold. I found there were women and children on one side and men on the other side of the plane. They were saying, "they are taking us to Mogadishu". The Kenyans who brought me there were still here. I was crying and screaming and telling them to let me go as I had my passport and that I was from Dubai and they should send me back. One man tried me to keep me quiet by saying, "you are coming with us."

When we came down from the plane then I saw the faces of the people. After a few minutes, the plane that had brought us there took off and we were left in Mogadishu. After that they told us to make a line for women and children.

We were in Mogadishu airport. The airport was like the desert. It was barren. The security then took us to a place near Mogadishu airport and placed us in a room. The room they took us to was broken. We had to cover it.

In total there were 22 women and children. Apart from me and another lady, everyone else was three to eight months pregnant. The men were taken somewhere else.[31]

Kamilya Tuweni was one of many foreign nationals and Kenyan citizens placed on rendition flights from Kenya to Somalia. Not wanting to admit that these men, women and children had been detained on Kenyan soil, they sent them on rendition flights to Somalia so that they could be arrested in the territory of the conflict. Although unlike the others, Tuweni had not originally come from Somalia as a refugee, she was similarly placed on the flights to hide her illegal detention.

Among those sent to Somalia were four British citizens: Mohammed Ezzouek, Reza Asfarzadagen, Shahjahan Janjua and Hamza Chentouf. They had been detained without charge in Kenya, then sent to Somalia having been questioned by MI5. Again, the Kenyans did not wish to declare officially that they had been unlawfully detained, rather they felt it more prudent to send them to Somalia. Landing in Somalia with the other victims of the rendition flights, Mohammed Ezzouek described the base on their arrival:

I was put in the back of a truck with the other twelve people who had been on my plane. I could see the uniform of the officers escorting us through my blindfold. I knew they were Somalis not Kenyans as they were wearing Somali army clothes and blue army hats. All I could hear was Somali being spoken.

I did not know where we were being driven. In total we were driven for between five and ten minutes. The truck then stopped and we were all taken one by one off the truck. Our handcuffs were taken off us. Then our blindfolds, sandals, trainers and some clothes were taken off us. When my blindfold was taken off, all I could see was what looked like an army base. Next to us there were walls with bullet holes.

The Somalis opened the door and they said "go down". We all filed down into an underground cell It was pitch black. There were water bottles down there to pee into. The floor was dusty and dirty. There were rats and cockroaches. Water had dried on the dust like mud. It did not smell good. Where the bottles were it smelt like a very dirty toilet.

Half-an-hour later the Somalis came in with plastic mats to put on the floor for us. Then they brought us tea and samosas. That was our breakfast. All in the pitch black. The only time we saw light was when that door opened for them to go in or out. This was the area where there were Ethiopian and Somali troops. When I went up the stairs there were holes in the wall. I looked through the holes and could see Ethiopians and Somali soldiers standing outside, smoking and chewing khat. The uniforms of the Somalis were not the same as the Ethiopians, and the Ethiopians are also lighter in skin colour than the Somalis. In the distance I could see a big sign that had some Somali writing and it said Baidoa beneath that.

Everyone in the cell was talking to each other, asking what is happening. No-one had a clue what was going on.

The second or third day everyone except the Brits were taken out. We asked the Somalis where everyone had gone, we were told that they were being taken back home and that was the last we heard. Their clothes remained in the cell. After the third day, they came for us as well. We were chained and blindfolded outside and put on the back of a truck. There were troops in the back and they were armed. We were driven for about five minutes in a car before it stopped. We thought we were going to get it. I could hear big guns being cocked around us.

Hamza was taken out first and then Shah. A few minutes later it was me, and then Reza. They took me into a little room and made me sit down. Took off my blind-folds and I was in chains. I was in a room with a little mattress and a mosquito-net hanging up. In front of me was a white man in a white t-shirt. He said "hello my name is Darren. I am from the British consulate." Darren said, "I was meant to see you lot a few days ago. I was told you were not in the police station. I went everywhere looking for you."[32]

With the teams at Cageprisoners and Reprieve lobbying for their return while the British detainees were still in Kenya, the Foreign and Commonwealth Office was forced to act on their behalf. But the Kenyan authorities would only allow the British men to be brought back to Britain from Somalia. These men were fortunate to have teams working for their release, the others placed on the rendition flights to Somalia were not so fortunate.[33]

Seventeen-year-old Safia Benaouda, a Swedish citizen, was heavily pregnant with her first child when she was taken with the others from Somalia on a rendition flight to Ethiopia. The Ethiopians wished to claim that these men, women and children had been caught in Somalia as part of the conflict with the Union of Islamic Courts. Those rendered on the flights to Ethiopia were placed in a detention facility where they were held in cages very much reminiscent of those at Guantánamo Bay:

After a few weeks they started to interrogate Halima [Baduradine]. She was really destroyed after that. Several times a week they took her. Took her around fajr [morning prayer] and would keep her until night time. Sometimes her children went with her. She told us that it was Americans, French, Italians, Swiss, Israelis and later on the Libyans. She lived in Pakistan before and the Pakistanis also came.

Around sixteen days later they took a group of men, twelve of them, and the day after they took a group of women including me. There was an American man taking our fingerprints and DNA. He told us he was American, he said he was a specialist on taking DNA. He took DNA with a swab in my mouth. He did this to all the women I was with and later to the others. The later ones told me that even a seven month old was photographed and fingerprinted.

The same thing to all men, women and children except the Ethiopian women. One of the women was a resident in the UK. The other was a citizen of Ethiopia but both had lived in the UK. One of them had a son who was a one year old and he went with her to meet MI5. They went there two times.

A few days later they took my husband to investigate him. Then they were really harsh. They would not let us meet or talk or anything. I could see him as they built these new metal cages where the men were alone. One room for women and the Swedish men were there all the time. They were there permanently; the other men were going in or out. Swedish always there in little cages. I was in a separate room. I could not speak to him. There were Ethiopian guards walking around all the time. Some of the Ethiopians knew different languages.[34]

When the foreign detainees were brought before the courts, the prosecutors used terminology learned from Guantánamo Bay. According to Benaouda, the court was given a month to decide whether the detainees were "illegal combatants, prisoners of war, or others".

Since their unlawful detention, nearly all the foreign nationals have been released. However, apart from the few who were released in October 2008, the Kenyans also placed on the rendition flights to Somalia and Ethiopia remain missing to this day. The Kenyan government has tried its hardest to deny their existence and any implication that they may have sent their own nationals on rendition flights. This whole episode is eerily reminiscent of the tactics used by the US, its allies and Pakistan in kidnapping, interrogating and rendering detainees to Guantánamo Bay.

7

TORTURE AND ABUSE

"I stand for eight to ten hours a day. Why is standing limited to four hours?[1]"

Donald Rumsfeld—Secretary of State for Defence

The law against torture is one of the most universally recognised principles of international law. Despite the abhorrent practices of some countries, attempts to redefine the law against torture have failed. Article 5 of the Universal Declaration of Human Rights states, "No one shall be subjected to torture or to cruel, inhuman or degrading treatment or punishment." The rule is unequivocal, and as such has found reiteration in many pieces of international legislation such as the Geneva Conventions, the Convention Against Torture and the European Convention on Human Rights.

Since the attacks of 9/11 the US administration has made a plethora of statements claiming that the world has entered 'a new era'. On 26 September 2002, the former Director of the CIA's Counter-Terrorist Center, Cofer Black, gave testimony to the US Joint Investigation into September 11. When speaking about the 'operational flexibility' of the CIA's response to the attacks, he remarked, "This is a highly classified area. All I want to say is that there was "before" 9/11 and "after" 9/11. After 9/11 the gloves came off."[2]

The removal of the metaphorical gloves is the thing that has damaged the US most in its approach to counter-terrorism worldwide. In a bid to show the world that they would be relentless in their pursuit of Al Qaeda, the US authorities exposed a brutality that would fit the Zimbardo project[3]. The use of torture is only one aspect of this. The starting point was the process of demonization. The identity of the

Muslim 'other' has invoked fear of an unknown international ene-my—an enemy of any colour, language or geographical location. For Muslim terrorism suspects, the gloves coming off has meant the removal of due process, and more importantly, the degradation of their position as citizens of the world.

The profiling of Muslims worldwide has led to significant and some-times systematic abuse of detainees. For those who deem it permissible to use intimidation, references are often made to issues which directly offend Muslims. Insults against the Prophet Muhammad (PBUH) and the Qur'an have become widespread during interrogations, while other Muslim sensitivities are further preyed upon.

The descent into barbarism[4] during any conflict is something well known and recorded, and often the demonization process results in individuals over-stepping the mark in the treatment of those they detain. The War on Terror has ushered in a tragic new era, in which nuanced arguments can be made to permit the use of torture.

In the US the definition of torture changed considerably on 1 August 2002, when Assistant Attorney General Jay S Baybee sent a memo to White House Counsel Alberto R Gonzales. Within the memo Baybee explained that in order for any act to constitute torture, it must inflict pain, "equivalent in intensity to the pain accompanying serious physi-cal injury, such as organ failure, impairment of bodily function or even death".[5] Such a formulation went well beyond the internationally accepted understanding of torture, and significantly raised the thresh-old over which an act could be considered to violate the conventions relating to torture.

This policy was in place for less than a year when international pres-sure forced the administration to review its own position. On 4 April 2003, the *Working Group Report on Detainee Interrogations in the Global War on Terrorism: Assessment of Legal, Historical, Policy, and Operational Considerations* was issued to administration staff. The report reassessed the extent to which torture would be considered as having taken place. Now the standard definition was that of prolonged mental harm which had been caused by, "The administration or appli-cation or threatened administration or application of mind-altering substances or other procedures calculated to disrupt profoundly the senses or the personality."[6]

By using extremely technical readings of the US laws relating to tor-ture, the Working Group sought to bring about a standard that would be considered more acceptable to the international community, however by no means did it go far enough. Essentially the US position evolved to the extent that evidence of torture could not be considered unless there was evidence of long-term harm.

Between the legal wrangling regarding the definition of torture and the extent to which the US would fall foul, a series of memos were exchanged which would change the course of American history forever. On 11 October Jerald Phifer, Director of JTF-J2, outlined a request for approval of the techniques that the Commander for the Joint Task Force 170, James T Hill, was to incorporate. The Joint Task Force 170 was based at Guantánamo Bay, and the following exchange of memos related directly to the techniques that would be used against detainees being held there.

The commander requested from the chairman of the Joint Chiefs of Staff clarification regarding the forms of counter-terrorism interrogation techniques that could be employed against the detainees. Commander Hill reasoned that, "...despite our best efforts, some detainees have tenaciously resisted our current interrogation methods."[7] The techniques laid out in the memo from Phifer were as follows:

a. Category I techniques. During the initial category of interrogation the detainee should be provided a chair and the environment should be generally comfortable. The format of the interrogation is the direct approach. The use of rewards like cookies or cigarettes may be helpful. If the detainee is determined by the interrogator to be uncooperative, the interrogator may use the following techniques.

(1) Yelling at the detainee (not directly in his ear or to the level that it would cause physical pain or hearing problems).
(2) Techniques of deception
    (a) Multiple interrogator techniques.
    (b) Interrogator identity. The interviewer may identify himself as a citizen of a foreign country or as an interrogator from a country with a reputation for harsh treatment of detainees.

b. Category II techniques. With the permission of the OIC, Interrogation Section, the interrogator may use the following techniques.

(1) The use of stress positions (like standing), for a maximum of four hours.
(2) The use of falsified documents or reports.

(3) Use of isolation facility for up to 30 days. Request must be made through the OIC, Interrogation Section, to the Director, Joint Interrogation Group (JIG). Extensions beyond the initial 30 days must be approved by the Commanding General for selected detainees, the OIC, Interrogation Section, will approve all contacts with the detainee, to include medical visits of a non-emergent nature.

(4) Interrogating the detainee in an environment other than the standard interrogation booth.

(5) Deprivation of light and auditory stimuli.

(6) The detainee may also have a hood placed over his head during transportation and questioning. The hood should not restrict breathing in any way and the detainee should be under direct observation when hooded.

(7) The use of 20-hour interrogations.

(8) Removal of all comfort items (including religious items).

(9) Switching the detainee from hot rations to MREs.

(10) Removal of clothing.

(11) Forced grooming (shaving of facial hair etc...).

(12) Using detainees individual phobias (such as fear of dogs) to induce stress.

c. Category III techniques. Techniques in this category may be used only by submitting a request through the Director, JIG, for approval by the Commanding General with appropriate legal review and information to Commander, USSOUTHCOM. These techniques are required for a very small percentage of the most uncooperative detainees (less than 3%). The following techniques and other aversive techniques, such as those used in US military interrogation resistance training or by other US government agencies, may be utilized in a carefully coordinated manner to help interrogate exceptionally resistant detainees. Any of these techniques that require more than light grabbing, poking, or pushing, will be administered only by individuals specifically trained in their safe application.

(1) The use of scenarios designed to convince the detainee that death or severely painful consequences are imminent for him and/or his family.

(2) Exposure to cold weather or water (with appropriate medical monitoring).

(3) Use of wet towel and dripping water to induce the misperception of suffocation.

(4) Use of mild, non-injurious contact such as grabbing, poking in the chest with the finger, and light pushing.

The arguments put forward by the legal team assessing any potential breach of US torture statute revolved around the constant scrutiny of the system and detainees as part of the interrogation techniques, such policies being seen somehow as justifying the position that was being taken. Final approval for the memo was sought by William J Haynes, General Counsel for the Department of Defense, from Donald Rumsfeld. All the techniques listed above were given approval by the Defense Secretary except for the use of exposure to cold, water or simulated suffocation using a wet towel. In his reply approving the memo, Rumsfeld wrote the now infamous words, "However, I stand for 8–10 hours a day. Why is standing limited to 4 hours?"

These policies were continually practised in Guantánamo Bay and former detainees have described in detail many of the interrogation techniques that had been approved, but to an extent that went beyond the restrictions the US administration claimed to have put in place. It was not Guantánamo Bay, though, where these policies found their most troubling manifestations; that was in Iraq. On 28 April 2004, pictures were released in the US media exposing the abuse of detainees at the Abu Ghraib prison in Iraq. The policies that had been put in place for Guantánamo Bay had found their way to the Middle East and had resulted in the most shocking pictures yet seen of prisoner abuse by the US.[8]

Private contractors employed by the US in conflict zones have had a great impact on the way in which detentions and detainee abuse have taken place. After the abuses at Abu Ghraib were exposed, the US administration sought scapegoats to show the public that justice was being served. Jonathan Keith "Jack" Idema was an American citizen arrested for running a private interrogation facility in Afghanistan. Detainees captured by Idema's team were abused through techniques such as hanging them upside down for days at a time. According to Idema:

We were working for the US counter-terrorist group and working with the Pentagon and some other federal agencies...We were in contact directly by fax and email and phone with Donald Rumsfeld's office...The American authorities absolutely condoned what we did. We have extensive evidence to that. We're prepared to show emails and correspondence and tape-recorded conversations.[9]

The US acquiescence to torture has been troubling for the world. The legal manipulation of long-standing norms has not sat well with allied countries in the western world and they have found it impossible to find a legal avenue for such practices themselves. For all the US acceptance of certain practices which could constitute detainee abuse and torture, should they wish to go even further, they can outsource torture for those suspected terrorists that they wish to interrogate outside their military detention facilities. Part of the proxy detention program discussed in the last chapter is reliant on the third party country's willingness to use brutal techniques in order to extract confessions. Detainees such as Mamdouh Habib, Binyam Mohammed Al Habashi and Maher Arar were sent to Egypt, Morocco and Syria respectively in order to be tortured with methods that would go well beyond what the US had come to accept.

The outsourcing of torture has become an integral part of the entire system of global detentions in the War on Terror, with western countries relying heavily on their eastern counterparts to extract confessions that might not otherwise be possible. Although the US has led the way with such proxy forms of detention, other countries have been more than willing to rely on evidence gleaned from torture in their desire to prosecute suspected terrorists.

One of the countries that deemed it permissible to rely on such evidence was Britain. During the ricin trials, the British government spent years trying to build a case against the defendants and subsequently had to rely on testimonies sent from abroad. In 2004, the Court of Appeal in Britain accepted the argument brought by the government that information extracted abroad under torture could be used in British courts when dealing with suspected terrorism. The case was brought before the House of Lords on appeal the next year following outrage at the decision in the lower court.

Speaking before the House of Lords, Dame Eliza Manningham-Buller, the then director-general of the Security Service gave evidence before the House of Lords to justify the use of information gleaned from torture in third party countries. Her argument rested on the threat of Al Qaeda and international terrorism and gave this as the reason that there was, "...the need for enhanced international cooperation".[10] Manningham-Buller used the case of Meguerba from the ricin trial to highlight the cooperation that was taking place between countries; she claimed that, "The Meguerba case provides an example of full co-operation with our Algerian partners."[11] During the ricin case, the government had fed information to the US claiming that those involved had been collaborating with the Iraqi government. This resulted in the US making such a claim before the UN in a bid to get Security Council acceptance for its forthcoming invasion. It was later to transpire that there was no such link, no ricin and not one conviction for the plot.

The House of Lords was particularly critical of the way in which the government attempted to justify the acceptance of torture-based evidence. Lord Hope's scathing attack on the British government also made reference to the practices of the US and in many ways summarises the view of the international community:

Torture is one of the most evil practices known to man. Once torture has become acclimatised in a legal system it spreads like an infectious disease, hardening and brutalising those who have become accustomed to its use.... Views as to where the line is to be drawn may differ sharply from state to state. This can be seen from the host of practices authorised for use in Guantánamo Bay by the US authorities, some of which would shock the conscience if they were ever to be authorised for use in our own country.[12]

Abuse

The abuse of detainees and others within the War on Terror has often focused on religious sensitivities. Insults and profanities have often been directed at Muslim religious figures and symbols as part of the process of abuse. Abuse though, is not confined to suspected terrorists who are in the process of detention.

Counter-terrorism strategies in Britain have led to the widespread use of dawn raids across the country. Hundreds of homes have had their front doors smashed by police searching for suspected terrorists using new legislation brought in to allow for such actions. The raids have caused widespread anger and resentment amongst the Muslim community in Britain who feel that police powers go beyond what is acceptable. Tensions have been fuelled by incidents such as that in Forest Gate when, during the arrest of two young men one was shot in the shoulder, only for both to be acquitted later.

One of the cases to have troubled the Muslim community most, however, is that of Babar Ahmad. Ahmad was arrested on 2 December 2003 by officers from the Metropolitan Police Counter-Terrorism

Command under the Terrorism Act 2000. Six days later he was released without charge after the police and Crown Prosecution Service accepted that there was little evidence to suggest that he was involved with terrorism. Despite the lack of evidence, Ahmad was brutalised by police officers during the raid on his home:

During my first arrest at my London home on 2 December 2003, I was subjected to physical, verbal, racial and sexual abuse by the police officers. I had nothing to hide when I was arrested so I made no attempt to struggle or resist.

The police officers smashed my head through my bedroom window and punched me all over my body. They pulled my genitals and stamped on my bare feet with their boots. They forced me into the prostration position of prayer and mocked my religious rituals by asking me, sarcastically, "Where is your God now?"

The officers tortured me by deliberately scraping metal handcuffs along my forearm bones and applying tight pressure to my neck so that I had difficulty breathing. I sustained over seventy-three medically recorded injuries including bleeding in my ears and urine. Photographs of the injuries on my body can be viewed online at www.freebabarahmad.com which is a website for my campaign to obtain justice.

An investigation into the assault supervised by the IPCC (Independent Police Complaints Commission) not only cleared the police officers of any wrongdoing, but actually "commended" one of them for his "great bravery".

Having been messed around by the IPCC for over two years, I proceeded to sue the Metropolitan Police for assaulting me. Civil proceedings were formally lodged at the High Court in London in July 2007. A civil trial on this matter is expected to take place in early 2009 at the High Court.[13]

The mockery of Ahmad's religious rites caused deep resentment amongst Muslims who became enraged at his treatment. The abuse that Ahmad suffered satisfies conditions for such acts to be considered torture[14] and yet there was no attempt to account for the wounds he received. At the time of writing, raids are still taking place across Britain in which men, women and children are being abused in the worst possible ways. To make matters worse for many Muslims, dawn raids often find families who are still not fully clothed when the police enter their rooms—this in itself has an extremely negative impact, especially amongst those in the community who cover completely.

Coupled with the abuse of victims in raids has been the worldwide intimidation of campaigners, activists and families who lobby for the release of detainees. In Pakistan the security services make a point of visiting the families of detainees to ensure that they do not speak of the disappearance and to place pressure on activists to stop any campaign work. In March 2003, Aafia Siddiqui and her three children were allegedly detained at Karachi airport on their way to see family in Rawalpindi. Immediately after their detention, Aafia's mother, Ismet, was visited by a man on a motorcycle who told her not to raise any issue of her daughter's disappearance, or, he threatened, she would never see her grandchildren again.[15] Threats however are not the only means of discouraging activism. Far more brutal methods have been used to dissuade families from becoming involved.

Two years after her husband's detention, Nadja Dizderavic was actively seeking to end the plight of her husband detained in Guantánamo Bay. Boudella Haji was one of the Bosnian Algerians kidnapped and placed on a rendition flight to Cuba. Raising awareness of the illegality of his detention, Dizderavic herself became the victim of constant harassment and eventually of abuse by unknown assailants:

In May 2004 two people came with me at the front of my building when I was opening the door, someone approached me from behind and I turned to see who is coming and someone put their hand on my mouth and grabbed me and took me inside of the house and he took me to the main room. I can say that he knew my apartment well and after that a second man entered and I could not see anything except the ring on his finger. This man who was speaking poor Bosnian and he was from an English spoken area, the man who was beating me he was a foreigner. After all of this they took a picture of the man who was hitting me, they said that they could be found on Interpol, they said that they were French and British and that they had been prosecuted in the courts of those countries, but I assume that this was not true.

That man who was beating me, he was speaking English very quick and he was saying all bad words he was swearing. I started to fight against them and hit the man who was holding me between the legs and the other who was beating me I bit him on the hand near to the ring on his hand. When I kick the guy, he raised his head, his eyes were bloody like an animal he took my head and hit me on the wall three times and kicked me in the stomach. Last thing I remember, because the stomach hit was so strong I was about to lose consciousness, he said that I have 'salaam' from Bush.

I have all the medical records about what happened with this. I got injured in my stomach and I have to make an operation to take out two thirds of my stomach. For twelve days I was throwing up blood.[16]

Although the physical nature of the abuse that the detainees and others suffered is acute, in many ways it paled in comparison to the attacks on their religion. Guantánamo Bay established itself early as a site where detainees were subjected to religious mockery, and this was in fact deliberately used as a means of breaking their spirit. Former Guantánamo detainee Moazzam Begg explained the nature of the abuse that was used:

The ridiculing of the athaan (call to prayer); forcible shaving of the beard—as punishment; use of sexual enticement during interrogations; derision of the Prophet; withholding of food in Ramadan; prohibition of Quranic recitation, proscription of athaan and congregational prayer in Bagram, Afghanistan—a Muslim country; derision of Islamic rituals and supplications; forcible removal of prisoners while in the act of prayer, in addition to the degradation of the Qur'an have all been categorically reported by men formerly detained by the US military. The reports are far too recurrent, concurrent and consistent to deny, particularly as former US interrogators and soldiers have corroborated these reports.[17]

Knowing full well the position of the Qur'an in the lives of Muslims, Guantánamo Bay saw its systematic desecration as a means of causing grief to the detainees. This came to light in 2005 when *Newsweek's* April issue contained a report about the prison guards damaging copies of the Qur'an deliberately. Widespread protests around the Muslim world began and on 16 May 2005, Cageprisoners released a report which highlighted the systematic and institutionalised desecration of the Qur'an and other Islamic rituals through the testimonies of former detainees. A statement was given by the Tipton Three, Shafiq Rasul, Asif Iqbal and Rhuhel Ahmed who recalled:

We witnessed on numerous occasions US soldiers mishandling the Qur'an and also desecrating it. In Afghanistan, we witnessed US soldiers throwing the Qur'an in buckets that were used to urinate in, on purpose. In Guantánamo, the Qur'an was intentionally thrown on the floor, even after the soldiers were told not to do it, for the sole purpose of making the detainees angry and the soldiers knowing that they can get away with what they were doing. It was also stood upon, again thrown in the toilets, had obscene language written in them by the soldiers. I, myself mentioned this to the British delegate that used to come to visit us. He told me that he would mention it to whoever was in charge of the Camp but it seemed like nothing had happened because from the time we got there and just before we left we would hear of so many incidences where the Qur'an was mishandled purposely by the soldiers. There were also instances in which the interrogators would mishandle the Qur'an while interrogating detainees.[18]

Speaking more directly about an incident he witnessed, former Guantánamo detainee Martin Mubanga described in detail:

When I was in Charlie block in Camp Delta cell 33, and Rhuhel Ahmed was in cell 34, there took place an incident involving the Qur'an. Namely that when six or seven MPs [military police] came in to search my cell and search me, one of them picked up the Qur'an, searched it and then threw it on the floor whilst I was made to kneel with my hands on my head and face turned the other way. However, Rhuhel who was watching this informed me that they had thrown the Qur'an on the floor and he began to verbally reproach them. I was, at this moment in time, being restrained by four or five MPs and was unable to do anything.[19]

Varying levels of abuse have taken place which would fall foul of the conventions relating to torture, abuse or inhuman and degrading treatment. The process of demonising the detainees and Muslims in general has had a great impact on the way in which they have been treated not only by various police forces around the world, but also by the way that governments respond to their rights. Debates surrounding national security have overwhelmed any considerations relating to the individual, while the negative impact of such policies has not only affected Muslims, but also civil society at large.

Torture

For many years now western democracies have occupied the moral high ground in terms of judicial administration through adherence to fair trials and the rule of law. It was from this superior ground that they were able to criticise those countries that have put in place measures which prevent due process from taking place. One of their most important features was the complete denial of torture as a valid technique in the process of interrogation—decades of judicial and legislative precedent protected their citizens from such brutality.[20]

The international norm established against torture has been placed in a category known as *jus cogens* (compelling law). The principle of *jus cogens* requires that the norm cannot be deviated from due to its importance in maintaining international legal order. As explained by the academics Hilary Charlesworth and Christine Chinkin:

All the violations of human rights typically included in the catalogues of jus cogens norms are of undoubted seriousness; genocide, slavery, murder, disappearances, torture, prolonged arbitrary detention, and systematic racial discrimination.[21]

With the exception of slavery and genocide, the War on Terror has made its way through most of these protected norms in various permutations around the world. The way in which the war has been conducted has resulted in numerous violations. Amongst the most serious is America's espousal of torture as an acceptable means of extracting information.

Nihad Karsic and Almin Hardaus were detained in metal shipping containers in Bosnia. Being suspected of terrorism, the two men were interrogated by US forces and tortured in order to extract information. Karsic described the conditions they were kept in:

When I went to the toilet once, the US soldier beat me on my leg and back. They would constantly kick me over and over again. They put a bucket over my head and with a stick they hit it over and over again. It caused a great noise. I opened my mouth in order to help the noise escape otherwise my ears would break. They were hitting so hard that the stick broke from the force.

Another time another soldier beat me. When the interrogator entered the cell, I had to stand up and turn my face to the wall, when they entered into the cell, I stood up slowly, the guard ran over and hit me hard over my head. This one particular guard would abuse me all day long. This American was dark skinned and he kept on beating me, he had a moustache. They took shifts, but this particular one abused me, the others would just shout and swear at us. Four times, this same guard beat me with a steel rod on my shoulder and back.

In this container they made a line, they said if we cross the line, we will have problems, it was in middle of the container, later they shortened this line so we had even less space to walk. They took our photos, our hair, our DNA, spit, fingerprints and voice.

When they placed me in that cell, they took all my clothes and shoes and my underwear, and my shirt which was a little bit long just made from paper. They did not allow me to sleep as it was regulation. Any time the guard entered the cell, I had to turn to the wall. I had to stand up every time they came in and turn to the wall. They were putting me through sleep deprivation. This went on for many days. In the first few days it was very intensive, soldiers were coming, they were shouting at me terrorist and so on.[22]

Days after their initial kidnapping and secret detention, the two men were simply released back on to the streets of Sarajevo without any apology or compensation for the treatment they had received. Hardaus explained the difficulty that they felt in speaking about their treatment:

We were never given a formal apology from anyone; the US said that we had been in the wrong place at the wrong time. We were scared for a long time after, we were scared to say anything to anyone, we only spoke to our close families because we thought something big was happening in Bosnia.[23]

The use of torture by the US has become commonplace as those it deals with have a history of violence towards detainees, and especially suspected terrorists. Abou Elkassim Britel was detained by the Pakistanis, handed over to the US and then sent to Morocco. At all stages of his detention he suffered at the hands of his captors, but in an environment where foreigners were treated particularly poorly, the Pakistanis subjected him to torture before his transfer to US officials:

Kassim still finds it difficult to relate what he's been through. Even though he does speak about it now, he is not up to telling the whole story.

My husband was psychologically tortured with death threats against him and threats of violence against the female members of his family. They told him that the Italian ambassador was not interested in him "because he was a terrorist".

As for the physical torture, I know he was beaten severely, with a cricket bat at times. The handcuffs he wore around his wrists were tied behind his back with chains and he would be hung from the prison bars or off the ceiling for a long time. He would be blindfolded and his hands and feet would be chained so that he could not defend himself nor predict where he was going to be hit. The cell did not include a toilet and he was not allowed to relieve himself except once every twenty-four hours, when he was given a bucket. For three days he was sleep deprived, while tied to a gate.

When I saw him again after eleven months, he still had patches of yellow on his skin where he'd been severely beaten. This treatment, inflicted on him by the Pakistani police and secret services, lasted a very long time. At the beginning of April 2002 after another violent interrogation, Kassim was in critical condition, exhausted and continuously prone to fainting, so they gave him medical attention for about a week.[24]

The conditions of detainees being held as part of operations against suspected terrorists has resulted in some of the most brutal forms of torture. A sad consequence of the way the US and her allies have conducted military operations has been the endemic abuse of those in custody. In 2008, Alex Gibney released his Academy Award-winning documentary *Taxi to the Dark Side* in which he retraced the death of a detainee named Dilawar at Bagram. Only five days after his arrest, Dilawar died from the constant beatings and torture that he received from his guards.

Officers in the US military have occasionally been exposed for their roles in the abuse, though often with quite worrying levels of impunity. But it is not just US soldiers that have been found to be in breach of their duty to those detained as part of military operations. In Septem-

ber 2003, a captain of Queen's Lancashire Regiment (QLR) was killed
in Basra. What then allegedly took place, was that the QLR somehow
felt that the civilian employees of a hotel they knew were responsible
for the incident, and began to hurt them. Among the nine employees
that the British soldiers attacked, was Baha Mousa, who died as a
result of his injuries. The lawyer for Mousa and the other eight men
was Phil Shiner from Public Interest Lawyers in Britain. He explained
what took place:

Baha Mousa was hooded, tortured, beaten, kicked, you name it, it was done
to him and the other eight men. Baha Mousa died and another man Keefa
Taha Al Muttari was beaten and tortured to the brink of death and he suffered
with acute renal failure and needed immediate kidney dialysis. He could not
have that in Basra as the equipment wasn't available and he was treated with
conservative measures, and miraculously he recovered.[25]

The result of the case brought against the British military was that
on 19 September 2006, Corporal Donald Payne pleaded guilty to the
war crime of inhumane treatment. On 27 March 2008, the British
defence secretary Des Browne was forced to admit that there had been
substantial breaches of the European Convention on Human Rights,
and finally the Ministry of Defence paid the Mousa family £2.83 million in compensation. Although some have attempted to pass these off
as isolated incidents, Phil Shiner's work with Iraqi detainees uncovered
further abuses. He represented a further nine Iraqi civilians who had
been taken to Camp Breadbasket by British troops where they were
detained, abused, humiliated and tortured. An order was given that
was tantamount to collective punishment after it was found that food
had been disappearing from a depot as part of the UN Oil for Food
program. The soldiers allegedly began to detain individuals from the
surrounding countryside and take them to the interim camp. It was
there that they were systematically humiliated using different techniques that have been witnessed elsewhere. Shiner explained the similarities between the abuse carried out by British soldiers and the
practices of the US:

I have compared everything that I could find on US torture policy in
Guantánamo, Abu Ghraib and Camp Bucca, with what I know from my cases
in respect of what UK forces were up to. There are remarkable similarities in
terms of our approach to systematic humiliation of Muslim males, the use of
sexual humiliation, and the use of stress techniques and weird and wonderful
interrogation techniques, all of which emerge clearly from the witness statements of Baha Mousa's colleagues.

One speaks of a game involving footballers' names, they were told as Iraqis that they had to remember the names of what turns out to be last century Dutch footballers such as Van Basten and Ruud Gullit, and if they did not remember those names they were beaten. Another game involved kickboxing. A hooded detainee would be surrounded by a number of soldiers who would take it in turns to compete on how hard they could smash that detainee against the walls of a ring.

There were many other techniques and practices during the detentions in other cases. This raised real questions on how we could have possibly gone to war, and at the same time, in the same country, with different forces from the US, and just as a matter of coincidence, come up with exactly the same approach to interrogation and techniques. It looks to me like this is not a coincidence, and is something that needs to be investigated by the Attorney General and an independent investigative body.[26]

Outsourcing

The outsourcing of torture has been a key weapon in the arsenal of western countries who wish to circumvent their own principles on due process and the rule of law. As discussed in the previous chapter, the process of using proxy countries has become more common. Along with the proxy nature of the detention, the main aspect that requires outsourcing is that of abuse or torture. It is through the outsourcing of torture that information can be gleaned which otherwise may not be available.

After the bombings of 7 July 2005 in London, Alam Ghafoor, a British citizen, was detained by the authorities in Dubai and told that the British had requested his detention. After denying any involvement with the bombings, he was put through a process of sleep deprivation and beatings in order to confess to crimes that he did not commit:

At this point, they took me into another room, and put me through sleep deprivation for four days straight. I was slowly losing my mind as it seemed as if the walls were closing in, literally I thought the walls were caving in. I told them, "I have told you everything that I know, there is absolutely nothing else that I can tell you, give me a piece of paper, and I will write down for you everything that you want me to write." I wrote for them a confession, that I am involved with the London gang. The guy interrogating me asked me if the statement was true, I said "it doesn't matter if it is true or not, this is what you want." I said, "You want to show the world that you are fantastic in this War on Terror." I said to them, "You have done it, you have caught me, I am the mastermind."

He looked at me and said, "You are a supporter of Osama bin Laden and a supporter of Saddam Hussein and you know the Taliban." He then said to me, "I understand why you are a supporter of the Taliban, because you have two stripes on your face, because Taliban means two students, and those two stripes mean you support the Taliban." The guard rushes out of the room and calls his senior who asks me again if what I have written is the truth. I say again that, "It doesn't matter if it is the truth it's what you want." At this point I had been for four days and nights without sleep under bright halogen lights. I was going out of my mind. He said that they will put me under the lie detector machine to see if I am lying. I said, "You didn't believe me when I told you the truth before, why would you believe me now?" At the bottom I said I want a trial before a British judge in a British court.[27]

The tangible link to British security services in the case of Ghafoor is somewhat weak, the mere statement of the UAE security services does not mean that there was complicity by the British, however, in other cases complicity was rather more obvious. Adam Brown was questioned about things that could only have been known in Britain while being interrogated by the Syrian authorities. It seemed clear to him that information was being fed to the Syrians by the British authorities in order to enhance his interrogation:

First they were made to strip down to their underpants and they were beaten; first on the soles of their feet and on their back and then on their legs, then they were told to lie on their backs and then were beaten across their chest which was basically lacerating their skin and they were beaten head to toe apart from the face, if they were hit in the face it would be like a punch or a slap. When they returned to the cell they weren't able to walk because of the way their feet were swollen. They lifted up their tops and their skin was sort of blackish blue and lacerated and bleeding from all of the cables and this was meted out not only to the young guys but there was one guy who I'm not sure how old he was but he didn't have a coloured hair on his head. We heard him screaming and he came back black and blue from being beaten with cables. Another detainee that was with me was threatened with this thing called 'the chair', where they basically put you into a chair, I think face first and basically try to break your back.

There was a guy who left my cell before I got there I was told of his story, that they broke his back he was only sort of in his early twenties and they beat him until he basically became like a two year old. He lost his memory and became like a vegetable. They beat him with cables and all the rest of it as well. But that was sort of the worst they did to him.

In Fara' Falastin, it was no more than being slapped and being taunted and being threatened with sort of worse torture. The worst torture happened in the other prison. They were asking me if I was a Salafi, and what types of books I read. They were saying to me "you extremist", "don't think that you can ever beat America because America has all this technology". They kept saying why do you want to go and fight in Iraq, and I kept saying that I'd been living there for a year, if I wanted to do that I would have gone a long time ago, and that I had no intention of going anywhere. But they wanted me to admit that.

I got taken for one interrogation and they said that "you're a liar, you wanted to go to Iraq, and we gonna put it plainly to you now that you have to admit that you wanted to go to Iraq," and he said if you speak the 'truth' we will be fine with you, no-one will say anything to you and no one will touch you but if you lie then we will beat you and we will be bad to you, very very bad to you, and as he was saying this there was someone being tortured and screaming. I wasn't worried for myself because I didn't want to admit anything that I hadn't done, but I was fearing that they were going to take my wife and use her, and beat her or my son as well. So that is what he wanted me to admit so I just admitted it, and I felt when I said that that was all he wanted me to say, and then from that the interrogations finished. I was only approached once more after that to be asked some routine questions.[28]

Fara' Falastin is one of the most well known prisons in the entire process of outsourcing torture. As described earlier in this book, a number of Canadian citizens were detained there. While Maher Arar was sent to Syria by the US, other Canadians such as Abdullah Almalki, Muayyad Nureddin, and Abou Ahmed El Maati were detained and tortured while in Syria. During their interrogations, very much in the same way as Adam Brown, they realised that information was being fed to their captors by their home country as the information about their life was too detailed to have come from any other source. All the men experienced severe levels of torture for months at the hands of the Syrians.

Another country that used Syria as part of the outsourcing process was Denmark. Umm Hadigah describes the abuse of her husband, Mohamed Hamid, in Fara' Falastin where he was detained after having travelled to Syria for a family visit:

Yes, the men they were told psychologically again and again that they would never leave this place, the prison. At the beginning the three men were put in the same cell, but then after a while the Syrian police they put my husband in a different cell, away from the other two family members. So from that day they didn't hear anything from him, and he was beaten to the extent that his clothes were ripped apart, and there was blood on it. These clothes when he travelled back to Denmark he bought it with him and the police they used it in the investigation, and have now finished with it. So now I have the clothes in my house, so I have it as evidence—what happened with him. In the prison when they changed him from the first cell to the second cell he was put in a cell filled with people to the extent that they nearly lay on each other, and it was totally dark, no light at all.

They arrested him as it was requested from the Danish authorities and the Syrians said to my husband they have no interest in keeping him, and they themselves made an investigation in Syria and they didn't find anything on him, because the questions they asked him—he answered them and they (the Syrian authorities) checked it up and everything was fine. They didn't have interest in keeping him, but they were told by the Danish authorities to keep him back, and send him to Iraq, but they didn't say why. That was just the request from the Danish authorities, but the Syrians didn't they just released him, as they said we have no interest in keeping you, we have no interest in sending you to Iraq.

The process of proxy detention and the outsourcing of torture often involves western agencies playing a background role in the interrogation of a suspect. However in some cases, the security services of the home nation will actively participate in the process. Their aim is often to extract information but also to offer ways out to the suspects through cooperation.[29]

MI5 complicity in the secret detention of individuals often results in their turning a blind eye to the abuse and torture of detainees being held in foreign countries. Ashraf Hossein was detained in Bangladesh by the Bengali security services after he had travelled there to get married and also to visit his native town in Sylhet. Just a month after marrying his wife, Hossein was arrested and taken into custody from the village of his in-laws. Agents from the Rapid Action Battalion and Directorate General Forces Intelligence for Bangladesh took him into custody where he was kept in secret detention. Hossein claims that there were two 'white' men who had balaclavas over their heads who were also present at the raid. He alleges that these were the same men from MI5 who would come to interrogate him later. He was detained between 1 December 2005 and 29 May 2008, during which time MI5 interrogated him many times:

When I saw some British faces, I was so relieved; I believed I will get some justice now, some law and order.

As I sat down Liam told me to relax, they were trying to show they are my friend, all smiling and happy. Andrew then said to me, "I hope our Bangladeshi friends are treating you fine," this with a smirk on his face.

Liam says, "From our findings we see you are a highly trained individual aren't you, so why have you obtained all this training?" He then says, "Ahh so you are the mastermind for the atrocities in the UK, aren't you? So you know about the July 7 bombings" saying this very calmly but with a sharpness coming from his throat.

At that point I told Liam and Andrew, "it's not true, it's all been a mistake, I am innocent, I don't know why I am arrested, please tell me why am I here for, what have I done, please help me I am a British citizen." These guys have been abusing me for the last three weeks or so, beating me and threatening me that they will rape my wife. Whatever I have said or wrote is all made up; I did all this just to please the Colonel. The MI5 men just turned around and looked at the Colonel and shook their heads in disappointment, Liam said, "I think we need a break." It seemed both Liam and Andrew were disappointed with my demonstration of innocence.

I look at the Colonel's face and he is fuming with anger his face gone all red.

Both Liam and Andrew laugh after I spoke and Andrew says, "they haven't done a very good job on you have they", I was gob smacked, I thought what is he saying, so he knows what is happening to me, but he is doing nothing about it even though I am a British citizen, my head started spinning I felt a little dizzy.

Liam then says, "Colonel I believe you need a ten minute break now."

The Colonel replied, "Fine", calls an officer from outside who takes me and escorts me to an empty room near the interview room that I was just in.

The officer shoves me in the room with him waiting inside with me; the Colonel comes in a minute or two later, he first slaps me in the face, I am shocked he then punches me in the back really hard, I was about to go down when he grabs me by the testicles so hard he keeps me standing, I am in pain, I have tears coming down my cheeks, I was finding it hard to breath, he says, "what are you playing at, you think this is a game, this is not the movies," he lets my testicles go and I go straight to the floor huffing and puffing with pain, he orders the officer to beat me on my body, but he tells him don't break any bones, just give him pain. He says, "Not the face."

The officer knew exactly how to hit me and where so no bones are broken.

Andrew and Liam knew exactly what was happening. They left the room and arranged for me to get a beating. They got me beat up so I was compliant.

Andrew says, "Are you okay, I hope you are okay and the break has done you some good." Liam says, "where were we, so you are a trained person from my notes I see you trained in Kashmir, bomb expert", I just agreed with him, he carried on asking me about training, my involvement with July 7 bombings in UK, fighting in Afghanistan, the assassination attempt of General Pervez Musharraf, he kept asking me about why I came to Bangladesh, to be with JMB, HUJI, I was funding them, training them, training western people to make bombs so they can go back to the west to bomb places, he said, "so you are Al Qaeda, they have sent you here, your boss is Osama Bin Laden", I just agreed, Liam told me, "so you were with Sheikh Abdur Rahman, and Bangla

Bhai, you are funding them and working under their protection, these were the leaders of JMB, they have been executed by the government of Bangladesh, even though I have never seen them or met them in my life.[30]

The situation for Ashraf Hossein became far worse after his eventual release back to his family in Bangladesh. MI5 and the Bangladeshi security services used their position to interrogate him for months on end and attempted to buy his cooperation with them. It would be many months before Hossein would find his way back to Britain and to safety.

The torture of Rangzieb Ahmed, very much like Hossein, was conducted with the full knowledge of western security services. While secretly detained in Pakistan, Ahmed was subjected to torture in between rounds of questioning by US and UK officials. Rangzieb recalled one particular incident involving his torture and the way in which his US interrogators responded to his treatment:

I recall that on the 7th day of my detention I was taken to the interrogation room using the same routine. I was asked questions repeatedly about Al Qaida. I kept denying any involvement or association following which I was beaten with a stick by the male who was the heavy smoker also that this was common for all detainees. He was the main aggressor, torturer. After approximately fifteen minutes he rang the bell and requested someone to bring in the 'box'. I recall that three people came into the room with a box which was one foot square. I was still in handcuffs and my arms were forced on the table in front. Each arm was held down by an individual and the one who stood behind me he held my back by putting his arm around my neck and pulling back. At this point the male who was the heavy smoker got up and opened the box and took out a pair of pliers.

He began to ask the same questions and I replied that I did not know anything. My left arm was held down at the wrist at which point the smoker got hold of my small finger of my left hand and he gripped my nail with the pliers and began to pull it back, not forward. I was in extreme pain and he asked the same questions to which I replied I would tell you and when he stopped pulling I replied with the same answer namely that I did not know anything at which point he began to pull the nail back again. This happened a few times after which he pulled out the entire nail. This ordeal in the interrogation room took approximately half-an-hour to forty-five minutes.

Another person was called into the room that was in civilian clothing and gave me an injection on the left arm and bandaged my finger. I recall the following day there was no interrogation. However the following day, the day after, I was taken back into the interrogation room and the same persons were present. The same questions were put and I replied with the same answers. Again the same routine was carried out whereby I was held down and my hands were held down to the table and another fingernail was pulled out. Again I received an injection and my second finger was bandaged. I made no confessions during this torture of any involvement in any activities. However the next day the same routine whereby another nail was pulled out and I received a further injection and the injury was bandaged. I was not subject to any further interrogation up to the thirteenth day of detention when I was taken out of this building to a secret location to be met by UK officials. I was brought back the same day and the following day I was seen by Americans.

The Americans were aware of my treatment as I told them what happened to me and also that I could not sit straight as I had been hit on my back with a wooden instrument by a male with curly hair. They laughed when they heard this. They also saw my fingernails had been removed.[31]

8

SECURITY

The profile exists. It is this one manifest truth in the global struggle against terrorism that has led to the multitude of ill-conceived responses seen around the world today. Terminology such as 'radicalisation', 'Islamist' and 'jihadist' are all used in a plethora of expressions to highlight the ideology or individual the War on Terror seeks to defeat. The great difficulty arises though when it is realised that the number of divergent opinions and factions that exist within communities is far greater than the number of counter-terrorism measures that can be envisaged. In such circumstances fear takes root within governments who are often keen to show their strength in the face of such threats. Suspicion of a section of the public evokes the type of 'quick fix' legislation seen in the past—and, ultimately, to the abandonment of the rule of law.

In many ways it is the rule of law that always comes under attack in such circumstances. An extraordinary situation is said to require an extraordinary response, and because of this thought process, the norms of just and civil societies are abandoned in favour of public security. Whether purposeful or not the policies directly criminalise communities and make them feel as if they are under constant surveillance, in today's case introverting Muslims and further increasing their mistrust and dissatisfaction with the political process.

Prior to the War on Terror, detention without charge already existed in communities in the third world. Political opponents and activists were often rounded up and imprisoned without charge or trial due to the instability of the countries they resided in. The global War on Terror has provided those countries with an excuse to continue their programs of unlawful detention without the close scrutiny of the international community, many of whom have become complicit in such activities.

Detention without charge is not something that can be simply introduced in western countries. The rule of law as understood by those people who live under it dictates that such a mechanism cannot arbitrarily be brought into commission. With philosophical restraints such as habeas corpus being placed on western governments such as Britain, Canada and US, new methods of bypassing the rule of law are invented in order to secure the detention of suspected terrorists. It is, however, not just the issue of detention without charge. Other ethical considerations have been manipulated in order to bring in counter-terrorism measures which seem legal and humane, but which really contribute to the climate of fear. The treatment of foreign nationals in the three countries mentioned is testimony in itself to the way in which legislation has been used in order to attack the most vulnerable first. Whether it was the PENTTBOM detainees, those detained as part of the ricin plot or those under the Canadian security certificates; the law was completely changed in order to bring about their detentions.

In a speech to the Fabian Society in 2006 Gordon Brown suggested a day to celebrate Britishness to help solidify a set of national values.[1] The BBC conducted a poll asking respondents to name the one event in history that best defined Britishness. The winner was the signing of Magna Carta. It is bizarre that habeas corpus, a 'civilising' concept exported to the rest of the world, is suspended in 2009 in the name of national security measures. At a time when a unifying national identity is sought as a panacea for radicalisation, the one characteristic—the right to be free from authoritarian detention—that best defines the national conscience is the one that is being eroded and lost.

The positions taken by the western world have resulted in the erosion of human rights to such a degree that now we are in a situation akin to that before the signing of the Universal Declaration of Human Rights. The value of what the rule of law means has been diminished by the actions of governments who seek to present the security debate as one that takes precedence over all norms of behaviour. Nothing has been more evident of this than what took place in the prisons at Guantánamo Bay.

It is Guantánamo that has established itself as a primal force in the removal of due process from the psyche of the international community. Looking at the policies and procedures that have been put into place at the US naval base, there is little doubt that those detainees exist far beyond the reach of recognised law. Even the word Guantánamo has been given nominal, verbal and even adverbial forms in its usage as the world has come to consider the prison a reference point for unlawful detentions.

Despite the images that are shown, the testimonies that have been taken and the legal challenges that have been brought, the reality is that Guantánamo is one of the most humane faces of the War on Terror. With Guantánamo there is a feeling that at least the prison was in the open, that its location was known and that the detainees were known. It is however elsewhere in the global network of detention sites that some of the most horrific abuses have taken place. Families are constantly left wondering as to the location of their loved one and detainees are left with no understanding of how to contact any individual to assist their situation. The detainee is completely at the mercy of the captors, and it is nearly always the case that in such circumstances abuse takes place.

The US and her allies have established a system of cooperation with countries such as Libya, Syria, Egypt, Algeria and Morocco in the detention of suspected terrorists. This cooperation is on the understanding that the western governments will be permitted to keep their own hands clean while the suspect is brutalised by these regimes. The extracted confessions are then used in order to bring cases against those once placed within the secret detention system.

All human beings are ultimately accountable for their own actions—indeed it would be very difficult to say that a torturer was not culpable for the abuse against his or her victim merely because an order had come from above. However the world we live in today has been greatly affected by those in control; the policies that we see every day have been manufactured within a climate of fear created by the suspected threat of terrorism. It is in pursuit of those known or unknown terrorists though that internationally recognised standards of behaviour and the most fundamental norms of civil society have been decimated. Torture and arbitrary detention have become prevalent in a world where there is no leader to turn to.

The United States of America and the United Kingdom were at one time the benchmark for all others in terms of their recognition as leaders in human rights. The War on Terror has drastically changed that status quo to another where great latitude has been given to all those claiming to be involved in counter-terrorism efforts. The rendition of Maher Arar from the US to Syria, their allied efforts with Ethiopia in the Horn of Africa and other relationships formed with the worst human rights offenders signal an era where human rights are to be completely sacrificed in the name of the global War on Terror. What has been lost in the last eight years is not only the moral high ground that these countries once occupied, but also the right to give protection to those seeking fairness in their treatment. The fundamental norms of human behaviour have disintegrated and those who would accuse the US and its allies of hypocrisy and double standards, have now found much evidence to back up their claims.

The hope to see a world leader emerge who could reverse the trend of the last eight years has been the desire of millions around the world—a leader who would ignore the policies of the past and signal a new intent for global human rights. The presidency of Barack Hussein Obama is one that has the heavy responsibility of bringing about the change that the world hopes for—a poll conducted by the BBC World Service suggested that sixty-seven percent of people across seventeen countries questioned about the new president felt that he would strengthen US relations abroad but also indicated that he would remove US troops from Iraq and broker a deal in the Middle East. The order to close the detention camps at Guantánamo Bay and CIA black sites announced to the world an important step in reversing the trend of the Bush era, however the continuation of Robert Gates as Defense Secretary and the use of renditions has indicated that the desired change may be very short lived.

It is still early days for the new administration, and there is much that needs to be tackled, however the Obama government has been given the opportunity to prove to the world that it has the capability to bring about tangible change to crises around the world, so on behalf of all those still being held in secret detention facilities around the world, we are keen to see how the new administration will respond.

There are fundamental norms that exist which transcend all cultures and societies for all time. These norms exist not because of positive legislation enacted in order to give them value, but rather because of the inherent morality that is intrinsic to their being. Nearly all societies understand the rights of all human beings to their life, their possessions and to their honour.

Throughout history there have been references to these norms. John Locke's 'Second Treatise on Civil Government', a work that some may regard as seminal on civil government, raises particularly important questions about justice and the place of law. What is particularly interesting is Locke's definition of the nature of law, that being: no one ought to be harmed in their life, health, liberty or possessions. While reading Locke's work, a formulation in Islamic law known as *al-Maqaasid al-Shariah* (the aims of Islamic law) comes to mind. Imam Al-Ghazali, the universally respected Islamic jurist formulated the aims of Islamic law as being "to promote the welfare of the people, which lies in safeguarding their faith, their life, their intellect, their posterity and their wealth."[2] The common ground between the statements reinforces the concept of fundamental norms of behaviour that go beyond the details of any particular system.

Fundamental rights exist because their essence is understood by all people. Removing the emphasis from these norms does not just harm those individuals detained, but rather harms everyone through the erosion of the global conscience. When the emphasis on human rights becomes a secondary or tertiary consideration, then abuses begin to manifest themselves in the most horrible ways. The policies that the United States of America and United Kingdom have implemented in Afghanistan, Iraq, Guantánamo Bay and their own domestic legislations have led the world in the way it deals with suspected terrorists. While the US and UK may not specifically torture suspected terrorist detainees held in Ethiopian prisons, the climate it has created has allowed for such practices to take place without challenge.

Counter-terrorism measures need not equate to the removal of civil liberties and human rights. Past examples of genuine conflict resolution have, in nearly all circumstances, been through dialogue, often with the most unlikely parties. During the apartheid years of South Africa, the government was forced to enter into dialogue with Nelson Mandela in 1985 when he wrote to the minister of justice Kobie Coetsee.[3] For the majority of his struggle, Mandela had been referred to as a terrorist and it was only when genuine channels of dialogue were opened with the ANC that a resolution to the conflict could be found.

Similarly, the Irish Republicans had their own chance to bring a resolution to the 'Troubles' when the British government finally agreed to open up to discussions with Sinn Fein. On 12 October 1984 the IRA detonated a bomb at a Conservative Party conference at the Grand Hotel in Brighton, and UK Prime Minister Margaret Thatcher was fortunate to escape. At this point in time there seemed no hope for an end to the IRA campaign until, just a year later, a change of policy within the British administration led to the Anglo-Irish Agreement which was signed on 15 November 1985.[4]

Governments around the world must pay attention to the history of political violence and learn from the positive results that dialogue has achieved. Any claim that the threat of Al Qaeda and the extent of violence are unprecedented is false. The current threat is one that is very much akin to others in the past and thus opens the door for discussions between various parties.

One clear difference between the current threat of terrorism and other examples from history is the lack of a tangible entity with whom to begin the dialogue. Al Qaeda does not have offices or a known base from which to operate and so cannot be easily contacted or approached. But this does not necessarily need to be a bar to opening a channel to its leadership worldwide. The age of the media has very much opened the world to communication and so messages can be relayed without any formal meeting.

In many ways one of the greatest failings of the War on Terror's counter-terrorism policies has been the complete lack of understanding of Islam and the way in which authority is understood. For those who follow the *fatawa* (religious edicts) of the Al Qaeda leadership, it is the *fatwa* (edict) issued from a prominent figure which is of the greatest importance. If there was no *fatwa* which permitted the targeting of innocent civilians, then no action could be taken by those who would choose to rely on such authority. By governments opening dialogues with groups who feel a sense of political outrage, there will come the opportunity for the cessation of hostilities and more importantly the bringing about of actual safety for the innocent.

Such comments are not new; in very small ways they have already been recognised and implemented. During the hostage-taking of Norman Kember by an armed group in Iraq, the British government turned to those of religious and political authority within the Muslim world in order to attempt to bring about his release. On 7 December 2005, the Jordanian cleric Abu Qatada, detained in Britain since 2002, made a televised appeal for the release of Kember. After much debate between the Home and Foreign Office the video message was facilitated and it went on air.[5]

A Freedom of Information Act (FOIA) request was made in relation to the video appeal and subsequently the Home Office revealed all communication between government agencies regarding the video and its impact.[6] Understanding that Abu Qatada was issuing a religious edict was recognised by an official at the Home Office in one correspondence on the morning of the video's release:

I understand that it was only 5 minutes long and included a clear plea for the release of the kidnapped 4. He said that they were men of peace and shouldn't be attacked. Attacks should be confined to people who attack you (ie his audience). The 4 had no link with criminal governments. The rest was his legal opinion as to why the peaceful should not be attacked.[7]

Although the move by Abu Qatada was seen quite cynically by the British press as an attempt to help bolster his case against deportation, there was clear recognition in an internal Home Office memo that his video had carried the necessary weight to aid the four hostages by helping to extend the deadline of the captors' demands:

...The Abu Qatada video had attracted a lot of attention and was considered a success from a media perspective. Some media had linked his appeal to the extension of the deadline.[8]

The significance of a cleric such as Abu Qatada in this circumstance is undeniable. Having faced a period of internment in Britain, the threat of deportation to Jordan, a further period of detention, and then an oppressive control order, Abu Qatada has been through a process of detention that has made the most of his status as a foreigner. He has been accused of being a danger to British society despite having categorically stated that he does not believe it permissible to launch attacks in Britain.[9]

It is with such figures that governments across the globe will be able to begin the process of repairing much of the damage that has been done. Without doing so, the attacks will continue unabated until the various religious authorities around the world have the space to debate and even re-think their fatwas regarding the permissibility/impermissibility of violence in specific contexts.

The need for dialogue is not limited to governmental levels though. There currently exists a climate of terror amongst the Muslim communities in Britain and US making them think that they cannot speak about certain issues. Jihad has become a taboo word in mosques as elders are concerned such talk could lead to criminalisation. Such policies based on fear only have the result of creating a vacuum around issues which concern many Muslims. The lack of opportunity to discuss these and other issues in Islamic centres forces those still interested to attempt their own research without any real guidance.

To genuinely counter terrorism, the mosques must be able to hold seminars and conferences on the subject of jihad without the concern that by doing so they will be automatically criminalised. And these debates must be free from government interference, involvement would inevitably mean a complete loss of confidence in the whole process. Without scholars with religious authority in their communities taking up such issues, a correct discourse cannot be effectively achieved.

Counter-terrorism measures will never work as long as they continue to be reactionary and devoid of understanding of the group that they seek to tackle. The ignorance and the malicious policies that have been undertaken since 9/11 have had a devastating and negative impact on any attempt to actually bring about a peaceful solution to the current crises in the world. By trying to first understand the perspective of both sides there is the hope that there can be dialogue; and with that hope comes the hope for change.

NOTES

INTRODUCTION

1. Cageprisoners interview with the jurors from the ricin trial, 20 Sept. 2005.
2. US Secretary of State addresses the UN Security Council, 5 Feb. 2003, http://www.whitehouse.gov/news/releases/2003/02/20030205-1.html.
3. Pincus W., 'London Ricin Finding Called a False Positive', *Washington Post*, 14 Apr. 2005.
4. Prime Minister Tony Blair, *PM's Press Conference*, 16 Nov. 2001.
5. Murphy S.D., 'Contemporary Practice of the United States in International Law: Decision Not to Regard Persons Detained in Afghanistan as POWs', *American Journal of International Law*, vol. 96 No. 2 pp. 475-480. See also Wedgewood R., 'Al Qaeda, Terrorism, and Military Commissions', *American Journal of International Law* vol. 96 p. 328 and Fleischer A., *Special White House Announcement Re: Application of Geneva Conventions in Afghanistan*, 7 Feb. 2002.
6. President George W. Bush, Presidential Address to the Nation, 7 Oct. 2001.
7. UN Security Council Resolution 1373 states, 'Reaffirming the need to combat by all means, in accordance with the Charter of the United Nations, threats to international peace and security caused by terrorist acts', this does not however constitute an immediate allowance for military action.
8. Royston, 'Until What? Enforcement Action or Collective Self-Defence?' 85 *American Journal of International Law* (1991) 506.
9. Cassese A., *International Law*, Oxford University Press, 2004. See also Gray C., *International Law and the Use of Force*, Oxford University Press, 2008.
10. Steiner H., 'Securing Human Rights: The First Half-Century of the Universal Declaration, and Beyond', *Harvard Magazine*, 1998. Lauterpacht H., *International Law and Human Rights*, Stevens & Sons, 1950. There is a difference between international human rights law and international humanitarian law that must be clarified. Human rights relates to the

freedoms and basic rights that all human beings are entitled to—whether it be the right to liberty, life, possessions, association, religion, etc. International humanitarian law, also called the law of armed conflict, is the normative system of law which governs the conduct of hostilities during an armed conflict—when conflict breaks out, these laws become automatically applicable to combatants, non-combatants and civilians.

11. Humanitarian intervention and its other formulation, pro-democratic invasion, are contentious concepts in international law. There has been a wealth of literature written about these concepts and the extent to which they have any basis in reality. Opponents of humanitarian intervention often cite political motivations as being the key components for intervention rather than any genuine humanitarian concerns, hence why there have been very few statements regarding the need for intervention in the African continent compared to other regions of the world. Examples of the language of humanitarian intervention being referred to without being legally accepted include Indian intervention in East Pakistan (1971), Tanzanian intervention in Uganda (1978), Vietnamese intervention in Kampuchea (1978), Northern and Southern Iraq (1991) and Kosovo (1998)—all examples show that there has never been any legal basis for claiming that humanitarian intervention is an acceptable practice—see Chesterman S., *Just War or Just Peace? Humanitarian intervention and International Law*, Oxford, 2003. The argument is taken further by Franck and Rodley in their piece, After Bangladesh: The Law of Humanitarian Intervention by Military Force, (1973) 67 *American Journal of International Law* p275— where they analyse historical examples of intervention on the basis of humanitarian reasons but where strong political motivations were present. Also see Reisman M., Coercion and Self-Determination: Construing Chater Article 2(4), 78 *AJIL*, 1984 and Schachter O., The Legality of Pro-Democratic Invasion, 78 *AJIL* 1984-US intervention in Grenada, Nicaragua and Panama during the 1980s led to a series of discussions by scholars on both sides of the divide who argued about the place of humanitarian intervention, again political motivations were exposed in all examples.

12. Campbell D., 'US interrogators turn to "torture lite", *The Guardian*, 25 Jan. 2003.

13. This is within the context of the War on Terror—references to terrorism are widespread around the world in a variety of contexts including Sri Lanka, left-wing organisations in Europe and South America and even references are made to 'narco-terrorists' in Colombia and Bolivia.

14. '*Inside Africa's War on Terror*', Cageprisoners report, Mar. 2007.

15. 'Police "did not identify Menezes", *BBC website*, 31 Oct. 2008, http://news.bbc.co.uk/1/hi/uk/7702776.stm.

16. Schedule 7 of the Terrorism Act 2000 gives rights to the police and immigration staff to detain anyone entering or exiting, for nine hours. During the period of questioning the individual being questioned is not permitted the right to a lawyer and can be charged for not answering questions. Returning from the Berlin Film Festival, the actors from the documentary

Road to Guantánamo, were detained under the Terrorism Act. The film had won the Silver Bear award at the festival but on their return to the UK the British actors were verbally abused by the police and questioned about their activities—see BBC *website*, 'Guantánamo actors held at airport', 21 Feb. 2006, http://news.bbc.co.uk/1/hi/entertainment/4736404.stm.

17. The detentions of Adam Brown, the Nairobi 4, UK Guantánamo detainees and many others all point to the use of detentions outside legal parameters for the purposes of interrogation.

18. Article 520 bis (1) and (2) of Spain's Code of Criminal Procedure maintains that terrorist suspects can be held in incommunicado detention for up to five days.

19. Detainee U is a detainee in the UK, his name cannot be used due to legal proceedings.

20. Applebaum A., 'Hollow Rhetoric on "Rule of Law"', *Washington Post*, 21 Dec. 2005.

21. See President Pervez Musharraf, *In the Line of Fire*, Simon and Schuster, 2006.

22. Statement by Abdullah Almalki to Cageprisoners stated that he saw very young children being detained at Fara' Falastin prison in Syria. There are also statements by former Bagram detainees regarding the detention of 11-14 year olds such as Omar Khadr.

23. See Moazzam Begg, *Enemy Combatant*, Simon and Schuster, 2006; also see Murat Kurnaz, *Five Years of My Life: an innocent man in Guantánamo*, Palgrave Macmillan, 2008.

24. Cageprisoners report, *'Enforced Disappearances in Pakistan'*, 14 Oct. 2006.

25. References during the course of this work to the way the US and UK have derogated from established norms relate to the way in which attitudes have changed domestically through legislation and the overt manner in which human rights have been affected. This is not to ignore or belittle the activities of both countries over the twentieth century which resulted in the abuse and deaths of hundreds of thousands of innocent people. The colonial countries such as UK, France, Germany, Italy and the US, particularly after World War II, have been heavily involved in the complete abandonment of human rights during their colonisation/pseudo-colonisation of the third world. For detailed discussions regarding the past abuses see: Blakeley R., *State Terrorism and Neoliberalism: The North and the South*, Routledge, 2009.

26. McCarthy R., 'Why did Baha Mousa die in British custody?', *The Guardian*, 21 Feb. 2004.

27. Randall D. and Gosden E., '62,006-the number killed in the War on Terror', *The Independent*, 10 Sept. 2006 cites the number of people that have been estimated killed since the attacks on the World Trade Centre. The article also goes on to state that 4.5 million people have been made refugees since the start of the War on Terror.

1. MUSLIM

1. 'Searches to target ethnic groups', *BBC website*, 31 Jul. 2005, http://news.bbc.co.uk/1/hi/england/london/4732465.stm.
2. Dodd V., 'Asian Men Targeted in Stop and Search', *The Guardian*, 17 Aug. 2005.
3. Federal Bureau of Investigation, Directorate of Intelligence, *FBI Intelligence Timeline*, http://www.fbi.gov/intelligence/di_timeline.htm.
4. The Federal Bureau of Investigation http://www.fbi.gov and Report to Congress on Implementation of Section 1001 of the USA Patriot Act (as required by Section 1001(3) of Public Law 107-56) 17 Jul. 2003, Office of the Inspector General.
5. Testimony of Glenn A. Fine before the Senate Committee on the Judiciary concerning *The September 11 Detainees: A Review of the Treatment of Aliens Held on Immigration Charges in Connection with the Investigation of the September 11 Attacks*, 25 Jun. 2003.
6. See Nguyen T., *We Are All Suspects Now: Untold Stories from Immigrant Communities after 9/11*, Beacon Press, 2005.
7. Peirce G., *Was it like this for the Irish?*, 10 Apr. 2008.
8. Hillyard P., *Suspect Community: People's Experience of the Prevention of Terrorism Acts in Britain*, Pluto Press. 1993.
9. Cageprisoners report, *Citizens No More*, Jul. 2007.
10. Cageprisoners interview with Nihad Karsic and Almin Hardaus, 19 Jun. 2007.
11. Cageprisoners interview with Emina Lahmar, 17 Jun. 2007.
12. Perlez J., 'US Seeks Closing of Visa Loophole for Britons', *New York Times*, 2 May 2007.
13. Chertoff M., *The Daily Telegraph*, 4 Apr. 2007.
14. Adam Brown's name has been changed to protect his identity.
15. Arar was placed on a rendition flight from the US and he was detained in Jordan and Syria where he was held for many months. Eventually Arar was released with the help of the Canadian government only for it to transpire that they had been complicit in his detention. Arar was later to be awarded twelve million Canadian dollars in compensation for his detention by the Canadian government.
16. Cageprisoners interview with Adam Brown, 13 May 2007.
17. 'Syria—*International Religious Freedom Report*', US Department of State, 2007.
18. US Congress, Congressional Record—H9422, 15 Oct. 2003.
19. The ideological links that the Syrians attempted to make follow a pattern for a specific reason. By first identifying whether an individual is a *Salafi*, then further identifying him as a *Takfiri*, they are able to place him within a specific Islamic tradition. Finally, they ask him whether or not he is an *Irhabi*, which is the term used for 'terrorist' in the Arabic language.
20. Cageprisoners interview with Tanweer Sheikh and Mohammed Suleman Latif, 11 Sept. 2006.

21. Cageprisoners interview with Tanweer Sheikh and Mohammed Suleman Latif, 11 Sept. 2006.
22. Cageprisoners interview with Tanweer Sheikh and Mohammed Suleman Latif, 11 Sept. 2006.
23. Statement of Rangzieb Ahmed to Cageprisoners, 28 May 2008.
24. 'Human Rights Ignored in the War on Terror', Amnesty International, 28 Sept. 2006, www.amnesty.org.uk.
25. Statement of Rangzieb Ahmed to Cageprisoners, 28 May 2008.
26. Testimony of Alam Ghafoor to Cageprisoners, 11 Aug. 2005.
27. Testimony of Alam Ghafoor to Cageprisoners, 11 Aug. 2005.
28. Cageprisoners interview with Detainee E, 15 Apr. 2008.
29. Cageprisoners interview with Mouloud Sihali, 15 Apr. 2008.
30. Cageprisoners interview with Mouloud Sihali, 15 Apr. 2008.
31. Cageprisoners interview with Detainee DD, 08 Apr. 2008.

2. GUILTY

1. Oborne P., 'The politics of fear (or how Tony Blair misled us over the war on terror)', *The Independent* 15 Feb. 2006.
2. Gray C., *International Law and the Use of Force*, Oxford: OUP, 2008 second edition.
3. International Humanitarian Law has never recognised the legal term 'unlawful combatant' or indeed 'enemy combatant'. The terms of reference for unlawful activity in the context of warfare are one of two: either you can be a combatant who acts illegally by targeting civilians or not distinguishing oneself, or you can be a civilian who acts unlawfully by taking part in hostilities. In either case, there are strict laws which apply to both scenarios and more than adequately cover both the Taliban and Al Qaeda. The term enemy combatant does not allow for recourse to international humanitarian law and prisoner-of-war protection due to its unknown status in legal language. See: Aldrich G.H., 'The Taliban, Al Qaeda, and the Determination of Illegal Combatants', *American Journal of International Law*, vol. 96 No. 4 p. 894; Garraway C.H.B., *Interoperability and the Atlantic Divide—A Bridge Over Troubled Waters*, US Naval War College, International Studies Series p. 5; Wedgewood R., 'Al Qaeda, Terrorism, and Military Commissions', *American Journal of International Law*, vol. 96, p. 328.
4. Cageprisoners interview with Nihad Karsic and Almin Hardaus, 19 Jun. 2007.
5. Harding L., 'Afghan Massacre haunts Pentagon', *The Guardian*, 14 Oct. 2002.
6. Cageprisoners interview with Nihad Karsic and Almin Hardaus, 19 Jun. 2007.
7. Cageprisoners interview with Emina Lahmar, 17 Jun. 2007.
8. Cageprisoners interview with Nadja Dizderavic, 17 Jun. 2007.

9. Elliot M., 'The Next Wave', *Time*, 16 Jun. 2002; CNN, 'Bin Laden suspect held in Bosnia', 26 Oct.2001; 'Man linked to Bin Laden arrested in Bosnia', *The Guardian*, 8 Oct. 2001.

10. Cageprisoners interview with Kobilica Anela, 14 Jun. 2007.

11. Cageprisoners and Reprieve interview with Omar Syed Omar, 09 Mar. 2007.

12. Cageprisoners and Reprieve interview with Omar Syed Omar, 09 Mar. 2007.

13. Combined Joint Task Force Horn of Africa, *Factsheet*, http://www.hoa. africom.mil/AboutCJTF-HOA.asp.

14. US Department of State Country Reports on Human Rights Practices: Ethiopia, 2005.

15. 'US Begins Training Exercises With Ethiopian National Defense Forces', *Addis Tribune*, 11 Jul. 2003, http://www.hartford-hwp.com/archives/27c/ 422.html.

16. Nicaragua v USA *ICJ Reports* (1986) 4 p. 104. Near the end of the Cold War, the Reagan Administration in the US helped to train and equip the El Salvador contras fight a border war with Nicaragua, the ICJ condemned the US for the role that it played in interfering with Nicaragua's sovereignty.

17. England A., 'Many dead' after US strikes on Somalia', *Financial Times*, 9 Jan. 2007.

18. Cageprisoners and Reprieve interview with Halima Hashim, 1 Mar. 2007.

19. Cageprisoners and Reprieve interview with Fatima Ahmed Abdur Rahman, 2 Mar. 2007.

20. Cageprisoners and Reprieve interview with Shaykh Mahmoud Adam Salat, 6 Mar. 2007.

21. Cageprisoners and Reprieve interview with Safia Benaouda, 5 Apr. 2007.

22. Cageprisoners and Reprieve interview with Millie Mithounie Gako, 2 Mar. 2007.

23. Cageprisoners and Reprieve interview with Millie Mithounie Gako, 2 Mar. 2007.

24. Cageprisoners interview with Anna Lucia Pighizzini, 9 Jan. 2008.

25. Cageprisoners interview with Amir Muneef, 4 May 2005.

26. '*Tunisia—Country Reports on Human Rights Practices*', US Department of State, 6 Mar. 2007.

27. Cageprisoners interview with Souad Zeroual, 30 Aug. 2007.

28. Cageprisoners interview with Umm Anas, 4 Apr. 2007.

3. THE RULE OF LAW

1. Attorney General John Ashcroft, *Testimony before the Senate Committee on the Judiciary*, 6 Dec. 2001.

2. Article 9 of the Universal Declaration of Human Rights.

3. Article 10 of the Universal Declaration of Human Rights.

4. 'Setting an Example?': Counter-terrorism Measures in Spain', *Human Rights Watch*, January 2005 Vol. 17, No. 1(D)),1.

5. The UK government has introduced: Terrorism Act 2000, Anti-Terrorism, Crime and Security Act 2001, Extradition Act 2003, Prevention of Terrorism Act 2005 and the Terrorism Act 2006. They are now working towards trying to pass the Terrorism Bill 2008.

6. Press Association, 'Crushing defeat for Blair over 90-day plan', *The Independent*, 9 Nov. 2005.

7. Steele J. and Smith M., 'MI6 grenade fired from public park', *The Daily Telegraph*, 19 Jul. 2001.

8. Branigan T., 'Britons would trade civil liberties for security: ICM poll finds backing for anti-terror laws', *The Guardian*, 22 Aug. 2005.

9. The European Commission against Racism and Intolerance (ECRI) found that the climate of fear in a post 9/11 UK was causing further alienation in the Muslim community, see Morris N., 'Ethnic minorities face climate of fear, says race watchdog', *The Independent*, 15 Jun. 2005.

10. Section 77 Canadian Immigration and Refugee Protection Act.

11. Herman S., 'PATRIOT Games: Terrorism Law and Executive Power', *JURIST*, 26 Jan. 2006. http://jurist.law.pitt.edu/forumy/2006/01/patriot-games-terrorism-law-and.php.

12. Cageprisoners interview with Khadija Podd, 8 Jan. 2008.

13. Cageprisoners interview with Detainee G, 21 May 2008.

14. Cageprisoners interview with Detainee G, 21 May 2008.

15. Cageprisoners interview with Mahmoud Abu Rideh, 28 May 2008.

16. Ibid.

17. Home Office, *Control Orders*, http://www.homeoffice.gov.uk/security/terrorism-and-the-law/control-orders/.

18. Cageprisoners interview with Detainee W, 2 Apr. 2008.

19. http://www.homeoffice.gov.uk/security/terrorism-and-the-law/control-orders/.

20. Cageprisoners interview with Cerie Bullivant, 2 Apr. 2008.

21. Cageprisoners interview with Sophie Lamarche, 21 Jul. 2008.

22. Lichtblau E., 'US Will Pay $2 Million to Lawyer Wrongly Jailed', *New York Times*, 30 Nov. 2006.

23. Berkowitz P., *Terrorism, The Laws of War, and The Constitution: Debating the Enemy Combatant Cases*, Hoover Press, 2005.

24. Junod T., 'Innocent', *Esquire*, 1 Jul. 2006. http://www.esquire.com/features/ESQ0706JLINDH_106.

25. Cageprisoners interview with Frank Lindh, 3 Apr. 2008.

26. United States v Lindh 212 F.Supp. 2d p. 556.

27. Cageprisoners interview with Frank Lindh, 3 Apr. 2008.

28. Goodman A., 'From Paintball Practice to Prison: A Look At One of the Most Controversial Terrorism Cases in the Country', *Open Democracy*, 16 Jun. 2004.

29. Cageprisoners interview with Souhail ben Kahla, 29 Jul. 2008.

30. Cageprisoners interview with Souhail ben Kahla, 29 Jul. 2008.
31. Cageprisoners interview with Farhat Paracha, 1 Oct. 2006.
32. Sister Prejean H., *The Death of Innocents*, Canterbury Press, 2006.

4. FOREIGN EXCHANGE

1. Chahal v United Kingdom European Court of Human rights Reports 1996-v, judgement of 15 Nov. 1996.
2. 'Timeline: Guantánamo Bay Britons', *BBC website*, 27 Jan. 2005. http://news.bbc.co.uk/1/hi/uk/3545709.stm.
3. Lieutenant Commander Charles D. Swift before the US Senate Committee on the Judiciary on the Subject of 'Detainees' 15 Jun. 2005.
4. 'UK residents "still held in Cuba"', *BBC website*, 11 Jan. 2005. http://news.bbc.co.uk/1/hi/uk/4165841.stm.
5. Gutman R., *A Witness to Genocide: First Inside Account of the Horrors of Ethnic Cleansing in Bosnia*, Element Books, 1993.
6. 'Arms Shipments to Bosnia from Islamic Countries', 1996 Congressional Debate, Senate, 9 May 1996.
7. Izetbegovic A., *Inescapable Questions*, Islamic Foundation, 2002.
8. The Dayton Peace Accords, 21 November 1995-Annex 1 A: Agreement on the Military Aspects of the Peace Settlement, Article III (2).
9. 'Report on the Status of Human Rights in Bosnia and Herzegovina', Helsinki Committee for Human Rights, Br: 02A-02/2008.
10. Cageprisoners interview with Abdelilah Daudi Karrache, 15 Jun. 2007.
11. Cageprisoners interview with Sabiha Delic, 19 Jun. 2007.
12. Cageprisoners interview with Abu Hamza Emad Alhusin, 14 Jun. 2007.
13. Cageprisoners interview with Abu Hamza Emad Alhusin, 14 Jun. 2007.
14. Cageprisoners interview with Abu Hamza Emad Alhusin, 14 Jun. 2007.
15. Cageprisoners interview with Fadhil Al Hammadani, 15 Jun. 2007.
16. Cageprisoners interview with Abdelilah Daudi Karrache, 15 Jun. 2007.
17. Cageprisoners interview with Abu Hamza Al Masri, 17 Apr. 2008.
18. Special Immigration Appeals Commission Act 1997 had a Procedure manual produced in 2003 with further amendments in 2007. The various forms of the Commission have resulted in the current form which is used in order to provide an unethical appeals process for those facing deportation.
19. Jordan signed the Understanding in Amman on 10 August 2005 and Libya signed a similar document on 18 Oct. 2005-http://www.fco.gov.uk/resources/en/press-release/2005/10/fco_npr_181005_libyamou. Algeria refused to sign the agreement.
20. Raustiala K., 'Form and Substance in International Agreements', *AJIL* vol. 99, No. 3 (Jul 2005) pp. 581-614.
21. Cageprisoners interview with Faraj Hassan, 28 Aug. 2007.
22. Cageprisoners interview with Detainee DD, 8 Apr. 2008.

23. Although the men have been cleared through the SIAC process, a small number remain on UN sanctions which effectively serve as a further form of detention. Without the ability to earn or hold on to any significant sum of money, the men and their families are placed in an extremely difficult situation. The sanctions system does not require any evidentiary standard, only that the home secretary suspects the individual may in the past, present or future be involved with terrorist activities. The system is not limited to the Libyans but has also affected a number of British citizens who have been attempting to challenge the orders against them.
24. Tribunals Service: Special Immigration Appeals Commission, 'About us', http://www.siac.tribunals.gov.uk/aboutus.htm.
25. All those returned to Algeria were detained on their arrival by the security services of Algeria. Despite the UK's insistence that it is safe for detainees to return with a signed Memorandum of Understanding, the reality is very much the opposite.
26. Cageprisoners interview with Detainee G, 21 May 2008.
27. Cageprisoners interview with Detainee Z, 01 May 2008.
28. Cageprisoners interview with Umm Hadigah, 16 Jan. 2008.
29. Cageprisoners interview with Sophie Lamarche, 21 Jul. 2008.
30. Brownlie I., *Principles of International Law*, Oxford, Sixth Edition, p. 313, 2003.
31. State v Ebrahim 31 ILM 888 (1991), Supreme Court of South Africa (Appellate Division).
32. R v Horseferry Road Magistrates' Court, ex parte Bennett [1993] 3 All ER 138, House of Lords.
33. 'Extradition Act 2003 undermines fundamental rights', *Liberty*, 30 Nov. 2006.
34. Cageprisoners interview with Babar Ahmad, 7 May 2008.

5. GUANTÁNAMO BAY

1. Lieutenant Commander Charles D. Swift giving evidence before the Senate Committee on the Judiciary on the subject of 'Detainees', 15 Jun. 2005.
2. De Zayas A., 'The Status of Guantánamo Bay and the Status of Detainees', The Douglas McK. Brown Lecture, University of British Columbia, Vancouver, 19 Nov. 2003.
3. Harding L., 'Afghan massacre haunts Pentagon', *The Guardian*, 14 Sept. 2002; see also, Doran J., 'Afghan Massacre: The Convoy of Death', *Channel 5* (UK); Smucker P., 'Afghan War Crimes a Low Priority', *Christian Science Monitor*, 12 Sept. 2002.
4. Mofidi M., '"Unlawful Combatants" or "Prisoners of War": The Law and Politics of Labels', *Cornell International Law Journal*, 2003.
5. Gibney A., *Taxi to the Darkside*, Revolution Films, 2007—the documentary details the death of Dilawar through interviews with the guards involved with his death.

6. EPW (Prisoner of War) cards were issued to detainees in Guantánamo and Kandahar initially but were soon removed once the implication of POW status was realised by the US forces.

7. Sands P., *Lawless World*, Penguin, 2006.

8. See White House Press Release, 'President issues Military Order', 13 Nov. 2001.

9. Verkaik R., 'Guantánamo treatment is 'monstrous', says law lord', *The Independent*, 26 Nov. 2003.

10. Sands P., *Lawless World*, Penguin, 2006.

11. Rasul v Bush (03-334) 542 US 466 (2004).

12. Hafetz J., 'Modest Improvements Cannot Save an Inherently Flawed Process at Guantánamo', *findlaw.com*, 27 Jul. 2007.

13. Moeckli D., 'The US Supreme Court's "Enemy Combatant" Decisions: A "Major Victory for the Rule of Law"?', *C&S Law*, Mar. 2005.

14. The Uighurs are an ethnic minority in China who are predominantly Muslim in their belief. Human rights organisations have documented their harassment by the Chinese authorities due to their adherence to Islam.

15. 'Reprieve deplores unjust Guantánamo "war crimes" trial', *Reprieve press release* 7 Aug. 2008.

16. Executive order—'*Review and Disposition of Individuals detained at the Guantánamo Bay Naval Base and Closure of Detention Facilities*', The White House, 22 Jan. 2009.

17. Cageprisoners interview with Lieutenant Commander Charles D Swift, 14 Dec. 2004.

18. Ibid.

19. Ibid.

20. Cageprisoners interview with Lieutenant Colonel Yvonne Bradley, 21 Mar. 2007.

21. Ibid.

22. Ibid.

23. Ibid.

24. Cageprisoners interview with Clive Stafford Smith, 28 Sept. 2004.

25. Kassimeris G (editor), *Playing Politics with Terrorism: A User's Guide*, Hurst, 2007.

26. Ibid.

27. Ibid.

28. Cageprisoners interview with Bernard Docke, 2004.

29. Cageprisoners interview with Emina Lahmar, 17 Jun. 2007.

30. Cageprisoners interview with Nadje Dizderavic, 17 Jun. 2007.

31. Cageprisoners interview with Zahra Paracha, 1 Oct. 2006.

32. Johaina Aamer, *My Story*, Cageprisoners, 9 Jan. 2006.

33. Cageprisoners interview with Zaynab Khadr, 1 Aug. 2005.

34. Cageprisoners interview with Amani Deghayes, 3 Mar. 2005.

35. Cageprisoners interview with Airat vakhitov, 21 Dec. 2005.

36. Ibid.

37. R (Binyam Mohamed) v Secretary of State for Foreign and Commonwealth Affairs [2008] EWHC 2048 (Admin).
38. Cageprisoners interview with Murat Kurnaz, 17 Jul. 2008.
39. Cageprisoners interview with Christopher Arendt, 23 Dec. 2008.

6. DARKNESS

1. President Pervez Musharraf, *In the Line of Fire*, Simon and Schuster, 2006.
2. Nowak M., foreword from *Beyond the Law*, Cageprisoners, Dec. 2006.
3. 'Summary of the High Value Terrorist Detainee Program', *Officer of the Director of National Intelligence*, Washington DC. http://www.dni.gov/announcements/content/TheHighValueDetaineeProgram.pdf.
4. 'As New Evidence Emerges that War on Terror Prisoners were Held on Diego Garcia, Reprieve Demands Immediate Action from the British Government', *Reprieve Press Release*. http://www.reprieve.org.uk/documents/2008_08_01DiegoGarciascandal-ReprievedemandsimmediateactionfromUKgovernment.pdf.
5. Ibid.
6. Categorisation agreed by Amnesty International, Cageprisoners, Center for Constitutional Rights, Center for Human Rights and Global Justice, Human Rights Watch and Reprieve in *Off the Record*, 7 Jun. 2007.
7. Testimony of Rangzieb Ahmed released to Cageprisoners, 28 May 2008.
8. 'Secret prisons: Obama's order to close "black sites"', *The Guardian*, 23 Jan. 2009.
9. Greenberg K.J., 'Obama's Guantánamo? Bush's Living Legacy at Bagram Prison', *tomdispatch.com*.
10. 'US Policy on Counterterrorism', *Presidential Decision Directive* 39, The White House, Washington, 21 Jun. 1995.
11. 'Remarks upon her departure for Europe', Statement by US Secretary of State Condoleeza Rice, http://www.state.gov/secretary/rm/2005/57602.htm 5 Dec. 2005.
12. See Council of Europe Committee on legal Affairs and Human Rights, 'Alleged secret detention in Council of Europe member states', AS/Jur (2006) 03 rev, 22 Jan. 2006.
13. 'Ending Secret Detentions', *Human Rights First*, Jun. 2004. Also see 'The Captives' *New York Times*, 5 Jan. 2004.
14. 'Ending Secret Detentions', *Human Rights First*, Jun. 2004. Also see *US News* and *World Reports* 2 Jun. 2003.
15. 'Britain "ordered torture of 9/11 suspect"', *The Guardian* 24 Jan. 2006.
16. Miller G., 'Obama preserves renditions as counter-terrorism tool', *Los Angeles Times*, 1 Feb. 2009.
17. Hasnain G., 'How Pakistan's Sacked Judge Became a National Hero', *Time*, 8 Mar. 2007.
18. Cageprisoners interview with Amina Masood Janjua, 2 Oct. 2006.

19. Cageprisoners interview with Sohail Faraz, 4 Oct. 2006.
20. Cageprisoners interview with Rabia Yaqoob, 2 Oct. 2006.
21. Amnesty International, Cageprisoners, Center for Constitutional Rights, Center for Human Rights and Global Justice, Human Rights Watch and Reprieve in *Off the Record*, 7 Jun. 2007.
22. Cageprisoners interview with Anna Lucia Phigizzni, 9 Jan. 2008.
23. Cageprisoners and Reprieve interview with Khalif Abdi Hussein, 7 Mar. 2007.
24. Cageprisoners and Reprieve interview with Khalif Abdi Hussein, 7 Mar. 2007.
25. Arar v Ashcroft US District Court, 22 Jan. 2004.
26. Cageprisoners interview with Adam Brown, 13 May 2007.
27. Testimony of Alam Ghafoor to Cageprisoners, 11 Aug. 2005.
28. Statement of Rangzieb Ahmed to Cageprisoners, 28 May 2008.
29. Cageprisoners and Reprieve interview with Mohammed Ezzouek, 16 Feb. 2007.
30. Cageprisoners interview with Kamilya Mohammed Tuweni, 09 Apr. 2007.
31. Cageprisoners interview with Kamilya Mohammed Tuweni, 9 Apr. 2007.
32. Cageprisoners and Reprieve interview with Mohammed Ezzouek, 16 Feb. 07.
33. 'Mass Rendition, Incommunicado Detention and Possible Torture of Foreign Nationals in Kenya, Somalia and Ethiopia', *Cageprisoners and Reprieve report*, 22 Feb. 2007.
34. Cageprisoners and Reprieve interview with Safia Benaouda, 5 Apr. 2007.

7. TORTURE AND ABUSE

1. Donald Rumsfeld reply to William J Haynes II, General Counsel for the Department of Defense, 'Action Memo Re: Counter-Resistance Techniques' 27 Nov. 2002 taken from Greenburg K. and Dratel J., *The Torture Papers: The Road to Abu Ghraib*, Cambridge University Press, 2005.
2. Statement of Cofer Black, Joint Investigation into September 11, 26 Sept. 2002.
3. Zimbardo P., *The Lucifer Effect*, Random House, 2007. The Stanford Prison Experiment was a two week investigation when students were requested to play the roles of prisoners and prison guards. The experiment was shut down prematurely after only six days when some of the guards developed sadistic tendencies and those imprisoned began to display signs of depression and extreme stress.
4. Kassimeris G (ed.), *The Barbarisation of Warfare*, Hurst, 2006.
5. 'Re: Standards of Conduct for Interrogation under 18 U.S.C. 2340-2340A', US Office of the Assistant Attorney General Memorandum for Alberto R. Gonzales Counsel to the President, 1 Aug. 2002 taken from Greenburg

K. and Dratel J., *The Torture Papers: The Road to Abu Ghraib*, Cambridge University Press, 2005.

6. Working Group Report on Detainee Interrogations in the Global War on Terrorism: Assessment of Legal, Historical, Policy, and Operational Considerations, 4 Apr. 2003 taken from Greenburg K. and Dratel J., *The Torture Papers: The Road to Abu Ghraib*, Cambridge University Press, 2005.

7. 'Subject: Counter-Terrorism Techniques', Commander of JTF 170 James T. Hill to Chairman of the Joint Chiefs of Staff, Washington, DC 20318-9999, 25 Oct. 2002, taken from Greenburg K. and Dratel J., *The Torture Papers: The Road to Abu Ghraib*, Cambridge University Press, 2005.

8. Further analysis of the Abu Ghraib scandal can be read in Mayer J., *The Dark Side*, Doubleday; 2008, Sands P., *Torture Team*, Allen Lane, 2008; and full documentation of memos from Greenburg K. and Dratel J., *The Torture Papers: The Road to Abu Ghraib*, Cambridge University Press, 2005.

9. Campbell D., 'Rumsfeld knew all about me, says American 'jailer' held in Kabul', *The Guardian*, 22 Jul. 2004.

10. A and Others v Secretary of State for the Home Department, Statement of Eliza Manningham-Buller in the House of Lords 20 Sept. 2005.

11. Ibid.

12. A and Others v Secretary of State for the Home Department, 20 Sept. 2005.

13. Cageprisoners interview with Babar Ahmad, 7 May 2008.

14. Nowak M and McArthur, 'The United Nations Convention Against Torture: A Commentary', *Oxford Commentaries on International Law*, Oxford University Press.

15. Ozment K., 'Who's Afraid of Aafia Siddiqui?', *Boston Magazine*, Oct. 2004.

16. Cageprisoners interview with Nadja Dizderavic, 17 Jun. 2007.

17. Cageprisoners report, *The Systematic and Institutionalised Desecration of the Qur'an at Guantánamo Bay*, 16 May 2005.

18. Ibid.

19. Ibid.

20. There is a body of evidence that cements the position that torture can never be an acceptable tool, see: Nowak M. and McArthur E., 'The United Nations Convention Against Torture: A Commentary', *Oxford Commentaries on International Law*, 2008; Sands P., *Torture Team: Uncovering War Crimes in the Land of the Free*, Allen Lane, 2008; Greenberg K.J., *The Torture Debate in America*, Cambridge University Press, 2008; Levinson S., *Torture, A Collection*, OUP, 2006.

21. Charlesworth H. and Chinkin C., 'The Gender of *Jus Cogens*', 15 *Human Rights Quarterly* 63 (1993).

22. Cageprisoners interview with Nihad Karsic and Almin Hardaus, 19 Jun. 2007.

23. Ibid.
24. Cageprisoners interview with Anna Lucia Phigizzni, 9 Jan. 2008.
25. Cageprisoners interview with Phil Shiner, 6 Aug. 2005.
26. Cageprisoners interview with Phil Shiner, 6 Aug. 2005.
27. Testimony of Alam Ghafoor to Cageprisoners, 11 Aug. 2005.
28. Cageprisoners interview with Adam Brown, 13 May 2007.
29. Cageprisoners interview with Umm Hadigah, 16 Jan. 2008.
30. Name has been changed in order to protect the identity of the victim. Cageprisoners interview with Ashraful Hossein, 2 Aug. 2008.
31. Cageprisoners interview with Rangzieb Ahmed, 28 May 2008.

8. SECURITY

1. Brown G., 'The future of Britishness', *Fabian Society*, 14 Jan. 2006.
2. Imām Al-Ghazālī 'Al-Mustafa min 'Ilm Al-Usul'.
3. Memory for Justice, *Biography*, Nelson Mandela Foundation. http://www. nelsonmandela.org/index.php/memory/views/biography/.
4. The CAIN project archive on the Anglo-Irish Agreement.
5. 'Terror suspect's Iraq kidnap plea', *BBC website*, 7 Dec. 2005, http://news. bbc.co.uk/1/hi/uk/4506970.stm.
6. 'Abu Qatada's Norman Kember video appeal', Home Office, FOIA request, 30 Jun. 2006, http://www.homeoffice.gov.uk/about-us/freedom-of-informa-tion/released-information/foi-archive-crime/2422-Norman-Kember1?view =Standard&pubID=361963.
7. 'RE RESTR; KEMBER: ABU QATADA', email correspondence from Home Office official to Foreign Office official, 7 Dec. 2005.
8. 'Kidnapping in Iraq', Internal memo between Home Office officials, 8 Dec. 2005.
9. Moazzam Begg makes specific reference to Abu Qatada's fatwa regarding the targeting of civilians in the western world as being impermissible in his book, *Enemy Combatant*, Simon & Schuster, 2005.

BIBLIOGRAPHY

Books

Al-Ghazālī, *Al-Mustafa min 'Ilm Al-Usul*, 1111.

Begg M., *Enemy Combatant*, Simon and Schuster, 2005.

Berkowitz P., *Terrorism, The Laws of War, and The Constitution: Debating the Enemy Combatant Cases*, Hoover Press, 2005.

Best G., *Humanity in Warfare: the Modern History of the International Law of Armed Conflict*, Oxford University Press, 1996.

Brown C., *Sovereignty, Rights and Justice*, Polity Press, 2002.

Brownlie I., *Principles of International Law*, Oxford University Press, Sixth Edition, 2003.

Cassese A., *International Law*, Oxford University Press, 2001.

Chesterman, *Just War or Just Peace?*, Oxford University Press, 2001.

De Lupis I.D., *Law of War*, Cambridge University Press, 1987.

Dershowitz A.M., *Why Terrorism Works: Understanding the Threat, Responding to the Challenge*, Yale, 2003.

Dinstein Y., *War, Aggression and Self Defence*, Cambridge University Press, 2002.

Duffy H., *The 'War on Terror' and the Framework of International Law*, Cambridge University Press, 2005.

Evans M., *International Law*, Oxford University Press, 2003.

Fleck D., *Humanitarian Law in Armed Conflicts*, Oxford University Press, 1999.

Green L.C., *The Contemporary Law of Armed Conflicts*, Manchester University Press, 2000.

Greenberg K., *The Torture Debate in America*, Cambridge University Press, 2008.

Greenberg K. and Dratel J., *The Torture Papers: The Road to Abu Ghraib*, Cambridge University Press, 2005.

Gray C., *International Law and the Use of Force*, Oxford University Press, 2000 and Second Edition 2008.

Gutman R., *A Witness to Genocide: First Inside Account of the Horrors of Ethnic Cleansing in Bosnia*, Element Books, 1993.

Hillyard P., *Suspect Community: People's Experience of the Prevention of Terrorism Acts in Britain*, Pluto Press, 1993.

BIBLIOGRAPHY

Izetbegovic A.A., *Inescapable Questions*, Islamic Foundation, 2002.

Kassimeris G., *The Barbarisation of Warfare*, Hurst, 2006.

Kassimeris G. (editor), *Playing Politics with Terrorism: A User's Guide*, Hurst, 2007.

Khadduri M., *The Law of War and Peace in Islam*, Johns Hopkins Press, 1955.

Kurnaz M., *Five Years of My Life: an innocent man in Guantánamo*, Palgrave Macmillan, 2008.

Lauterpacht H., *International Law and Human Rights*, Stevens & Sons, 1950.

Levinson S., *Torture, A Collection*, Oxford University Press, 2006.

Margulies J, *Guantanamo and the Abuse of Presidential Power*, Simon & Schuster, 2006.

Mayer J., *The Dark Side*, Doubleday, 2008.

McCoy A.W., *A Question of Torture*, Metropolitan Books, 2006.

Murphy J.F., *The United Nations and the control of International Violence: A Legal and Political Analysis*, Manchester University Press, 1983.

Musharraf P., *In the Line of Fire*, Simon & Schuster, 2006.

Nguyen T., *We Are All Suspects Now: Untold Stories from Immigrant Communities after 9/11*, Beacon Press, 2005.

Nowak M. and McArthur, *The United Nations Convention Against Torture: A Commentary*, Oxford Commentaries on International Law, Oxford University Press, 2008.

Sands P., *Lawless World*, Penguin, 2006.

Sands P., *Torture Team*, Allen Lane, 2008.

Stafford Smith C, *Bad Men*, Weidenfeld & Nicolson, 2007.

Suskind R., *The One Percent Doctrine*, Simon & Schuster, 2006.

Wilson R.A., *Human Rights in the 'War on Terror'*, Cambridge University Press, 2005.

Worthington A., *The Guantanamo Files*, Pluto Press, 2007.

Zimbardo P., *The Lucifer Effect*, Random House, 2007.

Journal Articles

Aldrich G.H., The Taliban, Al Qaeda, and the Determination of Illegal Combatants, *American Journal of International Law* vol. 96, 2002.

Burmester H., The Recruitment and Use of Mercenaries in Armed Conflicts, *American Journal of International Law*, 1978.

De Zayas A., The Status of Guantanamo Bay and the Status of Detainees, *The Douglas McK. Brown Lecture*, University of British Columbia, Vancouver, 19/11/2003.

Draper G.I.A.D., The Status of Combatants and the Question of Guerrilla Warfare, *British Year Book of International Law*, 1971.

Franck T. and Rodley N., After Bangladesh: The Law of Humanitarian Intervention by Military Force, (1973) 67 *American Journal of International Law* p275.

BIBLIOGRAPHY

Garraway C.H.B., Interoperability and the Atlantic Divide—A Bridge Over Troubled Waters, *International Studies Series, US Naval War College,* 2004.

Megret F., "War?" Legal Semantics and the move to Violence, *European Journal of International Law,* 2002.

Moeckli D., The US Supreme Court's 'Enemy Combatant' Decisions: A 'Major Victory for the Rule of Law'?, *C&S Law,* March 2005.

Mofidi M., Mofidi M., 'Unlawful Combatants' or 'Prisoners of War': The Law and Politics of Labels, *Cornell International Law Journal,* 2003.

Murphy S.D., Contemporary Practice of the United States in International Law: Decision Not to Regard Persons Detained in Afghanistan as POWs, *American Journal of International Law,* vol. 96 No. 2 pp. 475–480.

Paust J., Legal Aspects of the Mai Lai Incident: A Response to Professor Rubin, *Oregon Law Review,* 1971.

Raustiala K., Form and Substance in International Agreements, *American Journal of International Law,* vol. 99, No. 3 (Jul 2005) pp. 581–614.

Reisman M., Coercion and Self-Determination: Construing Charter Article 2(4), 78, *American Journal of International Law,* 1984.

Roberts A., Judaic sources of and views on the laws of war, 37 *Naval Law Review,* 1988.

Royston, Until What? Enforcement Action or Collective Self-Defence? 85 *American Journal of International Law* (1991) 506.

Rubin A., The Status of Rebels Under the Geneva Conventions of 1949, *International and Comparative Law Quarterly,* 1972.

Schachter O., The Legality of Pro-Democratic Invasion, 78 *American Journal of International Law,* 1984.

Steiner H., Securing Human Rights: The First Half-Century of the Universal Declaration, and Beyond, *Harvard Magazine,* 1998.

Trainin I.P., Questions on Guerrilla Warfare in the Law of *War, American Journal of International Law,* 1946.

Wedgwood R., Al Qaeda, Terrorism, and Military Commissions, *American Journal of International Law,* vol. 96, 2002.

Media Reports

Addis Tribune, US Begins Training Exercises With Ethiopian National Defense Forces, 11/07/2003.

Applebaum A., Hollow Rhetoric on 'Rule of Law', *Washington Post,* 21/12/2005.

BBC website, Guantánamo actors held at airport, 21/02/2006.

BBC website, Police 'did not identify Menezes', 31/10/2008.

BBC website, Searches to target ethnic groups, 31/07/2005.

BBC website, Terror suspect's Iraq kidnap plea, 07/12/2005.

BBC website, Timeline: Guantánamo Bay Britons, 27/01/2005.

BBC website, UK residents 'still held in Cuba', 11/01/2005.

Branigan T., Britons would trade civil liberties for security: ICM poll finds backing for anti-terror laws, *The Guardian*, 22/08/2005.

Campbell D., Rumsfeld knew all about me, says American 'jailer' held in Kabul, *The Guardian*, 22/07/2004.

Campbell D., US interrogators turn to 'torture lite', *The Guardian*, 25/01/2003.

Charlesworth H. and Chinkin C., The Gender of Jus Cogens, 15 *Human Rights Quarterly* 63 (1993).

Chertoff M., *The Daily Telegraph*, 04/04/2007.

CNN, Bin Laden suspect held in Bosnia, 26/10/2001.

Dodd V., Asian Men Targeted in Stop and Search, *The Guardian*, 17/08/2005.

Elliot M., The Next Wave, *Time*, 16/06/2002;.

England A., 'Many dead' after US strikes on Somalia, *Financial Times*, 09/01/2007.

Goodman A., From Paintball Practice to Prison: A Look At One of the Most Controversial Terrorism Cases in the Country, *Open Democracy*, 16/06/2004.

Greenberg K.J., Obama's Guantanamo? Bush's Living Legacy at Bagram Prison, *tomdispatch.com*.

The Guardian, Man linked to Bin Laden arrested in Bosnia, 08/10/2001.

The Guardian, Secret prisons: Obama's order to close 'black sites', 23/01/2009.

Hafetz J., Modest Improvements Cannot Save an Inherently Flawed Process at Guantanamo, *findlaw.com*,, 27/07/2007.

Harding L., Afghan Massacre haunts Pentagon, *The Guardian*, 14/10/2002.

Hasnain G., How Pakistan's Sacked Judge Became a National Hero, *Time*, 08/03/2007.

Herman S., PATRIOT Games: Terrorism Law and Executive Power, *JURIST*, 26/01/2006.

Junod T., Innocent, *Esquire*, 01/07/2006.

Lichtblau E., US Will Pay $2 Million to Lawyer Wrongly Jailed, *New York Times*, 30/11/2006.

McCarthy R., Why did Baha Mousa die in British custody, *The Guardian*, 21/02/2004.

Miller G., Obama preserves renditions as counter-terrorism tool, *Los Angeles Times*, 01/02/2009.

Morris N., Ethnic minorities face climate of fear, says race watchdog, *The Independent*, 15/06/2005.

Oborne P., The politics of fear (or how Tony Blair misled us over the war on terror), *The Independent*, 15/02/2006.

Ozment K., Who's Afraid of Aafia Siddiqui?, *Boston Magazine*, 10/2004.

Peirce G., Was it like this for the Irish?, *London Review of Books*, 10/04/2008.

Perlez J., U.S. Seeks Closing of Visa Loophole for Britons, *New York Times*, 02/05/2007.

Pincus W., London Ricin Finding Called a False Positive, *Washington Post*, 14/04/2005.

BIBLIOGRAPHY

Press Association, Crushing defeat for Blair over 90–day plan, *The Independent*, 09/11/2005.

Randall D. and Gosden E., 62,006–the number killed in the War on Terror, *The Independent*, 10/09/2006.

Steele J. and Smith M., MI6 grenade fired from public park, *The Daily Telegraph*, 19/07/2001.

Verkaik R, Guantánamo treatment is 'monstrous', says law lord, *The Independent*, 26/11/2003.

Reports

Amnesty International, *Human Rights Ignored in the War on Terror*, www. amnesty.org.uk.

Amnesty International, Cageprisoners, Center for Constitutional Rights, Center for Human Rights and Global Justice, Human Rights Watch and Reprieve, *Off the Record*, 07/06/2007.

Cageprisoners report, *Beyond the Law*, 12/2006.

Cageprisoners report, *Citizens No More*, 07/2007.

Cageprisoners report, *Enforced Disappearances in Pakistan*, 14/10/2006.

Cageprisoners report, *Inside Africa's War on Terror*, 03/2007.

Cageprisoners report, *The Systematic and Institutionalised Desecration of the Qur'an at Guantánamo Bay*, 16/05/2005.

Cageprisoners and Reprieve report, *Mass Rendition, Incommunicado Detention and Possible Torture of Foreign Nationals in Kenya, Somalia and Ethiopia*, 22/03/2007.

Council of Europe, *Combating Torture in Europe: The Work and Standards of the European Committee for the Prevention of Torture*, 2001.

Council of Europe Committee on legal Affairs and Human Rights, *Alleged secret detention in Council of Europe member states*, AS/Jur (2006) 03 rev, 22/01/2006.

Helsinki Committee for Human Rights, *Report on the Status of Human Rights in Bosnia and Herzegovina*, Br: 02A-02/2008.

Human Rights First, *Ending Secret Detentions*, 06/2004.

Human Rights Watch, *"Setting an Example?: Counter-terrorism Measures in Spain,"* January 2005 Vol. 17, No. 1(D)), 1.

Liberty, *Extradition Act 2003 undermines fundamental rights*, 30/11/2006.

Reprieve Press Release, *As New Evidence Emerges that War on Terror Prisoners were Held on Diego Garcia, Reprieve Demands Immediate Action from the British Government*.

Reprieve press release, *Reprieve deplores unjust Guantanamo "war crimes" trial*, 07/08/2008.

US Department of State, *Country Reports on Human Rights Practices: Ethiopia*, 2005.

US Department of State, *Syria–International Religious Freedom Report*, 2007.

US Department of State, *Tunisia–Country Reports on Human Rights Practices*, 06/03/2007.

DETAINEES

Aafia Siddiqui
Abdel Hakim Khafagy
Abdelilah Daudi Karrache
Abdullah Almalki
Abdur Rahman Khadr
Abou Elkassim Britel
Abu Hamza Al Masri
Abu Hamza Emad Alhusin
Abu Qatada
Adel Abdel Bary
Adel Hamad
Ahmad Abou El Maati
Airat Vakhitov
Alam Ghafoor
Ali Al Marri
Almin Hardaus
Ashraf Hossein
Asif Iqbal
Babar Ahmad
Baha Mousa
Benaissa Taleb
Bensayah Belkacem
Binyam Mohamed Al Habashi
Boudella Haji
Brandon Mayfield
Cerie Bullivant
David Hicks
Dilawar
Detainee AN

Detainee DD
Detainee E
Detainee G
Detainee U
Detainee W
Detainee Z
Fadhil Al Hammadani
Faisal Faraz
Faraj Hassan Faraj
Farid Hilali
Fatima Ahmed Abdur Rahman
Habibullah
Hafsa Swaleh Ali
Hamza Chentouf
Halima Hashim
Hamad Ali
Haroon Rashid Aswat
Inigo Castillo Macazaga
Jamil El Banna
John Walker Lindh
Jose Padilla
Kamilya Mohammed Tuweni
Khalid Al-Fawwaz
Khalid Sheikh Mohammed
Khalif Abdi Hussein
Maher Arar
Mahmoud Abu Rideh
Mahmoud Adam Salat
Majid Khan

DETAINEES

Mamdouh Habib
Martin Mubanga
Masood Ahmad Janjua
Millie Mithounie Gako
Moazzam Begg
Mobeen Muneef
Mohamed Hamid
Mohammed Ezzouek
Mohammed Harakat
Mohammed Mrabet Fahsi
Mohammed Suleman Latif
Mouloud Sihali
Muayyad Nurredin
Murat Kurnaz
Mustafa Ait Idir
Mustafa Melki
Mustafa Setmariam Nasar
Nadja Dizderavic
Nihad Karsic
Omar Deghayes
Omar Dijid

Omar Khadr
Omar Syed Omar
Rangzieb Ahmed
Reza Asfarzadagen
Rhuhel Ahmed
Saber Lahmar
Sabri ben Kahla
Safia Benaouda
Saifullah Paracha
Salim Hamdan
Salim Mahmoud Adam
Sami El Hajj
Shafiq Rasul
Shahjahan Janjua
Sayfullah Ben Hassine
Shaker Abdur Raheem Aamer
Syed Talha Ahsan
Tanweer Sheikh
Uzair Paracha
Yaser Hamdi

INDEX

INDEX

INDEX

INDEX

INDEX